M. Edith Durham

Albania and the Albanians
Selected Articles and Letters
1903-1944

with an introduction by
Harry Hodgkinson

Edited by
Bejtullah Destani

GW00691910

Centre for Albanian Studies,
London, 2001

First published 2001 by
The Centre for Albanian Studies
e-mail: albastudies@hotmail.com

Designed and distrbuted by
Learning Design
English St., London E3 4TA
Tel. +44 208 983 1944
Fax +44 208 983 1932
Website: www.learningdesign.org

ISBN 1 903616-09-3

Cover illustration: a watercolour of a North Albanian scene,
painted by Miss Edith Durham in 1901, reproduced by kind
permission of Dr. James Hickson, Miss Durham's executor.

Contents

Contents

Contents

Acknowledgements

I am indebted to the following people and institutions for their invaluable assistance and encouragement during the preparation of this book:

The Board of Trustees and Director of Kosova Aid who made publication of this book possible; **James Hickson** (Edith Durham's executor, for permission to reproduce the watercolour on the front cover of a North Albanian scene painted by Edith Durham in 1901 which is held in the collection of the Royal Anthropological Institute, London); **Richard Mullen**, the editor of 'The Contemporary Review' for permission to reproduce articles written by M.Edith Durham and published in 'The Contemporary Review'; **Blackwell Publishers** in Oxford for permission to reprint articles written by M.E.Durham and published in the magazine 'Man'; **The Royal Society for Asian Affairs** (successor body to the Central Asian Society) for permission to reprint the article by M.Edith Durham, 'Albania Past and Present' published in The Central Asian Society Journal in 1917; **The Royal Institution of Great Britain** for permisssion to reprint the article 'Albania' by M.Edith Durham; to the **Folklore Society** for permission to reprint article 'Albanian and Montenegrin Folklore' written by M. Edith Durham; **Beverly Emery**, the librarian at the Royal Anthropological Institute; **Arkadiusz Bentkowski**, the Royal Anthropological Institute Photo Librarian; **J.C.H. King** who kindly introduced me to the Royal Anthropological Institute library; **the Newspaper Library** at Collindale; **staff at the London Library** and **Alexander Duma** for allowing me full acsess to his father's papers and photographic collection.

I am particularly indebted to **Noel Malcolm** who gave invaluable advice at every stage in the production of this book and who also very kindly proofread the final manuscript.

Futher thanks are due to **Ilir Hamiti** who compiled the index, to **Tony Wisewell** for technical assistance and to **Eddie McParland** for his patience during the design stages of the book.

Bejtullah Destani

Dedicated to
Dr. Ihsan Toptani

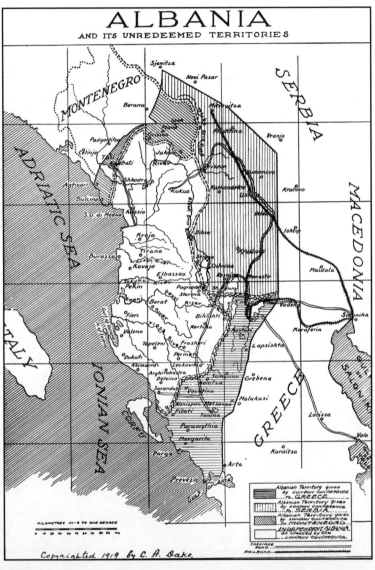

A map of Albania, published in 'Albania, The master key to the Near East' by Christo Dako, 1919, which shows the Albanian territories which were ceded to other countries by the Congress of Berlin, 1878 and the London Conference of 1912/13.

Introduction
by Harry Hodgkinson

In the London of peasouper fogs and hansom cabs, of Sherlock Holmes and Jack the Ripper, a fashionable surgeon called Arthur Durham owned an imposing house half way between Claridge's Hotel and Grosvenor Square. Durham came from Herefordshire stock; but his wife's family, behind the bland adopted surname of Ellis, was of Italian and French Huguenot origin.

William Ellis, Durham's father-in-law, was a Lloyd's underwriter, an economist and a pioneer of technical schools. He was a crony of John Stuart Mill, who praised his *"apostolic exertions"* for the improvement of teaching methods. He was also a friend of Garibaldi and had been involved with the Carbonare groups which made the early clandestine preparations for Italian unity.

One of the women of the family also stood godmother when the teenage Disraeli was baptised as an Anglican so that he could have a chance of climbing the greasy pole, as he put it, of British public life.

William Ellis had a reputation for a cool temper and a sharp tongue. There is a story of an exasperated visitor who, after storming and raging at him asked how he could keep his cool. *"One fool at a time is quite enough,"* said Ellis.

It is the authentic note of his eldest grandchild, Mary Edith, who was to become the uncrowned queen of the Albanian mountains.

With such a background, the Brook Street house could hardly have failed to be a breeding ground of talent; and at one time no fewer than four members of the family appeared together in 'Who's Who'.

One of the boys, Frank, was a civil engineer who worked in Russia and Eastern Europe. He joined up as a private in the First World War and rose to Lieutenant, Colonel and Chevalier de la Légion d'Honneur. He was Director of Works for the Imperial War Graves Commission and ended as secretary of the Royal Horticultural Society

Herbert followed his father's example, and specialised in tropical medicine. Wherever yellow fever, beri-beri and the tsetse fly beckoned, Herbert Durham was sure to respond. He helped Ronald Ross to indict

This Introduction was delivered as a lecture 'Edith Durham and the Foundation of the Albanian State' at Pembroke College, Cambridge in 1994.

the *genus anopheles* as guilty of causing malaria. He later became a research chemist for family friends, the Bulmers; and he ended up in Cambridge as a Fellow of King's. He even made furniture for the Combination Room there with his own hands.

Herbert seems to have been a rather opinionated and irascible, perhaps even curmudgeonly fellow; but this kept him hale and hearty for eight decades, and he died quietly in.his sleep. He left money to King's for research on sickness and health. On one condition: no woman was to have a penny of it. The courts, by the way, waived this androcentric proviso when King's went co-ed.

It is always dangerous to play the amateur psychologist - and often the professional psychologist, come to that - but it is hard to resist the conclusion that this posthumous macho outburst must have been a reaction to a lifetime's envy of and intimidation by his formidable sister.

Frances Hermia specialised on women's working conditions at the Ministry of Labour, and was the first woman in the Civil Service to be promoted Assistant Secretary.

Beatrice married a man who came within an ace of being one of the great seminal figures of world science, on a par with Charles Darwin. He was a geneticist before genetics existed; indeed, it was he who invented the word. Doing research in Cambridge into the how and why of heredity, he chanced on an article written forty years earlier in an obscure local scientific society's journal by a monk called Gregor Mendel. Working on the hybridization of green peas, Mendel had substantially discovered the laws governing the inheritance of characteristics in plants and animals, including humans.

Bateson, who had been moving towards the same discoveries, realised that his own research was now redundant, and devoted his own formidable talents to spreading the Mendelian solution. Inevitably, the man in the street was indifferent and the priest in the pulpit hostile. Oddly enough, so initially were the Darwinians. It took them time to realise that Mendel's and Bateson's genes explained, as nothing hitherto had done, how mutations produce their effects through Natural Selection.

With siblings and in-laws like this, what wonder that Edith, the eldest daughter, should kick against the traces when it seemed clear that she was destined as that Victorian victim, the daughter destined to sacrifice her own life looking after an ailing mother.

Born in 1863, she had indeed been sent to Bedford College, one of the earliest places to offer a decent education to young ladies. But Bedford did not yet offer degree courses; it was in fact little more than a glorified high school for girls of fourteen and upwards. Choice of subjects for study was happy-go-lucky and the atmosphere was rather prissy. Edith recalled having been reproved for speaking of an omnibus as merely a bus.

All Victorian young ladies were expected to dabble in water colours; but after Bedford, Edith went into painting seriously and secured a place at the Royal Academy Schools when she was twenty-two. She exhibited three pictures at the RA Summer Exhibitions,one of them mysteriously entitled *'The Decrees of Fate'*. In the Guildhall Art Gallery, there was a City of London townscape by her. She illustrated a Latin grammar and the reptile volume of the Cambridge Natural History.

She did not go on to become a professional artist; but her Academy training stood her in good stead for her own travel books and for the anthropological studies which began to occupy more of her time. She designed her own bookplate: an Albanian maintaineer seated, rifle across his knees, gazing at a bare landscape from which the rays of a rising sun are breaking forth.

In her late thirties, around the turn of the century Edith reached a crisis in health that we should now probably call psychosomatic. It must have been immensely frustrating for the eldest to watch her better qualified younger siblings achieving satisfying careers while she seemed destined to greet the twentieth century as a Victorian spinster. Her wise doctor told her to get away, as far as she liked, for as long as she could; and a form of peace treaty was drawn up in the Durham household whereby Edith would look after Mama for ten months of the year and have two at her own disposition.

It would be forcing the evidence, though, to present her as a Cinderella of the sick room, whose sisters went off, if not to princely balls, at least to the stimulation of public and academic life. Had she been so, no such bargain would have been struck. A photograph of the time shows a face neither plain nor pretty, the hair cropped boyishly, the eyes frankly and fearlessly appraising: an ikon of the emerging New Woman of Ibsen and Shaw and Mrs Bloomer, illuminated by an awareness of the feminism that was soon to break so rudely on the political scene, and which was to command her own loyalty.

So in 1900, at the age of 37, Edith Durham made her first sally into those Balkans which were to be her concern and glory - for the rest of her life.

She chose to go to Montenegro, which had great advantages for the European traveller. It was remote but accessible. You had to reach it by horse or on foot up a series of rough hairpin bends amid superb scenery and It was exotic but welcoming. Here, for the classically minded, was a race of Homeric warriors, wild in appearance - with even a touch of Rousseau's Noble Savage, perhaps - but not unamenable to the gold sovereigns and napoleons and kroner of the tourist.

The solid burgher of Mitteleuropa, in linen suits and Leghorn straw hats and his silken, bosomed spouse under her parasol, took a Lloyd Triestino liner. threading the Roman ruins and Venetian campanili en route, wondering at Zara whether to sip Ulahovi's maraschino or Lycardo's, and tying up amid the incomparable grandeurs of the Gulf of Kotor, at a quayside from which the rough road led off to the Black Mountain.

They took with them the 600 pages in 8 volumes of the guide issued by the Union of the Encouragement of Local Economic Initiatives of Royal Dalmatia. It contains everything, down to the Latin names of all the mountain flowers you will encounter; and when I began my own Balkan forays, Edith presented me with her own copy. One chapter included, for the more enterprising, details of an Optional Excursion into Montenegro.

At that time all rulers and most of the educated public were intoxicated by a highly self-serving vision of the ancient world: the British Empire as a liberalised re-run of the Roman - that sort of thing. The Montenegrin mountaineers were cast in the role of heroic warriors - *"beating back the storm of Turkish Islam"*, as Tennyson put it, rather as the ancient Greeks had preserved Athens from the Persian hordes.

Most of the time, these heroic battles were crossborder raids by Montenegrins into the Ottoman territory of Albania, in fact in search of maize and livestock to keep them from starvation. They had eaten their own during the winter. The Turkish government went by a simple principle: send a small army into Montenegro and it is massacred; send a large one and it starves. So leave the place alone if you possibly can; and let Mr Gladstone, if he so wishes, call on historians to celebrate the untamed liberty of the Montenegrin.

Thus in the early years it was the Slavs, rather than the Albanians who caught the attention of the surgeon's daughter from Brook Street. She travelled in Montenegro and Serbia, and her first book was the delightful 'Through the Lands of the Serb'. It is among other things the story of a woman who seemed fabulously rich because she could afford the train journey from England; and therefore desirable as a bride for Serbian army officers, Montenegrin policemen and the like, whose idea of a perfect career was to have enough money to sit in the gostiona and drink, smoke and play backgammon all day.

She learned to speak Serbo-Croat; and indeed never wholly mastered Albanian, not from lack of aptitude but because of the bewildering complexity of the various competing alphabets - from the banal to the positively hieroglyphic - in which Albanian was then written.

As she told the story, her first introduction to the Albanians came when she was doing relief work in Macedonia after the rising of 1903. She found that when gold had to be moved from one depot to another, it was always entrusted to an Albanian, who could be trusted to defend it with - literally with - his life. The Albanian mountaineer would neither steal the gold, nor allow it to be stolen from him, not on some generalised ethical principle, but because either would demean him ineradicably in his own eyes.

Of course there was clearly an element of idealisation in all this. If there is such a thing as *Original Sin*, then Albanians are no more exempt from it than the rest of us. But the human race, despite many rebuffs, never seems to abandon the quest for an earthly paradise; and Albania, hitherto remote in time and place, stunningly beautiful in appearance, and unparalleled in its concern for the guest, has long been high on the list of possible candidates. Nor, despite her down-to-earth character, did Edith Durham wholly lack this tendency - this psychological need, if you like - to idealisation.

My friend, Anton Logoreci, has schoolmastered in the mountains and seen the darker side of existence there: the murderous vendetta, the superstition, the intellectual and spiritual constraints, the use of women as beasts of burden. He gently sought to redress the balance somewhat in the mind of this revered old lady towards the end of her life. She listened. She fixed him with her eye. She spoke: *"Of course, you are a degenerate from the plains"*.

Edith's first disillusionment over Serbia came in 1903 with the murder of the headstrong young king Alexander Obrenovic and his older queen Draga. Their love affair had been an excuse for action by pan-Slav elements which resented the Obrenovic policy of amicable relations with Austria-Hungary. A clique of army officers hacked the royal pair to pieces, and threw the bodies into the palace courtyard under the complacent gaze of the Russian Legation. Edith was told that one of the conspirators thenceforth carried a piece of the queen's skin in his wallet as a momento of that heroic night.

Kings have been sickeningly murdered elsewhere than in Belgrade. But this act had a special, and as history has to show, a typical resonance about it. Here was a major act of policy, carried out behind a civilian and democratic facade by a well-organised, self-appointed and self-perpetuating cabal of army officers and their civilian hangers-on. For Edith Durham, this process became the sign manual of Serbian and later Yugoslav policy, first to the immediate neighbours of Serbia and then towards the non-Serbian nationalities of Yugoslavia. In the light of what has been happening in the last couple of years, it would be rash to write off that point of view.

She never quite lost, though, what it may be banal to call her love-hate relationship with Montenegro, as instanced by her personal dealings with its (in all senses) larger-than-life Prince and King Nicholas. Later Nicholas, or Nikita, as everyone called him, had already ruled for forty years. He succeeded an uncle who had been shot by a cuckolded husband; and there is a touching, idyllic picture of him as a twenty-year old, presented by Emily, Viscountess Strangford, an earlier women traveller in the Durham mould.

She had already written a book on the tombs of Syria, which earned her an offer of marriage from Strangford, a diplomat with Middle Eastern interests and a certain concern with Albanian philology. She shows us the young prince who could outshoot everyone else but who, being huge and heavy, couldn't match them with the skipping rope. He presides at the Senate of thirty old warriors, sitting under an oak and subject to heckling from the public gallery. This body was concerned with legal precedents, and at the time of Emily Strangford's visit was hearing the complaint of an old crone who wanted something to be done about her husband: he is a bore, and looks shabby. A perennial domestic problem you might say.

By the time Edith arrives in Cetinje, the lithe young prince is a weighty old man who tends to fall off his horse. He is notoriously greedy, rigging the Viennese bourse with calculated rumours and taking subventions from all and sundry. A German journalist has given him the name of '*King Baksheesh*'.

In her own crisp way, Edith says: *"He was a scallywag, don't you know?"* That tart Edwardian *"Don't you know?"* sprang to her lips whenever she wanted to underline a phrase.

All the same, these two remarkable people responded to something that each found in the other's personality. Here was the ruler of no more than a quarter of a million people, with ambitions to carry out a takeover of Serbia and marry his children into the major royal families. As Queen

Victoria had been called the Grandmother of Europe, so Nikita aspired to be its father-in-law.

One daughter he sent to St. Petersburg to be trained to marry the Tsar, but she died before the wedding. Two others he did indeed marry off to Grand Dukes, and they had the distinction of introducing the monk Gregory, alias Rasputin, to the Russian Court. The King of Italy became his son-in-law. and so did the King of Serbia. The boys didn't do half so well as the girls: one of them ended up as husband to the daughter of an east London tram driver.

No doubt as well as being intrigued by his pretentions. and wishing to keep an eye on his intrigues towards her beloved Albanian mountaineers, she was flattered when a crowned head, passing her on the road, would stop and ask her to step up into his barouche and talk politics.

For his part, her character interested and her true purposes mystified him. He admired her courage and her pertinacity. As to her motivation, he could hardly think, as the country folk did, that she was the sister of the King of England, sent out by him to redress their wrongs. But he knew she was a correspondent for *The Times* and *The Manchester Guardian*; and his Balkan mind would tell him that even if she did not have a direct remit from the British Government, it was more than likely that her observations and conclusions would find their way onto the desks of the Foreign Office clerks.

Again, he knew of her prestige among the Albanian mountaineers and could always hope to persuade her to use her influence with them, if not to serve his purposes directly - in rising against the Turks, for example - then in causing him the minimum of trouble. But he was rather jealous of her love affair with Albania. One day he asked:

"Miss Durham, why are you wearing the jewellery of my worst enemies?"
"Because, Your Majesty, they are my best friends."

Nikita even asked her once to keep an eye on a Montenegrin stand at a White City exhibition. This was not an unmitigated success. The Montenegrins were appalled how, in capitalist London, men did not appear to realise that it is not consonant with masculine dignity to engage in anything so humiliating as work. And when they saw the natives working as blacksmiths they could only conclude that the English were a nation of gypsies.

King Nicholas would have been right to assume that Edith Durham's despatches were brought to the attention of the Foreign Office, for she had made a perfect choice in her timing and her sphere of activity. The Balkans had become, as every journalist said, the powder keg of Europe; and they were also the least well-known corner of Europe.

It was clear by around 1900 that the Turk, described by the Tsar Nicholas I, fifty years earlier, as *"a very sick man"* was now on his deathbed. The sickroom was filled with self-appointed heirs each keeping a beady eye on the others - the rival Balkan nationalities he had ruled for four hundred years, and their backers among the Great Powers.

The Balkans were now the fault line between two geopolitical systems; and it is along such fault lines that volcanic action expresses itself. On the face of it, this was a perennial contest between the Teuton drive south to the Aegean and the Slav drive west to the Adriatic. But this local rivalry was by now built into a wider system of relationships created primarily not to make but to prevent wars to maintain a balance of power in Europe to keep in check the rise of Germany to primacy as an industrial and military force. Hence the Great Powers were divided into two groups, the Triple Alliance of Germany, Austria-Hungary and Italy, and the Triple Entente of Britain, France and Russia.

The problem for the Foreign Offices of Europe was how to prevent some local conflict between the Balkan nations - over, for example, which of them should have Macedonia - from setting this mechanism of wider alliances into operation, and so producing general war. Which is of course exactly what happened when the assassination of the Archduke in 1914 did release the fully wound clockwork of disaster. War could be averted after the Balkan wars in 1913 because there was any amount of someone else's land, especially historic Albanian territories, for the powers to dole out among their clients. By 1914 this resource had dried up. The focus of action was Bosnia, for six years now an integral part of the Hapsburg empire.

In the dozen or so years that led up to World War I, thetefore, intelligence from the Balkans was at a premium among opinion-formers in Europe. The old reliance on reports from consuls and professional diplomats was not good enough, and a new breed of observer emerged to cover the places and movements and trends the others couldn't reach.

We have seen in the last few years how abysmally Europe and America have been served in the matter of identifying these underlying trends: how our statesmen spoke of their determination to keep the old ship Yugoslavia afloat long after the wretched hulk had been gnawed away by the worm of nationalism, and was already gently settling on the seabed of oblivion. Of course, wishful thinking has always been growth industry in politics, and especially in democratic politics; and statesmen have never tended to underestimate their power to deflect reality by a judicious dose of rhetoric. But, as we are seeing in Bosnia, reality has a habit of getting its own way in the end.

In the 1900s, of course, public opinion did not have the advantage of the present-day circus of cameramen and observers, politicians and negotiators, who follow the circuit of successive crisis. And the task of keeping it informed devolved on devoted and experienced individuals: journalists like the legendary J.D. Bourchier of *The Times* in Bulgaria, and amateur travellers of intelligence and courage like Edith Durham.

Nowhere could their findings be more welcome than in the British Foreign Office. This was already undergoing a major shift in the scope of its operations and the status of its permanent staff. Until Lord Salisbury retired as Foreign Secretary in 1898, the office had been staffed by young gentlemen whose handwriting was legible, who possessed a private income and whose family connections were known to, or could be vouched for by the Minister himself. These men had many social advantages, and they were not overburdened with work, in either volume or in power, to tax the brain. Indeed, one of their major jobs had been to write out despatches for Queen Victoria, who had no time for these new fangled typing machines. They remained in fact, as they were formally described, clerks. The Foreign Secretary told them what to write, and to whom; and they wrote it. He didn't tell them what to think; that is what he was there for; and a flair for thinking on their own account would have been superfluous, an embarrassment even.

With the turn of the century all this changed utterly. Under the Liberal Government of 1906, and encouraged by the Foreign Secretary, Edward Grey, thinking on the part of the permanent officials became fashionable as never before and, to the same degree at least, never afterwards.

Consider what was at stake. For about a century, certainly from Waterloo in 1814 and perhaps even from Trafalgfar nine years earlier, the status of Britain, had never been seriously questioned. Now, with the German Naval Law of 1903 and the evident challenge to British seapower, even her very existence might be in the balance.

Did one seek an accommodation with Germany? Could one indeed reach an accommodation which an ebullient, self-confident Germany would observe? Could one come to a balancing understanding with France and Russia: France with whom colonial rivalries were endemic, Russia who was regarded as Enemy No. 1 by the India Office and loathed as a tyranny by British liberal opinion? But again, if we did not make a deal with France and Tsarist Russia, might they not, aware of their weakness in isolation, themselves come to an understanding with Germany, leaving Britain on her own and facing, at best, a steady attrition in authority and status?

These questions were now argued backwards and forwards by a group of senior Foreign office personnel of high intelligence and farsighted patriotism. Reading today their often agonised memoranda, one can only admire the way they argued the case, even when it went against the grain of their personal predilections.

The material collected by Edith Durham, and presented in her forthright style, was manna to these people. The Kosovar historian, Bejtullah Destani, who is rapidly earning a special place for himself as an expert on British policy in the Balkans, has lately pulled out a succulent plum from the Public Record Office. This consists of two letters sent from Scutari towards the end of 1908 outlining, as no one else was then in a position to do, the situation between Turks and Albanians, and Christians and Muslims, following the introduction of the Young Turks' new Constitution, and exposing its weakness. The letters run to around 3,000 words, about three newspaper columns, and much of what she says is used again in her books.

The significant thing, though, is to see from the minute sheet to whom these letters were circulated; and there is no difficulty in identifying the recipients from their initials. First comes John Tilley, who later wrote a standard book on the F.O.; then R.P. Maxwell, who had been a member of a committee to reform Foreign Office procedures. He now described Edith as *"a remarkable woman with a great command of strong language."* Maxwell was followed by Charles Hardinge, the Permanent Under-Secretary; and below him are the initials E.G. - Edward Grey, the Foreign Secretary himself. In terms of influence and prestige, this was the apogee of Edith Durham's career in Balkan politics.

One only needs to say that to invite the countervailing comment that influence and prestige do not of themselves determine policy. It was, I think, the first Duke of Marlborough who said that *"interest never lies"*. He might more correctly have said that perceived interest never lies for nations and their rulers are not impeccable in their perceptions of long-term interest. What he meant, though, and what is undeniable is that nations act for reasons of advantage and not for abstract rational or moral considerations. You make war over Kuwait, which produces oil; but not over Bosnia, which doesn't. So when, as they say, the chips are down, local Balkan realities, however convincingly described by an Edith Durham, had to give way to the wider compromises involved in sustaining the entente with France and Russia. This was made quite explicit at the time of the Montenegrin capture of Scutari at the end of the First Balkan War in the Spring of 1913. It had been suggested that Britain should put pressure on the Russians to force the Montenegrins to withdraw. Arthur Nicolson, then Permanent Under-Secretary, wrote:

"We have promised the Russians our diplomatic support and we cannot now withdraw. Moreover were we to abandon the Russian standpoint we should be heading straight towards a serious breach in our understanding with Russia, and this would be simply disastrous to us. Scutari is not worth running such a risk. Scutari, that is, could be thrown to the wolves, whatever the lady with the strong language thought about it."

In the end, Albania hung on to Scutari; but only as a result of horse-trading between the Powers. Albania, with German backing, was not prepared to see the Slavs gain an outlet to the Adriatic; but Austria had to yield in return when the Albanian lands were sliced in two. The western half received an initially precarious existence; the eastern (Kosova and part of Macedonia) was handed over to Russia's protegee Serbia.

The siege of Scutari deserves a moment's attention on its own account. It provided Edith Durham with the subject for her book 'The Struggle for Scutari', which for me is her finest achievement in terms of narrative and political comprehension. It was the first of the great Ottoman fortresses to be attacked and, defended by both Turkish and Albanian troops, was the last to fall. It had moreover strategic lessons to teach which could have prevented the later massacres of the Western Front. But the general staffs of the Powers were hardly inclined to think there was anything to learn from a little Balkan sideshow like this.

Readers of Proust will remember the almost euphoric spirit with which military people anticipated war before 1914. The gilded N.C.O.s with whom the Narrator shares claret and roast pheasant explain how the cavalry will break through the enemy lines, and the fighting will be over in a fortnight. Presumably the Germans would be dictating peace in Paris and the French in Berlin. And a good thing too, no doubt.

What the strategists had not reckoned with, though, was the lethal combination of barbed wire and the machine gun. This omission was to condemn to death, on the battlefields alone, six million men and eight million horses.

Edith had watched the Turks, helped by German advisers, laying a complicated network of barbed wire, mile upon mile of it, around the perimeter of the city. For reasons of security, only Muslim civilians were employed; but this being Albania, the Christian Paul who was turned away today came back tomorrow as Muslim Mehmet and earned his few piastres.

Back in Cetinje, Edith tried to disabuse her hosts that they were not going to have the walkover they counted on. *"Lady* (said a senior Montenegrin army officer) *do you know what we will do with your barbed wire?"* and he made a snipping gesture with a couple of fingers. How many Montenegrins were needlessly impaled and riddled by machine gun fire on this contemptible barbed wire will never be known.

Edith followed the Montenegrin forces along the eastern shore of Lake Scutari, watching the soldiers dying for lack of even the most primitive medical amenities; and marvelling at the women who brought meals for their men, robbed the Albanian villages of food and blankets, and even pulled down - for no apparent reason except that it happened to be there - the telegraph wire their own army had just put up.

Towards the end of 1912, as the Balkan War broke out, a group of friends in London headed by Aubrey Herbert, an MP, Turkish speaker and specialist in Balkan affairs, set up a committee which was to develop into the present Anglo-Albanian Association. Originally it aimed, as did Albanian nationalists in general, at securing for Albania autonomy within the Ottoman Empire. When the Ottoman Empire collapsed, Herbert and Durham turned their attention in personal contacts, press information and memoranda for the use of policy-makers, to pressing the case for Albanian independence. This was achieved in 1913; but, as we have seen, only in part - Kosova remained outside - and only under pressure from Austria-Hungary.

The problem which now arose was how to implement this award, given the non-existence of an Albanian national army or civil service, in the face of the predatory neighbours who hoped to carve up Albania. The Serbs, in their urge to reach the Adriatic, sought to make agreements with local Albanian chieftains to create petty vassal states. The Italians fomented reactionary Islamic plots against the Prince chosen to rule Albania. And the Greeks brazenly sent into Southern Albania, which they christened Northern Epirus, regular army units disguised as local patriots clamouring for union with the *'Motherland'*.

In those days, no new European state was complete without a monarch chosen from the unemployed minor royal families of Germany, and related to the Great White Queen Victoria. He was thought to add prestige, a degree of political stability; and he gave a certain reassurance to foreign investors.

The candidate chosen for Albania was William of Wied, head of a minor princely family from the Rhineland. No one, by the way, quite seems to know whether to call him Prince or King of Albania; and indeed the philologists tell us that his title, Mbret, is a variation of the Latin word for emperor. Wied got the job as a result of persistent lobbying in Vienna by his aunt, the eccentric Queen Elizabeth of Romania. She wrote execrable poetry, rather on the style of Ella Wheeler Wilcox, she moved around her palace, robed in what looks in photographs like a spiritualist medium's ectoplasm; and she eventually retired to Venice with a favoured lady-in-waiting.

Another relation, the Queen of the Netherlands, persuaded her government to provide Wied with a contingent of Dutch troops. These came to form a state within a state, and even went so far as to arrest and send into exile Wied's Minister of War, the notorious Essad Pasha. They proved, however, the only forces on which he could rely during a six months' reign in 1914, when he was in effect besieged in his capital Durazzo.

The Kaiser had tried to dissuade Wied from taking on the job on the grounds that he knew nothing about the Balkans; but the Kaiser, equally implausibly, favoured a Muslim King for Albania. This was hardly feasible in the atmosphere of the time, and given the determination of the new Albanian leaders to link their fortunes with the West.

Edith Durham found Wied a high-minded political innocent. Or, to put it in her own words in a letter to Aubrey Herbert: *"He is a blighter ... a feeble stick, devoid of energy or tact or manners and wholly ignorant of the country. The Queen's only idea is to play the Lady Bountiful, distribute flowers, put medals on the wounded and make fancy blouses of native embroidery."* They were both very royal and kept people standing in their presence.

The Queen irritated Edith by constantly quoting the Romanian aunt as a fount of wisdom; so that eventualy, she told me, she was provoked into commenting: *"Albania is not Romania, Ma'am"*.

Edith tried to persuade Wied to make a gesture that would capture the imagination of his subjects. Let him get on horseback and show himself to them. But he remained in his palace, beleaguered by the quarreling interests outside. And when he did go riding, the experience proved disastrous for his reputation. The news spread among the mountaineers that he had been seen actually helping a woman, his wife, to mount and dismount. What more was needed, eighty years ago, to call in question his virility?

it was left to Edith Durham to follow her own advice to Wied: to get on a horse and show herself around. She went off to the south, which the Greeks were trying to annex. On the principle that every true Greek is Orthodox in religion, the Greeks (in their day the inventors of logic) deducted that all the Orthodox must therefore be Greek, even if they did not speak Greek, and described themselves as Albanians, Macedonians, Bulgarians, or what have you.

So the Greek government sent regular army formations into Southern Albania early in 1914, pretending they were local *'Epirots'* demanding union with *"the Motherland"*. They, and their ecclesiastical fellow conspirators, dragooned the population to meetings at which resolutions calling for enosis with Greece were submitted, and telegrams sent to the Conference of Ambassadors in London which was deciding on the frontiers of Albania. Edith watched this charade at Korca. Berat was the nearest place out of Greek control, where she could herself send a telegram to the Ambassadors warning them to take no notice of the tendentious messages they had been receiving. She wrote to me once that this had involved her in a forced march of three days across the mountains, sleeping two nights on the bare ground. And she added, with a touch of justified pride: *"This telegram saved Korca."*

I am told there is a project to erect a statue to her in Korca. If so, who will say there is no gratitude in politics.

It was on this recce of the south, by the way, that she was one stopped by a Greek officer who threatened to shoot her if she advanced another step. *"You can't,"* she replied, *"I'm English."*. Those, as they say, were the days.

On this heroic trip, she was accompanied by one of the most distinguished journalists of the day, H.W. Nevinson. In his autobiography he has left this acutely admiring portrait of her:

'By courage and honesty she had won the hearts of a people distinguished for courage and honesty among all Balkan nations ... Kindly and generous she had, of course, shown herself, ready to undertake any journey and to work day and night to relieve sickness or distress ... But there was little of the sentimental nurse or philanthropist about Edith Durham. Her manner towards strangers and people whom she distrusted was abrupt to rudeness, and she would contradict her best friends with a sharpness that silenced dispute, if not opinion. Her

*language in conversation was even more racy than the style of her
books, and she had a way of hitting off affectation or absurdity with a
slashing phrase that was not exactly coarse, but made the cultured
jump. I have never known a woman to express facts or opinions with
such startling vigour, especially in disagreement.'*

'The Albanians,' he adds, *'had a simple faith in her absolute power and
bottomless wealth. They called her 'the Queen of the Mountains', and
indeed, Nevinson says, 'the Powers of Europe could not have done
better for the country than appoint her Queen, with me as her Grand
Vizier.'*

With the end of the First World War, Albania embarked on the most
dangerous phase of her modern history. The defeat of the Central
Powers, and in particular the disintegration of the Austrian empire,
removed from the scene the one deeply concerned champion of her
independence. The three traditional predators of Albanian territory -
Greece, Serbia and Italy - were now on the winning side. That an
Albanian state survived at all was something of a miracle. of course,
Albanians could and did appeal to the Wilsonian principle of national
self-determination; and without it their country would no doubt have
gone under. At one point during the Paris peace negotiations, President
Wilson did send an envoy to meet Edith Durham and get her views on
Albania's future. And at that time she certainly saw a United States
mandate for Albania as a feasible, and perhaps even desirable option,
given the looming threat from its neighbours.

National-self-determination was, however, a matter of principle rather
than of mandatory practice. Some nations proved more self-determined
than others, especially where the strategic interests - or, as it turned out,
the supposed strategic interests - of Britain and France were concerned.

Had the Wilsonian principle ruled across the board, Albania's frontiers
would have been widened to include Kosova and areas of western
Macedonia. But there was never any question of asking the Serbian ally
to give up these territories; and in the pursuit of the same strategic aim
- to build bulwarks against a renascent Germany, Czechs and Slovaks
were incorporated in a single state, and so were Croats, Slovenes and
Serbs.

We all know what happened to this pipe-dream in 1939 and 1941 when,
admittedly, the two Western powers had lost, first the will and then the
capacity, to sustain their creations of twenty years earlier. In the case of
Yugoslavia, it was evident from the beginning of the experiment that the
new state would not be a federation of equal partners, but a

centralised,autocratic monarchy operated by, and in the interests of a predominantly Serbian military, bureaucratic and diplomatic complex.

For Edith Durham there was never any doubt that Yugoslavia was an artificial creation which given the conditions under which it must operate, would never generate a genuine sense of cohesion. In particular, she believed that the Croats would break away from Yugoslavia the first moment they had an opportunity. Which indeed they did when Germany invaded the Balkans in 1941; and again, half a century later, when the collapse of the Soviet Union removed the last incentive to live together with what they had already began to call Serbistan; that reactionary clique of red fascists which has made Serbian rule a byword for civic incivility.

Behind Edith's point of view lay her conviction that it had been a mistake to break up the Austro-Hungarian Empire; and her belief that it should have been democratised and liberalised, particularly in relation to its Slav nationalities. It seemed to her that the breakup of that empire had been the work of a group of publicists who, behind a facade of scholarship, were, perhaps unwittingly, serving far from scholarly purposes; from a mixture of vanity, ignorance and undeniable idealism. All of which seem to make excellent bedfellows.

Her particular bêtes noirs were Seton-Watson of the School of Slavonic and East European Studies, and Wickham Steed of Northcliffe's Times. She invented a jingle about them.

'SW, WS. The two of them made the hell of a mess.'

To show that she was not a victim of persecution mania, it may be worth quoting a comment on the phenomenon of scholars in high places, made at the time of Philip Guedalla, a figure forgotten now, but relished in his days as combining something of the cool detachment of a Disraeli with the malice of a Max Beerbohm. Guedalla pictures the British Government as determined that President Wilson, himself an academic, shall be confronted at the Paris peacemaking by the embattled dons of England.

'The farce was produced on the largest and most magnificent scale ... Hastily equipped for a life of gay diplomacy ... they were set to the composition of brief but informing brochures on countries which they had never visited ... Fellows and Tutors followed Masters and Wardens overseas with the tragic, hurrying eagerness of the Children's Crusade; and once in Paris, they discharged their ridiculous duties with that solemnity which has never failed the older universities in a false position. England had need of them, and they took their place in the Hotel

Majestic as the last and most magnificent of the British Amateurs.'[1]

He might have added that some of them were even sent out to delimit the new frontiers; and Albania owes its loss of the natural market town of Debar to one such.

This is not the place, nor would there be times to go deeply into the rights and wrongs of the bitter arguments that flared up between Edith Durham and the SW camp. But it has to be pointed out, I think, what an imbalance of public recognition there was between the two sides. The Seton Watson school spoke with the prestige of the academic and political establishments, while Edith Durham, especially after the untimely death of Aubrey Herbert in 1923, was effectively working alone; and even the Anglo-Albanian Association was then more or less a one-woman band, going by Edith's indomitable will, her purse and her idiosyncratic typewriter. It was she who received and processed the reports of Serbian persecution of Kosovars, and forwarded them to the Foreign Office in letters which, while decorously addressed in proper form to the Rt. Hon. the Marquess Curzon of Kedleston, were written in the same pungent, fearless language of a woman defending her cause like a mother her child.

The fury of her opponents was compounded by their need to bend their genuine liberal and democratic principles to at least condone practices on the part of their protégés which could in no way be justified on liberal and democratic grounds.

It is enough to mention what would now be called the '*ethnic cleansing*' begun in Kosova in the 1920s by the Karageorgevic regime in Belgrade with - the habit was catching - the full approval of the Serbian academic establishment. Hundreds of thousands of Kosovar Albanians were kicked out of their homes and sent to Turkey, being classified as Turks merely because they were Muslims. This was official policy, about which no secret was ever made; and, as in the case of Hitler's '*Mein Kampf*,' detailed advanced blueprints were available of the monstrosities to follow.

Of course, things have not gone quite as the Serbs planned. The refugees from Kosova and also from Bosnia, have in their descendants a lobby of several millions of people inside Turkey. And Turkey is now a nation of fifty or sixty millions, and once again a major regional power, with a renewed concern over events in the Balkans. But that is another story.

Enough to say that the breach between Durham and Seton-Watson was absolute. He refused to meet her or debate with her. He was further exasperated when in 1925, she published 'The Sarajevo Crime'. In this she sought to assess the ultimate responsibility for the assassination of the Archduke. No one seriously denied that it had been organised by a backstairs group of military in Belgrade. This group intended to detach Bosnia from Austria-Hungary in the same way, and by the same means that the IRA hopes will despatch Northern Ireland from the United Kingdom. For them, the only question was one of timing.

I knew one of the Bosnian Serbs who were being trained for this purpose, and he told me they had been advised that matters must not be brought to a head until 1917, as the so-called Russian steam-roller would not be ready to pulverise the German army until then. (He later became one of Tito's ambassadors, by the way).

All this was quite consonant with an unofficial clique of army officers working clandestinely in touch with their Russian opposite numbers, as probably happened at the time of the murder of King Alexander Obrenovic.

Edith went further than this, however. Her thesis was that the Serbian politicians, and the military camarilla round the Regent, later King Alexander Karageorgevic were at least aware of what was going on, and prepared to profit thereby if they could get away with it.

For this she was bitterly maligned. Letters to the press accused her of being, and by implication of always having been pro-German, which was a far from friendly insult with the memories of the Western Front so fresh in people's minds One correspondent in effect told her that even if it were true, one ought to let bygones by bygones and look forward hopefully to the reign of peace and goodwill which was dawning.

I happen to possess Seton-Watson's copy of 'The Sarajevo Crime'. Every page margin, all the fly leaves are filled, in meticulous, tiny handwriting, with facts, statistics, quotations, comments. The text is profusely underlined. The whole effect is that of an exasperated dominie who despairs of his public. Such is his obsessiveness, that on the title page he writes in the day and month - 10th November - on which the book was published.

All this, one might say, is water under the bridge. Yugoslavia has gone down like the Titanic, and for much the same reason: her captain, crew and backers showed a haughty disregard for the icebergs of reality. The scholars who helped to install and then justified the regime between the wars and those who fawned on Tito in and after the second one, have come to their reckoning, and the kindest thing is to leave them to history. But it must be in order to point out that, in the light of recent events, Edith Durham can again be seen as very much centre stage and no longer the quirky, marginalised figure she was so long made out to be.

She went to Albania after the First World War in, I think, 1921. This was her last visit; which seems to call for some explanation since she was not yet sixty and was to live another twenty and more years. Although in far from perfect health she did get around, and her devotion to Albania remained undimmed. Alas, I was never bright enough to think of raising this subject with her.

I suspect that one reason, and perhaps even the major one, was a desire not to seem to be serving the purposes of the government in power, after the emergence of Ahmed Zogu, first as Minister of the Interior, then President and finally King, with, of course, the few months of the Fan Noli interregnum.

'I loathe Zog', she once wrote to me. And when he arrived in London after the fall of France, she gave me the news that she was feeling much better after an operation. *"But don't tell Zog,"* she said, or he would be wanting to come up to Haverstock Hill and pay her a visit.

The furthest she would go in accommodating herself to the Zog regime was to attend the National Day party at the Legation in Pont Street. Dervish Duma, who remained as First Secretary up to the time the Italians walked into Albania, used to send a cab for her, and she stood in as hostess since the Minister was unmarried. But afterwards she protested she was *"done up"* and took to her bed for a day or two.

One might argue that she underestimated Zog's political skills and overestimated the opportunities for manoeuvre open to him. For her, Zog remained the Mati chieftain rather than a representative, forward-looking national figure. But when, during the war, Fan Noli and Faik Konitza in America were prepared to work with Zog, as a symbol of national sovereignty, in an all-embracing national committee, she was prepared to throw her own weight behind them. (Incidentally, Fan Noli used to send her food parcels.)

The Foreign Office did not want to know. The head of the Eastern European department, when informally approached, replied: *"Zog! What is Zog but a brigand?"* Behind this brush-off was an imperial arrogance which assumed that when peace-brokering came round again, every option would be open and Whitehall would call the odds: an attitude of cynical pragmatism which landed us (not to mention the Albanians) for fifty years with the paranoid, pseudo-Marxist regime of Enver Hoxha.

Edith Durham died a year before the war ended. She did not see the bolshevisation of Eastern Europe. And even if she had done, she would have interpreted it, not in current political terms, but as another phase of the thousand year struggle, backwards and forwards, of Teuton and Slav.

Nor, fortunately, did she see the surrender of her beloved Albania to an alien and irrelevant ideology. But it already seemed to her, in that last year or so of her life, that all she had worked for was being swept away on the wilfully witless tides of history.

We know better; and although she is beyond our powers of reassurance, we can salute her memory and pay tribute to her unique achievement, and to the generous and disinterested spirit in which it was undertaken.

[1] Philip Guadalla, *'Men of War'*, Hodder & Stoughton 1927, pp 40 & 41.

Pall Mall Gazette, March 17th 1903
From An Albanian's Point of View
by M. E. Durham

"Englishmans," said the Tame Albanian, "silly mans! No understand my people. My people all one week like this," Here he waved his arms round violently. "Next week go back work. All quiet. Englishmans no understand that."

The Tame Albanian, as you perceive, is a very superior person; he has travelled much and speaks several tongues with fluent inaccuracy. In the days of his youth he was a Bashi-Bazouk, and had a sportive time sharp-shooting in the Balkans during the Russo-Turkish war Now he has settled down peacefully to a trade; but his eyes still gleam when he recalls the good old shot-and-powder times *"Reg'lar army all Mahommedan,"* he says with lofty contempt, *"I good Christian. I Bashi-Bazouk,"* from which I learned for the first time that Christianity and Bashi-Bazouks were connected, a fact which the latter's reputation had not led me to suspect. He enjoyed himself for a little while over pleasingly gory reminiscences. You may catch an Albanian and tame him, and dress him in the garments of Western civilization, and teach him a trade or a handicraft, and he will excel in it, for your Albanian is no fool, but - he remains always an Albanian.

He is tame in the sense that the domestic cat is tame. No self-respecting cat ever forgets that it used to be a wild beast, nor does the Albanian. This is, however, only my narrow Western view of the matter. The tame Albanian differs with me entirely According to him, it is we who are uncivilized. *"Now I tell you,"* he says, *"that London! I know him! Five million peoples! And what a lot of criminals! Oh, your people bad people. In my country all kind good mans. Perhaps you all alone, got no money, tired, hungry. You knock at door. 'Ullo, what you want?' 'I hungry.' 'Come in.' Then he give you bread, wine, tobacco, all what you want. Now, in London if you knock at door he says, 'You run 'way or I call a p'leece!'"* His words called up before me a vivid picture of the sufferings of a luckless foreigner adrift in our big city I admitted that we did not understand Oriental hospitality, and rejoiced him greatly, for he felt he had proved his point.

He expatiated on and waxed eloquent over the glories of his fatherland. *"What finest country in the world!"* he said. *"Now I tell you how fine. That Austria and them Italy, and that there Russia, and, and, all of 'em, they all wants my country"* (he swelled with pride at the thought); *"but they ain't going to have it. That Prince of Montenegro, he'd like it; if he thinks he'll get it, he's making a mistake."* Then, breaking off suddenly, *"You know them Montenegrins?"* he asked. *"Very well."* said I. *"Now, how much they make you pay for stay one night at X...?"*

I told him. Since he has taken to trade he pursues it with the same energy with which he formerly hunted Servians and Bulgarians, and his interest in prices is keen. When he learnt the amount of my very moderate bill he was filled with disgust *"What!"* he said, *"that all. You a British fem'le, and they only ask -? What silly, silly fools. Them Montenegrins don't know nothing!"* I steered him back to the subject of his own country. *"Then you would rather belong to the Turks?"* I suggested. He grinned. *"Isn't the government very bad?"* I asked. *"There ain't no government,"* said the Tame Albanian proudly. *"Surely the taxes are very high?"* *"Oo pay?"* asked he with a chortle; *"You tell me that, oo pay?"* He admitted that money had to be collected at intervals, but you always lived in hope that it would be raised off the next village and not yours, and if you displayed a proper amount of spirit, it usually was. A *"government"* that cannot govern is too charming a thing to be lightly cast away, and so long as the said *"government"* keeps itself well in the background, the Albanian, both wild and tame, is prepared to support it. Meanwhile, he swaggers about heavily armed and clad in the costume of a gentleman of the Middle Ages. The only modern things about him are his revolver and his well-filled cartridge belt; his ideas are as antique as his costume, and his habit of shaving all the hair off the front of his head and letting it grow long behind gives him an extraordinarily grotesque appearance. He made no concealment of the contempt he feels for the Turk, and he boasts of the greatness and the valour of his own people, and he intimates that the Turkish Empire owes its continued existence (in Europe that is) largely to them and that they control its destinies.

"And when will the war break out?" I ask the Tame Albanian. *"Things look pretty bad."* *"War?"* says the Tame Albanian, looking as wise as though the whole matter lay in his hands; *"There ain't going to be no war. Englishmans silly mans. No understand my people."*

Pall Mall Gazette, October 25th 1904
Slavonic Anglophobia
by M. E. Durham

Sir,

It is often of interest to see ourselves as others see us. Last spring, when on relief work in Macedonia, circumstances suddenly threw a vivid flashlight on the Pan-Slavonic attitude towards England.

I was stationed at Ochrida when the Russo-Japanese war was declared. The population, rather to my surprise, was intensely pro-Russian. News in Turkish papers is limited, but, as I received cuttings from the *'Times'* pretty regularly, Ochrida was kept well informed. The news of the Russian reverses was not at first believed. His Grace the Bulgarian Bishop characterised it as *"a pack of English lies."* When it proved true, there was much dismay, and the Bulgarian revolutionary party seemed to think their chances gone for the time being. Then a Russian newspaper correspondent arrived. He was making a round of the revolutionary centres, and his advent was a great event. I happened to have some business with the Bishop, and as I was entering the palace, I met the Russian coming out.

I found His Grace, who had been rather depressed, in a most valiant frame of mind. He attacked me at once. *"England,"* he said, *"had been fighting Russia under cover of the Japanese flag, with English vessels, English officers, English weapons. All Russia knew it was England that had to be dealt with."* He had a piece of news for me that I should be sorry to hear. Russia had beaten Japan, and would soon occupy the whole of it. England had always been the foe of the Balkan Slavs, and had attacked their only friend. Now she would pay for it! Christianity was the greatest power in the world, and would triumph in the end. England was not a Christian country and would soon be wiped out by Holy Russia - the sooner the better!"

As the peasants in the neighbourhood, his grace's flock, were living for the most part on British flour, I did not think this quite polite. He continued to pour out a torrent, but he was too ignorant a man to be worth arguing with. *"You will lose India,"* he cried. *"You will, you will! All the world knows you have no army. You are very proud of your navy. What is a navy? Nothing, I tell you, nothing! I have seen a navy and I know."*
"Your grace is doubtless thinking of the Bulgarian one," said I, after which I made my adieux.

Upon another occasion he had the kindness to tell me that it would be possible to take me and put me up to ransom, as they had done with Miss Stone. I laughed at him, and told him he would not get a single piastre for me. He thereupon added that Miss Stone might have been killed. I jeered at this, too, saying, *"You kill me, and you will have the whole of civilised Europe against you."*

We exchanged other amenities.

The present violent and unjustifiable attack on our fishing fleet has recalled this outbreak of Pan-Slavonic virulence to me very vividly. It was apparently derived from the Russian newspaper men, and perhaps is popular in Russia.

Yours truly,
M. Edith Durham
20, Ellesdale Road,
London N.W.

The Times, March 6th 1905
The Situation in Macedonia
by M. E. Durham

To the Editor of The Times

Sir,

In your interesting leader of to-day on Macedonia you observe that some statements made by Lord Percy in the recent debate in the House of Commons *"can only be read with astonishment"*. One of these is that the slow progress of the reform scheme had been and is at this moment due to the action of the Revolutionary Committee. From personal experience, I wish most emphatically to support Lord Percy's statement. During the five months that I spent last year travelling in Turkish territory, it was forced on me daily that no improvement could be expected till it was discovered what Power was supporting the Macedonian Committee and the committee was suppressed with a heavy hand. One of the several weak points in the reform scheme is that it demanded and obtained the release of all political prisoners arrested during the late insurrection, with no regard for the undoubted guilt of many of them. And it took no efficient means to grapple with the results. People in England little know the rule of terror exercised by that committee. The unhappy peasants told me everywhere the same dreary tale *"Some men from the committee came here. We were obliged to rise, or the committee would have shot us."*

A Bulgarian Bishop asked me repeatedly to supply food for brigand bands; agents of the committee had been levying blackmail under pain of death from persons very strongly opposed to the committee's plans. A man connected with the revolutionary movement told me, *"Next time we shall kill all the Consuls, and Europe will have to listen to us."* He seemed to imagine that the Powers could be terrorized as easily as the peasants. And on examination he did not pretend that the committee's action had any other purpose than the extension of Bulgarian territory.

It has been popularly supposed in England that the Macedonian Committee has been behaving with great discretion and has been holding its hand in order to give the reform scheme a chance. It has done no such thing.

It is true that it has abstained, for political reasons, from killing Turks, but it has organized a long series of murderous attacks on both Greeks and Serbs. These it can slaughter with comparative impunity, as, in deference to the wish of Europe, the Turks have not employed military force.

These are some of the facts that should be more widely known.

I am, Sir,

yours faithfully,

M. E. Durham
20, Ellerdale Road,
Hampstead,
March 1

The Contemporary Review, November 1908.
'Constitution' in North Albania
by M. Edith Durham

It is but two months ago that not only North Albania but all Europe was stunned by the proclamation of the Constitution in the Turkish Empire, and friend and foe alike were forced to wonder and admiration of the speed and sureness with which the almost bloodless revolution was effected.

Without stopping to enquire, and without having the faintest idea what manner of thing a *"Constitution"* might be, the bulk of the Sultan's subjects in Europe hailed it with enthusiasm - solely on the ground that any change must be for the better The most extraordinary scenes of rejoicing took place in the towns; Christians and Moslems embraced and swore brotherhood; streets rang with patriotic songs. The whole atmosphere was one of:*"Liberty! Freedom! Tyranny is dead! Fly hence - proclaim - cry it about the streets!"*

Even the most sceptical outsiders were temporarily swept along by the torrent of enthusiasm. Nor was the scene marred by any acts of rowdyism or ruffianism. The order maintained by the people themselves forced one to believe that, properly handled, they were capable of great things in the way of national development.

But to proclaim a new Government is one thing. To put it in working order is quite another. Moreover, the mass of different races that compose the Turkish Empire necessitates a somewhat different treatment for each district. The first wave of hope and enthusiasm is past, and the difficulties now begin.

It was my great good fortune to pass nearly three months travelling among the Roman Catholic mountain tribes of North Albania previous to the Constitution and to hear their views and desires. I was met everywhere by entreaties for help against the intolerable yoke of the Turkish Government. In the *'Great Mountains'*, complaints were most bitter against the Turkish Governor of the mountains, Shachir Bey - his tyranny and his injustice. The tribes were on the edge of revolt, and had already refused to obey several of his orders. In many cases only the women - and they don't count - still went into Scutari. The tribesmen everywhere vowed that they would acclaim any European Power that would step in and rule justly. It was everywhere reported and believed that a Moslem attack on the Christian tribes was to take place towards the end of September. All the border Moslem tribes and the Moslems of Kosovo vilayet had a few months previously been well armed - it was said

M. Edith Durham: Albania and the Albanians

by the Government - with Mausers and plenty of ammunition. The Christians, on the other hand, were very poorly armed with weapons of all patterns - often flint locks - and were unable to obtain others except at enormous price as contraband, a Mauser cartridge, for example, costing almost sixpence. In case of such an attack, they had not the means of defence.

In England, these tribes are usually described as free and content. But their condition was, and is, truly pitiable. Their so-called independence is merely nominal, and has been bought at a heavy price. They have retained it only by remaining isolated in the mountains, apart from all civilisation, leading wretched lives of poverty, squalor and suffering, greatly neglected by the Roman Catholic Church, whose children they are.

Their tribal laws are of a most barbarous description, and inflict cruelly heavy punishments, which are rigorously carried out. Remonstrance always bring the reply, *"We must; it is the law!"* or *"We cannot; we have no law for it!"* a reply that leads one to hope that, under better laws, justly administered, they would prove very much more law abiding than is usually reported; as is, indeed, shown by the fact that in other lands they make good citizens.

Some of the more enlightened wished for a joint occupation by the Powers (the Seven Kings, as they are usually called) after the plan of the Cretan occupation - to be withdrawn when order was restored and the people fit for independence. Others did not mind which of the Seven Kings ruled - provided he were not a Slav - so long as the present order of things was changed. The unanimous appeal through the Great Mountains, Pulati and Dukagini, was *"Save us from the Turks"*.

As my journey proceeded things became acute. Finally the Great Mountains drew up an ultimatum demanding the dismissal of Shachir Bey, and stating that, in case of refusal, the Turkish authorities alone would be responsible for the results. It was a threat of immediate insurrection. The wildest rumours were afloat - declaration of war, the intervention of a foreign Power at the people's entreaty. They were prepared, it seemed, to risk beginning a fight with an inadequate supply of ammunition, saying that, if no Power helped them, it was better to die than continue such a life.

And on to this red-hot material came the sudden and quite unexpected news of 'the Constitution'. Of course none of the tribesmen had the least idea what a 'the Constitution' might be. (Nor, indeed, to this day is it known how its terms will be applied to the peculiar conditions of tribal

Page 8

mountain life, which require special treatment.) All they grasped was that the much-desired change of Government was come. They asked eagerly which of the Seven Kings was coming - Austria, Italy or what other - and their hopes were greatly dashed when they heard it was only the Sultan over again. Of representative government they have no conception; *'Government'* means in their minds an absolute autocrat possessed of great wealth. *"The Turk,"* they said, *"is always a Turk."* and they hung back, hesitant.

They had immediate proof, however, that a change had come in the order of things, for their petition for the dismissal of Shachir Bey was granted almost as soon as presented; and, filled with high hopes, they flocked to Scutari and acclaimed a Constitution. So far their conduct has been highly creditable. They obeyed the command to hand over a man who had shot another in vendetta, instead of punishing him, as previously, by tribal law. But the fact remained that their hopes of a *"good time coming"* are of too extravagant a nature to be fulfilled at once: they are a child-people, and if disappointed will consider themselves deceived and betrayed. The situation is no easy one to manage.

The other tribes, both Christian and Moslem, not in this Scutari district, held festivals and proclaimed the Constitution at their various meeting centres.

The exceptions to this are the districts of Gusinje, Plava and Peja, inhabited almost entirely by very fanatical Moslems. They arranged to celebrate it by a festival, as had all the others, and I am told even began to assemble for the purpose; but a terrible dispute took place for right of precedence - Peja claiming first place as the largest town, Plava as the oldest, and Gusinje for being the bravest or best or some equally good reason. The meeting broke up in great disorder.

Of the Christians, the great Catholic tribe of Mirdita and its neighbour Kthela alone made no sign. Mirdita is in a unique position. It has an hereditary prince, Prenk Pasha, of the Bib Doda family. But he has been an exile in Turkish hands for almost thirty years, and the tribe has remained leaderless. When the Scutari Committee of Government sent to know the reason of the non-appearance of the Mirdites, they replied that they were waiting for their Prince, and could accept no new form of government without him. Moreover, that they do not belong to Scutari, and will hold any festival in their own territory. And there the matter had to rest. It was the first check. Prenk Pasha's return was arranged for shortly. He will re-enter his territory in a few days time, and developments on this point are of great interest, his own tribe and many others having the greatest veneration for him, his decision will probably be final.

Previous to the *'Constitution'*, the greater part of the vilayet of Kosovo had been for many years practically closed to travellers, and remained almost unvisited by Europeans. Such as penetrated it had to do so without Government knowledge or permission, and did so at their own risk - which was considerable. Or they were sent with a vast escort, which took care that they should see nothing. The Turkish Government, well aware of the constant persecution of both Roman Catholics and Orthodox Christians which was going on there, had the greatest objection to the true state of things being known. And no Power intervened. Any strangers found in certain districts were at once held up and turned back.

My previous effort via Gusinje had failed. But when the *'Constitution'* was not a month old I applied for and at once received Government permission to go to Prizren by any route I pleased, which meant that I was free of the whole vilayet. The district had sworn a *'besa' (oath of peace)* till the beginning of November and a considerable portion had accepted the Constitution. The authorities were only too pleased to find a solitary female who was willing to demonstrate the success of the new régime by visiting the most evilly reputed district without arms or armed escort.

I started for Djakova - travelling with some Moslem kirijees and a string of pack horses laden with hides. The slowness of travel gave plenty of time for conversation on the way. It all ran on the *'Constitution'*. At Puka they had had a great local festivity - had enjoyed themselves hugely; now they would like to know what it was about, what had happened, why nothing had yet been done. I counselled patience and good conduct, and hoped for the best.

Leaving the pack-beasts to follow another trail, I went on through the land of Hasi, a large, almost wholly Moslem, tribe of some 800 "houses" (a "house" is averaged at ten persons) or more. Towards mid-day we were hailed by a long, lean Moslem, who knew the kirijee. His surprise at seeing me was great. I do not think he had ever seen a woman *"Alla franga"* before. *"It is Constitution,"* he said, *"or you would not have been allowed here."* He civilly suggested we should come to his house for our mid-day halt, as he had water, and we should find none on the trail for two hours. So we followed him to a spot unmarked on the map, and found the promised water and repose, but were not asked into his house. His womenfolk - unveiled, as is the custom with all the Moslem hill tribes - looked at us from a distance, but were not allowed to approach.

Our host was completely mystified about *'Constitution'*. I was the first striking phenomenon connected with it that had as yet appeared. He plied us with questions as to *"What?"*, *"When?"*, *"How?"*, *"Where?"* and *"Why it was?"*; *"How long it would be?"* etc.; all most difficult to reply to, as he hadn't the faintest idea what he was talking about.

We arrived at Djakova in the evening, hurrying to get in before sundown. It is a large town, consisting almost entirely of Moslems of bad repute. I made an attempt to get there five years ago, but was sent back. My arrival now caused a good deal of sensation, as I was the first traveller in since *'Constitution'* and also, so I was told, the first foreign woman within anyone's recollection. The population was not at all pleased to see me. *"We have only had 'Constitution' a month, and the Giaours have already begun to come."*

The Roman Catholics have, by recent persecution, been reduced to 20 families. Of Orthodox Christians there are rather less than 100 houses at the other end of the town. They do not associate. Without the town are a number of Catholic villages, which were attacked last winter by the Moslems - 72 houses (many of them large *"family groups"* of even 50 persons) were burnt and plundered. The perfectly innocent inhabitants have received no compensation from the Government and no help from any foreign Power, and have to face the coming winter houseless and penniless. These people, it is hardly necessary to say, were all in a state of terror, and placed no faith in the *'Constitution'* at all. That order could easily be kept by a military force they all allowed. Also, that if the prestige of the fanatical leaders were broken they would have few followers. They did not believe a Turkish Government would do it, but were trying to hope, rather unsuccessfully.

I visited the Bimbashi, who, pro tem., is local Governor in place of the Kaimakam lately evicted. A local report said he had been evicted by mistake, being really a Young Turk; but that as soon as the ignorant Moslem population heard that the Constitution meant freedom for everyone they concluded there was no further use for Governors, and got rid of him. This tale is on a par with a remark I heard from a hill tribesman. He asked if the prison in Scutari had yet been pulled down, because if we were all to be free there would be no use for it.

The Bimbashi was very courteous and anxious to show that all was going on for the best under the best of Governments. Unluckily he only spoke Turkish, so we conversed by dragoman, and the whole room could hear. A large divan round two sides was full of squatting listeners. The Bimbashi said he was very busy reconciling blood feuds - he was, in fact, signing documents every other minute - and that he hoped peace would soon be established all round. With the best of intentions I said it was a very good work, and I, too, hoped for peace. At once a bearded, turbaned Moslem, with great pent-house eyebrows, shouted indignantly, and a murmur arose. *"Tell that woman,"* he said, *"she is not to meddle with our affairs. She has no right to speak. It is the Sultan's business."* He appeared extremely angry. My dragoman said we had better go. So after a few thanks and compliments I left, the Bimbashi giving me a Zaptieh as escort back, who hurried me through the stinking streets as fast as he could. The Christian who had accompanied me to the konak was so much alarmed by the remarks my appearance excited that he said he would not come out with me again for even £5 sterling. Indeed, he kept his hand on his revolver all the way, and I was only afraid that he might fire out of sheer nervousness. I believe myself he had greatly exaggerated ideas of the danger. But *'a scalded child dreads cold water'*.

There is no doubt, however, that the state of things around Djakova is very much *'in the balance'*. The neighbouring Moslems were mostly, it appears, sworn in under quite false pretences. Who is responsible I know not. I heard various tales as to what had occurred. One was that 40 battalions of Austrians were mobilised on the frontier - a man had seen them. The Constitution was to summon the people to war against them. A second tale was *'War with Russia'*. A third - generally believed - was that Shamsi Pasha, furious at not being invited to some large local festival, summoned the tribesmen to the railway station of Ferizovitch to fire on the train bringing guests, under the excuse that they were enemies. The scheme was frustrated by the skill of the engineer, who backed out his train; but the tribesmen remained to await the foe, and were promptly sworn in by the Young Turk Party, and remained under the impression that the *'Constitution'* was against the foe they had originally been summoned to combat.

The oath, however, holds good till the first week in November, and meanwhile the state of peace is quite unparalleled. I drove all over the plain of Kosovo in a local cart without arms or escort. Moslems even were going about unarmed. One man told me that he had never done so before, and that two months ago it had been very dangerous to go from Prishtina to the railway station, almost an hour's drive. Everywhere people said, *"It is like a dream - it cannot be true."* At Devich, a Servian monastery in a lonely spot among the mountains, a vast crowd of pilgrims came to the festival - over 2,000 - owing to the safety of travelling. All the land was peace. I had no adventures. But the net result was unsatisfactory.

Only by military force and a strong hand can peace be maintained. For by no means all desire it. The Slavonic peasants desire it greatly; they wish only to cultivate their land in quiet. The Servian leaders certainly do not desire it, as the establishment of law and order would effectually put an end to all their hopes of future annexation of territory, for the Slav population is very much in the minority, and in event of just treatment can have no further claim. The Moslems will resent any attempt to tamper with their rights, which include exemption from military service; and the Roman Catholics distrust all that hails from Stamboul, saying that only Christian rule will give justice to Christians.

I returned from Kosovo Plain and Prizren through a tract of wholly Moslem land, unknown and unmapped. I have since heard that it has not previously been crossed by a European traveller. The Austrians' staff map was hopelessly at fault, the course of both the Drin and its tributary the Mola being quite incorrectly given and most places not identifiable upon it.

Here things were very hopeless. Nothing but *'Constitution'* enabled me to get through it, and even with that talisman I doubt if I should have managed it but for the companion I picked up on the way, a man who was going up country to sell salt, sugar and coffee to a certain tribe, whose safe conduct he had. We met on the way the chief brigand, a celebrated holder up of travellers; but owing to the above circumstances he was quite cheery, and wished us *bon voyage*.

At our mid-day halt at a Moslem village, Suroji, however, we met his nephew and several comrades. He had evidently heard of us and had come to see. Being himself, when at leisure, in the salt and sugar trade he was much vexed at the presence of a rival. He demanded what right we had to come, and said I ought never to have been led through. If it were not for *'Constitution'*, I should not be allowed to set foot in the place. My salt and sugar man replied that I was under his protection, and that he was under the protection of Arnji, the tribe that had invited him.

The brigand's nephew objected to the Constitution if it meant the arrival of Giaours, and that anyone might come through and sell what he pleased. But he retired, grumbling, without molesting us. He was restrained merely by his *'besa' (oath of peace)*. An Albanian never breaks his *'besa'*. I knew I was in a land of reputed tigers, but I had sufficient faith in the strength of the leash that temporarily held them to proceed without fear, though I perceived they were straining upon it. It was advisable in these parts to ask no questions, but to be content with the remarks let fall.

Our next point - the salt and sugar man's destination - received us most hospitably as friends. We went forward with a guide picked up there. The only fact I learned about *'Constitution'* was that it undoubtedly meant war shortly; - with whom was unknown.

Our new guide turned nasty shortly after starting - picked a quarrel with the Moslem horse-boy, and applied bad names to him. Providentially, owing to *'Constitution'* the said kirijee had, for the first time in his life, left his revolver at home, a fact he deeply regretted; so we were spared a shooting affray which would otherwise have been inevitable.

The guide, at the early hour of 10 a.m., persisted in stopping at a friend's house to rest and eat. We remained outside until inspected, discussed and asked in. There was a large company of men, who appeared much displeased, and it was evident we were in a rather hot corner.

Knowing, of course, that we were "*Giaours*" (I and my dragoman), they asked the Moslem kirijee what news from Djakova and Prizren. He replied, *"All quiet."* Then they said, *"When will this Constitution be ready to begin? When are we to attack the Giaours? We are only waiting orders from Stamboul to drive out the lot."*

This was a new view of *'Constitution'*. It was an engine for the purpose of suppressing and exterminating the Giaours, who were getting too strong. They regarded it as part of the free Constitution scheme when the Moslems received the Mausers. (With regard to the Mauser story, I was told in one place that they were distributed by *"Old Turks"* who were nervous about the movements of the *"Young Turks"* and wished to secure fanatical followers, but they were outwitted by the *"Young"*.)

True, however, to the laws of Albanian hospitality, our hosts offered us food and drink; but I was not pleased when our guide proposed staying for the night - it was not yet mid-day - nor did I believe his tale that our destination was too far to be reached that day. I insisted on proceeding, and in spite of delay caused by his striking for his pay, shortly after starting, we arrived in almost two hours. He had possibly been instructed to impede our progress.

We found quarters among the small and rapidly dwindling flock of Roman Catholics in the large Moslem tribe of Luria - a tribe that has quite recently perverted. Luria's opinion also was that *'Constitution'* meant war. They wanted to know when it was to begin. The Moslem bairaktar (standard bearer) expressed it thus: *"We do not obey Sultan Hamid except when we choose - we are a free people. But this 'Constitution' is a war; we don't yet know if it is with Russia, Austria or Italy, but we shall flock like butterflies."* A Greek refugee, a handsome young assassin sheltering from justice, announced that he had seen war a few days ago in a glass of red wine. I wondered whether it were really a case of *in vino veritas*. It seemed hopeless to expect the Constitution to get much further without bloodshed.

Returning through Christian tribes, the situation was no more reassuring, though the difficulties were other. Everyone had a huge list of things - trifles such as railways, roads, factories and, above all, free schools - that were desired of the Government, and no one had the least idea that he himself had a duty towards the Government. The *'Constitution'* was a sort of *'magic dicky'* that was to create everything out of nothing. A rumour that they might have to contribute either work or money in order to attain these things caused great wrath. I vainly urged that in England also we paid taxes. They replied only, *"You are very foolish. You should make the Government pay. We won't have a poor Government. We want a rich one. If this Constitution is not rich enough to give us these things it can go to the devil."*

To my remark that railways could not be made at once and were costly, the reply was, *"My dear lady, they cost nothing. They are made by companies."* A man of Kthela, whose remarks were highly approved of, said, *"We have had this Constitution nearly two months, and it has given us none of these things. If by the end of six weeks it has not made security of property, established order and begun the other works, good-bye Constitution!"* His hearers thought him most reasonable. I said his demands were quite impossible to fulfil in the time. *"The Constitution,"* I was told, *"can do what it chooses. If it does not choose to do these things it had better go."*

To organise sufficient gendarmerie to keep order was alone, I urged, too great a task for six weeks. They promptly replied that they did not want any zaptiehs - were not afraid of them either. *"Our houses are of stone, and even with artillery the Turkish zaptiehs can't take them."* *"But you say you wish order kept, and then that you will resist an attempt to do so. How do you wish order to be made?"* *"By the Constitution."* We ended as we began. I retired exhausted.

So far the career of *'the Constitution'* has been quite unprecedented in the history of revolutions. If it is to succeed its actions must be still more unprecedented. Its path is beset with every kind of difficulty. Whether there are men capable of dealing with them remains to be seen.

At any rate, the skill with which the affair has so far been conducted gives hope that a return to the old order of things is impossible, and that the changes that must come will be changes for the better.

M. Edith Durham

The Contemporary Review, January 1909
The Serb and Albanian Frontiers
by M. Edith Durham

It is said, and with truth, in the Balkans that with every fresh generation a fresh upheaval takes place. The present one has arrived, with great punctuality, thirty years after the last *'settlement'*. That *'settlement'*, i.e., the Treaty of Berlin, is, indeed, responsible for it, as - while pretending to arrange for the benefit of the Balkan people - it ignored, possibly intentionally, all their national aspirations and the distribution of races. And, when one of these peoples is, by stress of circumstances, exasperated almost to the point of war, the newspapers of other and more fortunate lands say *"these turbulent little places must be made to understand that no breach of the peace will be tolerated"*.

Some years ago I was in the Zoological Gardens when an urgent message was received that a pet bear, that had just mauled a stable boy, should be at once removed from some neighbouring barracks. The old bear-keeper said to me: *"I know bears and I know boys - nasty little beasts. No one will ever know what that poor bear suffered before he turned on that boy. I'm all for the bear!"* In delimiting the frontiers it appears that either the *'boys'* of Berlin were entirely ignorant or that they drew the said lines with the deliberate intention of preventing the development of certain races and of fomenting race-hatred. Few are aware of the number of lives that have been lost on these frontiers and the amount of bitterness that has been created and fostered. During the past eight years I have yearly travelled the western half of the Balkan peninsula, and bit by bit have managed to see both sides of all the frontiers and get through all of the Debatable Lands of the Serbs and Albanians. I can only say that the whole arrangement of land distribution seems to have been planned with the intention of so weakening each race that it might speedily fall into Austrian power. And that, circumstances being so, Austria has, for the whole thirty years, been working steadily and quite unscrupulously to attain that end. No tricks have been too dirty to be employed, and money has been spent with extraordinary lavishness, though many parts of the Austrian dominions had in consequence to be starved.

Let us examine some of the frontiers. Perhaps that of the Herzegovina is the most unjust. The Herzegovina in English means *'the Duchy'*. It was the province of a certain Herzog Stefan, a mediæval Servian princeling. By blood, belief and superstition, by tongue and by custom, the Herzegovinians are one and the same as the Montenegrins. You can say that Montenegrins are Herzegovinians or that Herzegovinians are

Montenegrins. Montenegro was formed almost wholly of tribes from Bosnia and the Herzegovina that took refuge there in the mountains and managed to maintain independence against the Turks. Its boundaries were ever fluctuating, according to the fortunes of war. The tribes remaining in what is known as the Herzegovina, though under Turkish rule, managed in the mountainous parts to retain a certain amount of independence, their tribal system and internal tribal administration, and were in perpetual enmity with the Turkish Government. In 1876 they arose to struggle for freedom, and the stand they made was as heroic as any known to history. They were joined by their Montenegrin brethren - Prince Nikola himself is of Herzegovinian descent - and were the firebrand that ultimately kindled the Russo-Turkish War. Primarily to the Herzegovinians is due the fact that any of the Christian people of the Balkans were then freed from Turkish rule.

The combined Montenegrins and Herzegovinians fought their way victoriously right up to Mostar, and took Spitza, on the coast, as well as Antivari and Dulcigno. Spitza, entirely a Slav town, alone cost three hundred lives. If ever a people earned freedom the Herzegovinians did. What reward did they get? The English people, perhaps then more than at any other time, displayed its capacity for cant. After holding Christian meetings and preaching freedom for the South Slavs, it acquiesced in the handing over of these peoples to a foreign and most detested rule - that of Austria. Exhausted though they were with a long struggle, they again sprang to arms. It was only at the request of the Prince of Montenegro - so they themselves tell - that they finally laid them down, with the understanding (do not make any mistake about this) that the Austrian occupation was but to be temporary and preparatory to their freedom.

The frontiers delimited united a small portion of the Herzegovina to Montenegro, the stones and bare bones, for the line was so made that the cultivable plains went mostly to Austria. So carelessly was it drawn with regard to the rights of the inhabitants that, in one case at least, it passed between a village and its wood supply. The forest that belonged to it was beyond the frontier.

That this did not make for peace it is unnecessary to say. Nor was the frontier handled with tact. I have it from an Austrian official that in order to be sure that the soldiers guarding it should have no sympathy with the Slav inhabitants, a Hungarian regiment was sent there. The patrol meeting a Montenegrin with two sheep on their side of the border challenged him, and, not understanding his reply, shot him as a sheep stealer. It transpired - too late - that they were his own sheep that had strayed. He possibly did not know he was over the border. Shortly after the bodies of two Austrian gendarmes were found hanging on a tree in the grey of the morning. And this sort of thing was frequent. In 1882 a serious rising took place. The Herzegovinian has stood firm. He never wanted the Austrian, and he will not be one. He faces the Austrian authorities with a mule-like passive resistance which they cannot overcome. Even when they offer him - dirt cheap - iron ploughs, far superior to his ancestral wooden ones, he refuses to purchase. *"They may be better, but I will not be a Schwab!"* Lately the Herzegovinians have emigrated in great numbers to America. And all the time they have asked of Austrian rule: *"How long, oh Lord? Oh, Lord, how long?"*

Another Austrian official - more than one - has said to me: *"Our Government has never understood these people. The money spent on them is wasted. They hate us worse now than they did at the beginning."* The Slavonic lands of the Herzegovina were given to Austria, and bad blood was created. To compensate Montenegro, Albanian lands were given her, and, if possible, worse blood was created. The purely Slav town of Spitza was given as a port to Austria. The purely Albanian town of Dulcigno - which, though they took it, the Montenegrins failed to hold and which old records show never to have been Slav - was given to Montenegro.

The forced cession of Dulcigno to Montenegro was one of the most unpardonable pieces of political jobbery. It was engineered largely by Mr. Gladstone, who, never having visited it, seems to have believed it was Turkish. Spitza was close by, and was the natural port for Montenegro; but the Powers preferred intimidating a small and defenceless people - the Albanians - to depriving Austria of any of her ill-deserved booty. Dulcigno has never recovered its former position as a trading port, for its seafaring inhabitants left it almost en masse; the Montenegrins have failed to develop it, and its cession to this day keeps raw the hatred between Slav and Albanian. And Austria, counting on the ease with which she advanced before, counts on repeating the process.

The cession of Dulcigno was forced in place of that of Gusinjè, another Albanian town. Gusinjè being inland, the Powers were unable to *"navally demonstrate"* there, and could not enforce their foolish orders. The vague frontier there has never since been properly rectified. It trails somewhere over wild mountains, and neither side recognises it. The number of men shot on it in the past thirty years has been equal to a war. A large tract of valuable pasture is always in dispute. The Montenegrins claim that the Berlin Treaty gave it them. It has been the ancestral property of the Kelmendi, one of the finest of the Albanian Catholic tribes, for centuries. They say boldly *"If the Sultan wants to make a present of land let him give Constantinople, which belongs to him, and not the land of our forefathers. We can and will defend it."*

Only three months ago, when riding this frontier on the Albanian side, a woman begged leave to come with me along a certain part, saying she was terrified of the Montenegrin sharpshooters, and that they would not fire at a stranger. And on the Montenegrin side I found the same thing a year or two ago.

Continuing the Montenegrin frontier, perhaps the stupidest blunder of all is the drawing of it through the middle of the territories of the Vasojevich tribe. Vasojevich, a renowned Servian fighting tribe, was for long semi-independent and very strong. Thus divided, the portion left on Turkish territory is liable to constant persecution. When this happens, and it is of yearly occurrence, its brethren in free Montenegro are naturally wild to go to its help. Reprisals always take place, and, as has been picturesquely remarked, *"the frontier floats on blood"*.

I repeat emphatically that I find it hard to believe that the frontier drawers of Berlin can have been so badly informed as to have done these things in crass ignorance. Why shove the Austrian down on the Slav and the Slav down on the Albanian unless bloodshed and race hatred were desired?

Further along, where the Tara tears through a deep valley and makes a frontier all can see, less fighting naturally takes place. But the line is no more just. For it divides Montenegro from the Sanjak of Novi-Bazar, and thereby from union with Servia. The Sanjak was, in old days, the heart of the old Servian Empire, Rascia. Its line of kings, the Nemanja, sprang from the Zeta (now part of Montenegro), and the bulk of the people of the Sanjak are to this day Servian. I do not include, of course, the Turkish army, a certain number of which are quartered in it, much less the Austrian intruder. The so-called Turks in the district are almost entirely Serbs, whose ancestors were renegades. The remainder are Orthodox Christians. The number of Albanians in the upper part of the Sanjak is very small. The truly Albanian territory begins near Mitrovitza, which itself is a modern and mixed town. Had the delimiters of territories desired or intended the development of the Servian people, the obvious and only thing to do was to join them by this strip and give Servia - a fertile land - the chance of exporting her goods viâ Montenegro and Spitza as part of the coast line.

Berlin decreed that a path should be left for Austria to pass through, so it appears. And Europe is surprised because Austria has shown signs of intending to do so. Strangest of all, Austria was given the right to keep a large military force in the Sanjak *"to guard the Bosnian frontier"*. As though Germany kept soldiers in France *"to protect Alsace"*! A more anomalous position can hardly be imagined. The inhabitants of the Sanjak have not appreciated it, and dark tales are current of the number of Austrian soldiers who have foolishly taken a walk and been belated - and have never come back. The Sanjak arrangement has wholly paralysed both Servia and Montenegro, and Austria has lost no opportunity of trying to strangle each preparatory to swallowing it.

Austria has blocked the former trade route of Servia through Bosnia - which did considerable business - and has strenuously opposed any attempt at making a railway through the Sanjak. I have been repeatedly assured, and violently, by Austrians: *"We will never permit it."* A Hungarian once said to me frankly: *"Our policy is to cut the Serbs in pieces till they are powerless. They must never be allowed to unite or they will be too strong for us"*. And on this principle Austria has acted. No diplomacy is too low to employ to this end.

Servia has no outlet to West Europe save through Austria. Over Turkish territory to Salonika, and thence by sea, is a slow and lengthy alternative. Time after time has the Servian frontier been blocked by Austria, and the land practically besieged, as far as trade goes, in order to force the unhappy little land to comply with some outrageous Austrian demand, and no opportunity has ever been lost to blacken the character of the people. The press agencies of Vienna pour out sensational reports with the hope that no one will dare visit the place and learn the truth. Two men only have to quarrel over the price of a pig in a Servian market for the Vienna press to report: *"More riots in Servia! Serious disturbances! Police intervention!"* etc, etc. And the land is said to be constantly visited by Austrian agitators striving to excite revolution.

In Montenegro I know this to be the case, as I have frequently heard so-called Austrian commercial travellers in village inns haranguing the people as to the defects of the Montenegrin Government and the benefits to be derived from Austria. There was also an Austrian Vice-Consul who used to blacken the character of Prince Nikola, his family, and the Government; also the people in general - to English tourists. And he began this before he had been a week in the land. That the recent bomb affair in Montenegro was entirely an Austrian attempt to provoke a quarrel between Servia and Montenegro, few who have followed it can doubt. It was intended probably as a prelude to the advance on Salonika, which was to have been begun as soon as the Uvatz-Mitrovitza section of the railway was finished. The quite unexpected turn of events in Turkey upset this plan, but temporarily only, unless steps are taken to block the route.

Now Austria is trying to force the exasperated Serbs to declare war, and, not content with this, is striving to excite the Albanians to fight the Turks or the Montenegrins - she does not care who fights whom so long as some one will *"open the ball"* and give her the chance of intervening *"to maintain peace"*; this would, of course, require an army of occupation. The Albanians are told they will be helped if they will only begin.

Austrian plans are widely extended and embrace the whole of Albania. One must travel through the land to realise the great sums that have been spent on it - in hopes of buying the sympathies of the people - and the complicated network of intrigue.

The Roman Catholic Church in Albania is under Austrian protection, is subsidised and freely wirepulled. Quite recently, after having trained and installed Albanian priests in place of the Italians and Austrians who before prevailed, Austria realised that a united and patriotic priesthood might prove too strong for her, and has striven, by skilful intrigue, to split them into rival parties. The ground was almost *'salted'* - Austria was going ahead - when Italy interposed, with the result that the two Powers agreed to *"maintain the status quo in Albania"*, until, of course, one or other is in position to upset it. This means that one intrigues against the other, that the people are bribed and demoralised in consequence by both, and that their development and civilisation are greatly retarded.

The recognition of the Albanian nation and its emancipation from the toils of those who wish to absorb it is most earnestly to be desired. It was neither recognised nor considered by Berlin, but in any further arrangements must and will have a voice in the matter, for the Albanians are the oldest inhabitants of the land - were there before the arrival of either Serb or Bulgar. The Serbs were not settled in numbers till the beginning of the seventh century A.D., and the Bulgar invasion was yet later. Bulgar and Serb each in turn built an empire and swayed the Balkan peoples, and each empire in turn fell shortly after the death of the strong man that made it.

The empires of both in turn ruled almost all Albania for a brief period, but their frontiers were too fluctuating and their existence too short to be taken as precedents for fresh delimitation. And when both were overthrown and crippled by the Turk the day of the Albanian came. Space does not permit a detailed history. Suffice it to say that very shortly after the battle of Kosovo (1389), fatal to the Serbs, the Albanians began steadily to gain power, and continuously pushed the Serbs back and back. The fact that very many Albanians turned Moslem, and thereby acquired rank and position under the Turkish Government, aided this, but was not the cause of it. The Catholic Albanians also played a great part in it. Moreover, a large number of Slavs also became Moslem, but did not thereby acquire Albanian land.

At last, finding the situation intolerable, the Servian Bishop of Ipek, in 1690, accepted the offer of Austrian protection (Austria has long looked Balkan-wards), and migrated with a huge following of many thousand families to the strip of land north of the Save, where their descendants still live, and the bishopric was transferred to Carlovitz. They went; and they practically evacuated their former lands, which have since been for the most part re-settled by the descendants of the original inhabitants, the Albanians. The Serbs call the territory, fondly, Old Servia. The Albanians have as good a right to call it Old Illyria. It was Servian once; and Calais belonged to England. The conditions of the Middle Ages no longer exist. The fierce enmity between the two races on account of this territory is a cause of weakness to both, and renders more easy the entry of a foreign invader. Could they but come to an understanding over it, they could cry *"Hands off!"* to all comers, but this appears to be impossible.

As the territory has been but little visited of late by English travellers, some notes about it may be of interest. It consists mainly of two large tracts of undulating land, divided from each other by mountains, the plain of Kosovo and the district called Metohia. The Metohia is highly fertile and well watered by the White Drin and tributaries.

To the south of it lies Djakova, a purely Albanian town, almost entirely Moslem. The Kaimakam vaguely gave its population as *"between two and three thousand houses"* (a house is reckoned at eight inhabitants. No correct census has ever been made in Turkey). Of these houses rather less than a hundred are Orthodox Servian. Such Serbs as I spoke with mixed a great deal of Albanian in their speech, and used dialect forms of Servian. The land around Djakova is solid Albanian, the villages all being offshoots from various well-known mountain tribes, e.g., Shala, Fandi, Berisha - very many of them Roman Catholic. Immediately north of Djakova is a tract of rough uncultivated scrub land - goat pasture - sparsely inhabited. Following up the White Drin the land is fertile, and one comes to small palisaded Servian villages, where, I was told, the people were owners of their land.

A strip of scattered Serb villages, mixed with Albanian, extends up to Ipek, in the neighbourhood of which are many Serb peasants. The town of Ipek, as that of Djakova, has a very large Albanian majority. West of this Serb island - Dechani way - and the mountains beyond is Albanian. The people trace their origin from Shala. Crossing the White Drin and going westwards to the Monastery of Devich, I passed through Albanian-owned land, worked partly by Albanians and partly by Serbs, on the chiftlik system. Most of the people - they were not many - that we met spoke Albanian and were Moslem. Descending to Devich monastery we found a great concourse of Serb peasants, some 2,000. It was a feast day. The bulk of them came from the neighbourhood of Ipek, and a considerable number from near Mitrovitza. A few from near Prishtina.

The Serb *'island'* near Ipek is divided from the Serb Vasojevich district by the wholly Albanian mountain range between; the Rugova district is solid Albanian, which element extends northward to a considerable distance, I believe, but becomes more and more mixed with Serb.

From Prizren to Djakova all the villages passed were Albanian. Prizren itself, the former capital of Tsar Stefan Dushan in the days of Great Servia, surprised me. I had not expected to find the *"white city of the great Tsar"* so very Albanian. The large Servian theological school recently erected seemed a pathetic and useless struggle against the inevitable. The town is not Servian, and imported masters and even pupils - for boys from Montenegro often finish their studies here - cannot make it so. There is no such school in Montenegro, a wholly Serb land, and it struck me as a melancholy monument to a dead past.

The population as it at present stands is:
Servian: 950 houses
Catholic Albanian: 180 houses
Orthodox Vlach: 180 houses
Moslem (Albanian and Turk): 3500 houses.

The actual Turks are, I am told, in a considerable minority. I believe the figures to be fairly correct, as I tested them on various sides.

Driving from Prizren to Prishtina, with a Servian driver who was not likely to exaggerate the Albanian population, the villages were all wholly or partly Albanian, mostly wholly, e.g., Korisha, half-Serb, half-Catholic Albanians of Fandi; Suhareka, Moslem Albanian; Pechang probably also. At Grachanitza, by the magnificent old Servian monastery church, is a large Servian village; this lies east of the Sitnitza river. Roughly speaking, Kosovo Polje appears now to be mainly Albanian west of the Sitnitza and mainly Serb east of it. The village consisted of 75 houses, 15 of which are Albanian. The priest said regretfully: *"It was all Serb. But this is happening everywhere; there are so many Albanians."* The land was worked on the chiftlik system, and not owned by the Serb peasants.

Beyond Grachanitza is a Roman Catholic Albanian island at Janjevo. Following the railway, which goes up to Mitrovitza, it appears that the right side of it is Serb in the main as far as peasant population goes. The town of Prishtina, however, has barely a quarter Servian inhabitants, and is mostly Moslem Albanian, with some Orthodox Vlachs and Jews. North of Mitrovitza the Servians begin to increase (though Novi-Bazar has a large Albanian population), and soon form a majority.

In all these districts there are not enough real Turks to be worth counting. They consist mainly of officials and soldiers; in only a few cases do they form a real part of the population.

And neither the Servian nor the Albanian population appears to desire the success of the new Constitution. That this, under the circumstances, can last long seems doubtful. It is as well that others, besides Austria, should be prepared to act should a crisis occur; and it is to be hoped that in any further delimiting of territories that may take place the people most concerned may receive, at any rate, a little consideration, and that the conditions may be carefully examined on the spot.

M. Edith Durham

Folk-Lore Quarterly Review, Volume 23, 1912

Albanian and Montenegrin Folklore

Symbolic exlinction of household fire

In Montenegro, when the last male of a family was shot, it was customary for the chief woman of the house to throw water on the hearth and extinguish the fire as a symbol of the extinction of the family. The custom is not yet extinct among the peasants when the last male of a family dies.

Communal justice

There has been recently (about February, 1912) an extraordinary case of rude justice in the Fandi bariak of Mirdita. A certain family has long been a pest to its neighbours, robbing, shooting, and being generally objectionable. The local heads held a sitting and condemned the whole of the males of the family to death. Men were told off to ascertain the whereabouts of the various victims, and pick them off. On the appointed day the whole seventeen males were shot. Of them one was only five, and another twelve years old. To any protest against the brutality of killing a child in cold blood, the reply is, *"It was bad blood, and must not be propagated!"* It seems incredible, but I was assured that it was actually intended to shoot a wretched woman because she was *enceinte*, and might bear a male who would continue the inherited evil. Three shots, which missed, were fired at her. She then rushed to a man and called on him to protect her, and he took her in *besa (a peace oath)*, and she was spared.

Mourning custom

It is perhaps noteworthy that, whereas in Montenegro face-scratching as a sign of mourning is done by vomen, in North Albania it is only done by men, and it is not proper for women to do it. I was at a funeral at Skreli before Christmas, and all the men had already clawed their temples, which were red and inflamed with scratches; no women were clawed.

Divination

It is of interest just now to note what attention is being paid to the signs on bladebones and fowl breastbones. They are read eagerly, and, I am earnestly assured, foretell nothing but blood.

Folk-medicine

I was recently down on the plains of Bregu Mati distributing quinine to the luckless people who were penned on the plains by the troops throughout last fever season. I found a great many very bad cases of enlarged spleen. The local remedy for this is to take a sheep's spleen, lay it over the seat of disease, and then hang it by the fire and roast it all away, when the disease will disappear with it.

If you see a snake swallowing a frog, this is a most valuable opportunity to obtain a cure for epilepsy. You must throw a handkerchief, preferably a black one, over the snake. In its fright, it will disgorge the frog. Keep the handkerchief and, when any one falls down in a fit, throw it over the patient's head. The patient will then likewise disgorge the disease.

I am myself becoming the centre of a myth, and am supposed to have wrought a cure on a man I never touched. He was shot in the head during last year's revolution, and his recovery is entirely ascribed to me, and not to the doctor to whom it was due.

Taboos at childbirth

In Montenegro, though a woman expected, among the peasants, to be fit to carry wood and water three days after childbirth, she is not allowed to cook and make bread until she has been '*churched*'. I learnt this while living in a peasant house at Njegush, through commenting with horror on the case of a young married woman who, by carrying wood too early, brought on her death. I was told that fetching wood was quite a right and proper thing for her to do, but that, *of course*, she would not be allowed to make bread or cook. When I asked " *Why?*" I was told that bread so made could not possibly be eaten; it was not right; it was never done; and so forth. All the company agreed on this point.

I have recently learnt also that in Montenegro it is regarded as impossible for childbirth to be allowed at the house of the mother's parents. Should such a thing be permitted, it would bring the worst luck,- nay, absolute ruin,- on her brothers, who, of course, live in the parental home. I know of a case even among the upper and educated class. A young married lady went to visit her mother, and had to shorten her stay for the above reason. Her grandmother nearly drove her out of the house, and said on her departure,-" *Thank God! you have gone, and haven't brought evil on the house !* "

I have been making enquiries on the subject here in Scutari. I find that a mother is not allowed to visit a married daughter till after the birth of her first child. I enquired if under any circumstances the daughter could go to her mother's for such an event, but this seemed quite a new idea. People did not definitely say that it was impossible, but they did not seem to imagine that any such necessity could ever occur. The mother is not allowed to attend at the birth of her daughter's child, at any rate never the first time. Later on it appears not to matter so much, but there was uncertainty, and I gather that it is not done. Should no child be borne after a year of marriage, the prohibition of the mother's visit is removed.

It is customary to break an egg over the face of a newborn child. Therefore eggs are a correct present to take to a house after the occurrence of a birth. The breaking of the egg is, so far as I can make out, to avert the Evil Eye.

Foundation sacrifices

Cocks and lambs are still often sacrificed when foundations of houses are laid in North Albania. The citadel at Scutari is one of the many buildings of which it is told that a human being was built into the foundations. This particular event, according to an old and powerfully dramatic ballad, occurred early in the fourteenth century, when this place was under Serb rule. Devils destroyed by night what was built by day, and only after sacrificing the young wife of one of the three young Princes could the building be reared. The tradition of such burials in foundations has survived till recent years. An Austrian engineer in Bosnia told me in 1906 that some twelve years previously a panic was caused by a report that the Austrians were going to brick a child into the foundations of a bridge. This bridge was being built over the Lim, and, owing to the incapacity of the engineer, was so badly constructed that it fell twice. When the third attempt to erect it was made, the people took fright, and were only with difficulty persuaded that no human sacrifice would take place.

Objection to portraits

The late Mr. Holman Hunt has repeatedly told me that, when he began his painting in Palestine, he had the greatest difficulty in getting people to sit to him as models, owing to a belief that when the Day of Judgment came, the portrait might arrive first at the Gates of Heaven and be admitted, and the rightful owner of the name be dismissed as an impostor. A month or two ago I met again the aged man who was afraid lest my sketch of him might cause his death, as mentioned in Dr. Frazer's book. He had not forgotten the episode, and was glad to hear that the sketch was locked up quite safely.

Taboo on names

I have been for the last seven months engaged in distributing relief (clothing, roofing material, etc.) to the luckless Albanians whose property was entirely destroyed in the disturbances last year. This necessitates keeping a list of the families who have received relief, and it is usually. only with great difficulty that a woman can be induced to give her husband's name. She always gives her own maiden name. When pressed as to her husband's name, she very often says, *"Ask that other woman,"* pointing to a comrade, *"she knows."* The only reason I can obtain for this is,- *"Modesty; of course she is too modest to say to which man she belongs."* Even here in Scutari, until very recently, it was never the custom of a (Christian) man and wife to recognise each other in the street, and they very seldom, if ever, went out together. I was given the same reason,- *"She would not like people to know he was her husband."* The last ten years, however, have seen rapid changes. It was fortunate that I visited the Albanian mountaineers when I did, for that year (1908) was the last in which they were to be seen in their primitive state.

Burial customs

It is customary in the mountains of Shala, and Dushmani, and possibly elsewhere, to leave some iron article in a new-made grave until the corpse is brought for interment. It is unlucky to step over an empty grave.

Bridal customs

In the Crmnica valley in Montenegro (and possibly in other parts), it was, and among peasants may still be, the duty of the two djevers (bride-leaders) who came to fetch the bride to see that no one tied knots in the fringe of her strukka (a long straight shawl, worn like a Scottish plaid and with very long fringes at each end). Should some malevolent person succeed in doing this, the bride would either miscarry with her first child or bear a cripple.

Divine right

It is amazing how greatly the tribesmen believe in *"the divine right of kings"*. The hereditary chief of the Mirdites, Prenk Pasha, was looked on as but little short of a god when he returned from exile in 1908. Now, although after three years' experiences, the Mirdites and other tribes are disappointed in him, they still have a superstitious belief in his Power. I have frequently been told that *"The Mirdites 'cannot do [so and so], because Prenk will not allow them. They would like to of course. But what can they do ?"* When I have pointed out that one man cannot possibly prevent thirty thousand people taking separate action if they wish, I am always told, *"But he was born chief. He is sent by God. They have to do what he says."*

Edith Durham,
Scutari

The Near East, August 1st 1913
Albanian Affairs
(from our own correspondent, M. Edith Durham)

Valona, July 11

Servia and Albania

The new war may have serious effects for the new Albanian State, affecting as it does all our immediate neighbours. The Government, it is true, desires peace, but will it be able to restrain the people? Already the arrival at Valona of Sandansky, the famous Bulgarian freelance, has given rise to many rumours; for there is a disposition to regard the visit as official, and to see in it the beginning of a Bulgaro-Albanian entente. The conciliatory tone of the Bulgarian Press towards the close of the late war is remembered, and it is recalled that Bulgarians did not wish the Albanian boundary to be too restricted.

If it may be hoped that the Albanian Government will be wise enough to remain neutral, one hardly dare hope as much from the people. Apart from the desire for revenge and the hope of reconquering the territories that have been detached, there is another element to be reckoned with - the refugees from Kossovo. At the beginning of the war Servia and Montenegro pursued a fatal policy of extermination and terrorism. In the Ipek-Prizrend-Jakova district the villagers suffered the worst excesses at the hands of the invaders. This bad policy led to the flight of Albanians from Kosovo, and there are at the present time over 25,000 refugees in the Mallisia suffering from famine and want. Will they be likely to resist the temptation offered them by the outbreak of a new war?

Fully a fortnight ago skirmishes took place at Mat between the Albanians and the Servian troops, the latter wishing to take possession of strategic points in order to safeguard against action on the part of the Albanians. These incidents called forth a vigorous collective note from Austria-Hungary and Italy, addressed to the Servian Government, on the 3rd inst.

Government Activities

The Provisional Government is occupied with a scheme for the organisation of militia and a regular gendarmerie to replace the present irregulars. The Chief of the General Staff has just submitted a project to the Council of Ministers, but it has not yet been accepted. According to this project, the militia would comprise the citizens between the ages of twenty and forty, and the gendarmerie would consist of an up-to-date force under the command of young officers who received their instruction from the European officers of the reformed Macedonian gendarmerie. This military re-organisation is impatiently awaited, and the only difficulty that it is likely to meet is the shortage of necessary funds. It is hoped that the entry of General Said Pasha into the Albanian service will have a salutary effect upon the army officers. This skilful and energetic General has just placed himself at the disposal of the Government of his country.

Essad Pasha

The Provisional Cabinet appears to have found some little difficulty in dealing with *l'affaire* Essad Pasha. Essad, who has been credited with intentions more or less dangerous for Albania, arrived at Valona on July 1 in order to make his peace with the Government, and shortly afterwards it was announced that he had entered the Cabinet as Minister of the Interior. This reconciliation has been received with mixed feelings. It has been welcomed by those who are anxious for peace at any price; it has been condemned by those who would have wished to see portfolios in the hands of the men most capable of dealing with the situation. Following on the reconciliation, Essad Pasha set out for Italy and Austria, and it is said that he will subsequently take a cure abroad.

The Near East, August 1st 1913
Moslems of Albania

To the Editor of The Near East

Sir,

I am distressed to learn from your issue of July 11 that a report has been spread that I have been giving help mainly to *"Catholic Malissori"* here.

Mr. Christian has, I am glad to say, contradicted it. But I beg that you will allow me to state that both Serb and Montenegrin - having determined that *"when the land is once ours there will be no Mohammedan question"* (as I heard the Montenegrins repeatedly declare) - deliberately set to work with great savagery to make it impossible for the Moslem population to remain. They not only burnt down whole villages, but they tore down the walls of the houses, in many cases leaving only heaps of stones. They pillaged wholesale. Not a garment did they leave. Daily Montenegrin women streamed into Podgoritza bent double beneath huge packs of loot. A Bosnian volunteer who had witnessed the sacking that took place in Kosovo vilayet said, bitterly: *"A Montenegrin woman will march 100 kilometres to steal one shirt!"*. They were quite pitiless. When I protested to one that the children, whose garments she had looted, would die of cold in the winter, she replied: *"So they shall, God willing! They are Moslems! The more die the better!"*

Montenegro cried aloud to Europe that she required the fertile plains in the neighbourhood of Scutari to expand upon. When it was objected that these lands were largely already the private property of Moslem villagers, the reply was always, *"They will have to leave. Let them go to Asia."* In order to compass the ruin of these unfortunate people, their olive and fruit trees were felled. In some cases fire was made on the roots to ensure their not sprouting again. Hay, corn, tobacco, all stores, in fact, were looted; cattle and horses taken, gardens destroyed, vines cut.

Since my arrival here in April I have ridden from one devastated spot to another distributing such funds as have been entrusted to me by the Macedonian Relief Society, and such as I have managed to collect myself. Also several bales of clothing given me by friends in England and by the British Red Cross. But I keep finding and hearing of more and more burnt and ravaged districts. My fund is almost exhausted. Not a penny has been sent to this district by the British Red Crescent. Mountain men in most pitiable state - half-naked and half-starved - are now daily coming down from the track of the Servian Army - Mal-i-Zi and Kabasha Puka. Quite half of these are Catholics. All have suffered alike. They beg help for their starving, houseless families. I am forced to tell them to tell their neighbours, on their return home, not to come - as the fund is run out.

In addition to this, I have an urgent appeal for over 200 houses between here and the Montenegrin frontier - all burnt and plundered. These are Moslem. East of Scutari are a number of Catholic houses all plundered by the Montenegrins. But to houses plundered and not burnt I am forced to refuse all aid, though they are in a piteous condition. Quite three-quarters of those I have aided are Moslems - but I would appeal, too, for help for those Catholics who are in similar plight. And would point out also that the Orthodox armies have shown themselves in many instances as fanatical against the Catholics as against the Moslems. Any contributions, however small, will be of use. They should be paid into the Albanian Relief Fund, the Union of London and Smith's Bank (Swiss Cottage Branch), College Crescent, London, N.W.

I am sorry to have to add that in Montenegro I was forbidden by the Governor of Podgoritza to give either food or clothing to the Moslem villages on the frontier, which the Montenegrins had burnt. He also threatened some Catholic priests with imprisonment, and in one case with hanging, if they dare come to ask me to aid their flocks, who were in many cases in great want.

Refugees from the recently occupied districts of Gusimje and Plava all state that forcible *'conversion'* there of Moslems to the Orthodox faith has been going on. The means of persuasion are flogging and threats of death. Children have been taken to church and baptised without consent of their parents. Catholics, too, have similarly been *'converted'*. It is earnestly to be hoped that in delimiting Albania, the Powers will surrender as little as possible to the mercies both of Montenegro and Servia.

Trusting that you will publish this letter, for the facts should be widely known,

Yours, etc.,

M. Edith Durham
Scutari, Albania, July 23

The Near East, September 19th 1913
Albanian Affairs
from our own correspondent, M. Edith Durham

Valona, September 3rd 1913

The delimitation of the southern boundary, which is to be undertaken by the International Commission, is strongly exercising public opinion in Albania. According to the statements issued by the various agencies, the language of the inhabitants, and not their own desires, will carry most weight in regard to the delimitation. Now the districts whose fate was left in suspense by the Treaty of London are: Delvino, Premeti, Liaskovok, Kolonia, Rogou and Konitza. The first four of these have a purely Albanian population, with the exception of Delvino, in the south of which there are some Greek-speaking villages. As for the districts of Rogou and Koritza, their population is mostly Vlach, Hellenised to a great extent at Rogou. Therefore, there is, or should be, little anxiety, save with regard to Rogou. But will the Commission be able to guard against all the trickery that will be tried upon it? Already many reports from the regions occupied inform us that Greece is playing some strange tricks: hundreds of Albanians, both Christian and Moslem, are being deported from the contested area, and in their place hundreds - and thousands - of Greeks are being planted in the said areas, solely and simply with the object of distorting the truth.

The Hellenic Government, moreover, has recourse to more violent measures. Albanian inhabitants are forced to attend meetings from which are despatched messages demanding the annexation to Greece of Albanian regions. A couple of months ago Mr. Nevinson and Miss Durham were present at one of these meetings. The reports afterwards stated that it was a meeting of 25,000 Albanians, demanding union with Greece, while, according to Mr. Nevinson and Miss Durham, there were only three or four hundred people, gathered together by the police, who promised them addresses by the *"English visitors"*.

Certain journals have announced that the Hellenes of Koritza would oppose by force their separation from Greece. There is not, however, a single Greek at Koritza. The *"Greeks"* referred to can therefore only be Christian Albanians, and amongst them the national feeling is strongly developed, for the Christians have always been fervent nationalists, with their schools, their Albanian papers, and a society, *'The Orthodox League'*, which had for its object the emancipation of Orthodox Albanians from the Hellenising influence of the Greek clergy, under whom Turkey kept them. And what has taken place at Koritza has taken place also at Premeti, Laiskovik, and Argyrocastro. Nor should it be forgotten that beyond Cape Stylos there are over 100,000 Albanians (to be precise, 130,000), who have been torn from the motherland, without reckoning in those handed over to Servia - over a million.

The Albanians, both those of free Albania and those who are left under foreign rule, entertain lively feelings of gratitude towards the British Press for the fair and humanitarian attitude it has maintained throughout the crisis. It is, however, still necessary to bear in mind that the only way to make Albanian independent is to avoid letting it be too much whittled down, and thus weakened. Today the following memorial has been forwarded to Sir Edward Grey and to the French, Italian, German, Russian, and Austro-Hungarian Foreign Ministers by the representatives of the districts of Koritza, Kolonia, Leskovik, Konitza, Rogou, Argyrocastro, and Delvino:-

'Nous apprenons que les autorités grecques des régions albanaises occupées ont recours à la force pour exciter la population et leur faire faire des manifestations. Les Grecs commettraient des excés avant l'évacuation du pays qu'ils se proposent de détruire comme ils l'ont fait en Thrace et en Macedoine. Des villages entiers sont transplantés afin de fausser la verité dans la delimitation de la frontière. Nous vous permettons d'attirer l'attention du gouvernement de S.M. Britannique et le prier de prendre la defense de la vie et des biens de nos compatriotes.

Au nom des refugiés de Coritza, Kolonià, Leskovik, Conitza, Rogou, Permet, Argyrokastro, Delvina.'

Idoméné Kostouri,
Starré Caroli

The Near East, September 26th 1913
Albanian Affairs
from our own correspondent, M. Edith Durham

Valona, September 17th 1913

Dissensions in the Cabinet

At the moment when the International Commissions for the delimitation of the frontiers, north and south, are about to begin their work, the Albanian Provisional Government is passing through what might almost be described as a crisis. Notwithstanding the existence of unrest and discontent of which the Note of Protest presented to the Government (as mentioned in my letter of the 3rd inst.) was evidence, dissension has broken out in the Cabinet. As indicated in paragraph 6 of the Note referred to, there had been some internal trouble in the Cabinet, caused, apparently, by the vacillating policy of Ismail Kemal Bey, who, in difficult circumstances, has not shown such capacity as might have hoped. This state of affairs caused dissatisfaction amongst the Ministers, who had frequently had to complain of their President's conduct. Of the Ministers elected by the Congress at Valona last November, three - two Moslems and two Christian - had already been compelled to resign. And now we find Essad Pasha, the Minister of the Interior, formulating his complaints, somewhat brutally perhaps, and adopting a distinctly menacing tone.

As your readers will remember, after joining the Cabinet, Essad set out on his travels to Italy and Austria, and on his return to Valona he only remained in that town for a fortnight, after which he left for Tirana, his native place. From Tirana, he has addressed to Ismail Kemal Bey a demand for a reorganisation of the Cabinet, and for the strict observance of his own duties by each Minister, without interference on the part of Ismail Kemal. His attitude, not unnaturally, gives rise to considerable uneasiness, and already he is regarded with suspicion as a firebrand. It is still hoped, however, that no open rupture may take place, and the Progressives are doing everything possible to bring about a reconciliation between the conflicting interests.

Essad demands that the seat of the Provisional Government shall be transferred to some other town, Ismail Kemal being unable to shake himself free from certain disturbing influences at Valona, his native town. One section of the Government appears to believe that the difficulty will be surmounted by means of mutual concessions.

Public opinion in Valona and other towns is that all these difficulties will be smoothed over by the arrival of the Sovereign. And everywhere, therefore, there is much impatience for that arrival, which it is hoped will put an end to all the petty rivalry of the moment, and lead to the introduction of stable government.

A Pro-British Demonstration

The Hon. Aubrey Herbert, M.P., President of the London Albanian Committee, left Valona on the 11th inst., after spending four days here, for a tour, including Fier, Berat, Elbasan, Tirana, and Durazzo. During his stay here a large meeting was held to protest against the action of the Greeks in the Albanian districts that they have occupied, and the manifestants gathered in front of the house at which Mr. Herbert was staying, and gave cheers for Great Britain. In acknowledgement, Mr. Herbert made a short speech, which was much appreciated by his audience. A lengthy list of misdeeds committed by the Greeks was subsequently handed to him.

September 21st
Essad and the Cabinet

Essad Pasha, who passes his time between Durazzo and Tirana, continues to cause anxiety; but, fortunately, only the districts of Kavaja, Pekinje, and Kroya are with him; Scutari, Catholic Malissia, Elbasan, Berat, and the surrounding districts are partisans of the Provisional Government. Last week Essad organised a meeting at Tirana to protest against the Provisional Government, at which five demands were formulated, as follows:-

(1)   the transfer of the provisional capital to Durazzo
(2)   alterations in the constitution of the Cabinet
(3)   the convocation of a National Council
(4)   the despatch of a commission to Europe to induce the Great Powers to send the promised ruler
(5)   the rendering to the new Cabinet of an account of all that has been done by the present Government since the Declaration of Independence.

As counterblasts to this meeting, the students of Valona have sent Essad Pasha a telegram begging him to behave rationally and the day before yesterday a large counter-meeting was held here. It is now reported - though with what truth I cannot say - that Essad is showing signs of repenting his action and of a spirit of conciliation. Three members of the Cabinet of Valona are in favour of an agreement with Essad; but the President (Ismail Kemal) is reported to be opposed to it, and already the recruiting of gendarmes for use in an emergency has commenced.

Reported Montenegrin Outrages

From Jakova and Ipek comes news of an alarming character. The

Montenegrins are reported to be behaving with great ferocity. Ten villages have been the scene of their sanguinary exploits. At Cizi, all the members of the family of one Abdul Zekio were shut up in their home and burned alive. At Shipshaj, Musa Dervish, Aidin Kanber, Yussuf Selman, Sul Muslih, Rejib Fazli and Ismail Dervish were assassinated while tending their flocks. The whole of Doushkaja was destroyed; not a single house was left standing. The villages of Uizi, Fshaj, and Smach have been burned out; Maznik, Jablanica, Zhabel and Novosel have been sacked and pillaged, and most of their houses fired; at Streltza many houses have been burned and four people killed; and Popoch has been raided and many of its houses burned.

The Near East, October 3rd 1913
Albanian Affairs
from our own correspondent, M. Edith Durham

Valona, September 26th

The Albanians and Serbs do not appear to be able to live together in peace. From the very beginning it was said that Servia would have enormous difficulties in governing the 1,200,000 Albanians of Kossovo and Monastir; consequently very serious happenings were anticipated.

Of the conflict that has broken out at Dibra, I send the most accurate version that I have been able to obtain. On Friday the Servians proposed to evacuate Lower Dibra, which had already been assigned to Albania by the Conference of London, but before retiring they drove out the cattle of the Albanians, and when the shepherds showed resistance the Servians fired on them, and a fight followed, which gradually extended. Reinforcements arrived for the Servians, and a massacre followed, women, children, and old men being killed. The Albanians of the surrounding districts hastened towards Upper Dibra. But the Servians had taken thirty-eight notables of the town prisoners as hostages, with the intention of shooting them if the Albanians approached the town; but just as they were about to carry out their intention the Albanians arrived and saved all the prisoners but five, who were killed, among them being a sheikh.

At the time of writing a man has arrived from the country with the tidings that the Albanians have put to rout five battalions of Servians from Dibra, and have captured twelve guns, and that they are marching towards Stronga and Gostova.

The Boundary Commission
At the precise moment that the International Commission for the demarcation of the southern frontier of Albania is commencing its labours, the Greeks are attempting to consummate an Albanian entente. In that hope a deputation of six Albanians from the occupied districts has been sent to Valona by the Greek Government. This deputation remained five days, and departed yesterday; it has received its well-merited reply. That is to say, that the Albanians only wish to entertain good relations with the Greeks, their neighbours, at a time when the frontiers will be fixed, and no further differences exist between them; but at present, and as long as the Greeks intrigue in the occupied districts and do not evacuate these regions, an entente is quite impossible.

The Near East, October 31st 1913
Albanian Affairs
from our own correspondent, M. Edith Durham

Valona, October 24th

The Frontier Commissions

The International Commissions for the delimitation of the Albanian frontiers have begun their work: the Southern Commission at Kolonia (south of Koritza), whence it will work to the Adriatic; and the Northern Commission at Lin, on Lake Ochrida, whence it will work to Scutari. The former arrived at Koritza on the 16th inst., and left at once for Kolonia. The Northern Commission arrived at Elbasan on the 18th, where it had an enthusiastic reception, the townspeople turning out to meet it, bearing the flags of the six Powers. A schoolboy delivered a speech in French and Albanian welcoming the delegates in the town's name; and the President of the Commission made a suitable reply. But a little further on the procession was stopped by a young boy under a black flag, on which in white letters was the word *"Dibra"*. Here were the refugees from that hapless region - a great crowd of women, children, and men, presenting a sad spectacle. They had presented themselves to the Commission in order to expose Servia's systematic policy of exterminating the Albanians whom the London Conference had placed under her yoke.

These refugees numbered some 4,000 in the town of Elbasan; the delegates saw 15,000 more of them at Tirana; and their total is said to amount to 60,000. They presented a memorial to the Commission, setting forth the excesses committed by the Servians, etc., and imploring intervention on their behalf. But the Commissioners replied that they could not concern themselves with a subject that belonged solely to the diplomatists, their own duties being purely technical.

The Dibra Rising

As most fantastic rumours have been current concerning the insurrection at Dibra, it may be well to repeat that the rising was entirely spontaneous. It is utterly false to say that the Albanians were egged on by the Provisional Government, or that Austrian, Turkish, and Bulgarian officers led them; false, too, is the legend concerning Issa Boletinatz; and utterly ridiculous the story of the Albanians having used cannon and machine guns. The rising was the work of Albanians handed over to Serb domination, and no Albanian of independent Albania had any hand in it. The Albanians were driven to revolt solely by the policy of the Servians, who goad their new subjects on by every possible means, in order to obtain a pretext for getting rid of them.

The Commission of Control

At the same time that the frontier Commissions began their labours the Commission of Control assembled at Valona. Great Britain is represented by Mr. H. Lamb, C.M.G.; France by M. Krajevsky; Austria-Hungary by M. Petrovich; Russia by M. Pebriajeff; Germany by H. Winkler and Italy by Sig. Leoni. The Commission will make a tour in the country and draw up proposals for a code of laws. Naturally its views are not yet known.

Ismail and Essad

Ismail Kemal Bey is becoming more unpopular day by day. The 'National' bank, which has just been founded at Valona with Austrian and Italian capital, has given rise to much dissatisfaction by reason of certain of its articles, which do not correspond with the interests of the country. The creation of this bank has led to the resignation of the Minister of Finance, who disapproved of the conditions, and three other members of the Cabinet refused their signatures. This, however, did not prevent Ismail Kemal from passing the measure with a majority of two! The blunders of Ismail Kemal have encouraged Essad Pasha to push his daring so far as the proclamation of an independent Government at Durazzo.

Essad's Proclamation

In his proclamation, Essad vigorously refutes the intention attributed to him of wishing to split Albania into two parts, and declares himself forced to act as he has by Ismail Kemal's conduct of affairs. He adds that he will regard his Government as subject to the control of the International Commission, and that on the arrival of a Sovereign he will hand over the control of affairs to him.

'The Government of Durazzo' extends from the River Mat to the Shkumba, including Tirana, Kroya, Kavaja, Pegin, and Shiak. Each of these districts will return two representatives, who, under the title of 'senators' will govern the country, with Essad as President. Essad's action has created a very bad impression throughout Albania, and is blamed by all patriots.

The Near East, November 28th 1913

Albanian Affairs

from our own correspondent, M. Edith Durham

Valona, November 8th

The Servian Withdrawal

The Servians did not wait until October 26, the last date allowed them by the Austro-Hungarian and Italian Note, but retired across the frontier provided for by the Treaty of London on October 25. Before departing, however, they despoiled the villages they were abandoning to such effect that when the population returned to take possession of their houses they found neither crops, food, nor household goods. This spoliation may be described as official, for the army convoys transported the loot. I have received many letters assuring me that the Servians showed very little scruple or chivalry in their withdrawal.

The Commission of Control

The Commission of Control at Valona has made a division of its labours. The British and French delegates will occupy themselves especially with financial matters; the German and Austrian with the police and gendarmerie; the Italian and Russian delegates with judicial affairs. Filled with the best intentions, the Commission is seeking to find a modus vivendi for the Cabinet, which remains in a sorry state. For not only is there the problem of Essad Pasha and his 'Provisional Government;' at Durazzo, but now there is a fresh crisis in the Valona Cabinet between Ismail Kemal, the President, and members. Mufid Bey, Minister for Foreign Affairs in the Provisional Government, has just been elected Albanian member on the International Control Commission.

Valona, November 15th
Consuls in Albania

This week M. Pavloff has arrived here as Bulgaria's Consul-General, to the great satisfaction of the people here. It may be noted that the foreign consuls who have been in Albania since the days of the Turkish régime have not yet officially recognised the new Albanian State, since they have not yet received new credentials, and have not had any correspondence with the Provisional Government. Apart from Bulgaria, newly represented, none of the Balkan States has a consul here - those of Turkish days having quitted the country at the beginning of the last war - with the exception of Montenegro, who has sent her consul to Scutari again, to the great astonishment of all Albanians, who hardly look with favour on his return before the complete adjustment of affairs between the two countries.

The Gendarmerie Question

Sweden having declined the mission of organising the gendarmerie, the work will now be undertaken by Dutch officers. A few days ago, Colonel Wier and Major Thomassin, accompanied by two sergeants, arrived to begin the work, and when they have studied the requirements of the case they will be followed by a full staff of officers. It is thought here that Albania will have little difficulty in providing good officers amongst her own sons, as she has many officers who studied in the Military School at Constantinople and worked under the European officers who were charged with the reorganisation of the Macedonian gendarmerie. It appears, however, that the impression formed by the Dutch officers who have just arrived is far from favourable, probably because the officers who have been appointed by Ismail Kemal have been chosen for other reasons than efficiency and honesty.

The Near East, December 12th 1913
Albanian Affairs
from our own correspondent, M. Edith Durham

Valona, November 29th

Albania's 'Independence Day'

The national holiday was observed yesterday with great enthusiasm. It has, in fact, been decided that the anniversary of the proclamation of Albanian Independence - which took place at Valona, November 28, 1912 - shall be the national holiday. The holiday was celebrated at both Scutari and Elbasan, and throughout Albania with the exception of Durazzo, where it was observed two days earlier (26th), that having been the date on which the national flag was first hoisted in that town by order of the Valona Congress, which wished to proclaim Albania's national rights before the Servians entered Durazzo. The national holiday was the occasion of the official recognition of the Provisional Government by the Powers. The delegates of the Commission of Control and the three Consuls resident at Valona (Austrian, Italian, and Bulgarian) called on the President, Ismail Kemal, and the Austrian and Italian gunboats in Valona harbour fired a salute of twenty-one guns.

The Future Sovereign

The news that the nomination of Prince William of Wied as Sovereign will shortly be officially announced has created a very good impression here, all factions and parties uniting in acclaiming the new Ruler, whose arrival is expected about the middle of January. The question whether his title shall be 'King' or 'Prince' is occupying public opinion, the former being generally desired, as expressing Albania's complete independence more fully. Elbasan is generally regarded as being certain to be chosen as the capital, by reason of its situation and of other considerations.

The International Commissions

The South Frontier Commission, which had arrived at Leskovik, is just now at Janina, in consequence of the sudden death of Herr Bilinski, the Austrian member. The Agence Stefani states that Italy has agreed to the British proposal in regard to the frontiers, according to which the Commission will not have to conduct inquiries into the nationality of the population, but will endeavour to arrive at a modus vivendi between the proposals of the Triplice and those of Greece. It is already certain that Tepelena, Argyrocastro, Kolonia, Premetti, and Leskovik will be Albanian, while the cazas of Konitza and Pogoni will probably be Greek.

The Commission of Control will shortly visit Durazzo and Scutari. It holds four sittings a week with Mufid Bey, the Albanian delegate; but no results are yet perceptible.

The Dibra Refugees

The question of the Dibra refugees is a very serious one. These refugees numbered over 80,000, but, some having returned to the territories evacuated by the Servians, there are now some 50,000 of them menaced by starvation and death. The Albanian Government has provided some funds for their relief, and various subscriptions have been opened. It is thought here, however, that the best thing to do would be to repatriate these poor people - which could only be done if the Powers should charge a Commission to supervise the work.

The Near East, January 9th 1914
Notes from Albania
from our own correspondent, M. Edith Durham

Durazzo, January 1st

The Southern Frontier

Matters are growing complicated here. First of all, there is the question of the southern frontier. The Powers had fixed January 20 as the day on which the Greeks should evacuate the occupied districts. Now comes the news that the Greeks have already proclaimed a Provisional Government in the districts they ought to give up to Albania! Three hundred men of the gendarmerie organised by the Dutch officers have left for Starova in order to take possession of Koritza as soon as it is evacuated by the Greeks. Another force will be despatched to Argyrocastro for the same purpose. It seems, however, that things will not go off quite smoothly, and that the Greeks will have recourse to every possible strategy to delay their retreat.

The Provisional Capital

It seems almost certain that Prince William of Wied will make his entry at Durazzo. For the past week workmen sent by the Prince have been engaged under the supervision of an engineer in the renovation of the Government House at Durazzo, in order to make it more fit for the reception of the Sovereign. The choice of Durazzo as the provisional capital was rather unexpected, for it was generally believed that the Sovereign would make his entry at Scutari. However, it has produced a good effect, for, from the moment that Essad Pasha gave the choice his warm approval, the selection of Durazzo settled a difficult question in an agreeable manner.

The Potsdam Delegation

The delegation which is going to Potsdam to ask Prince William to accept the throne of Albania has not yet set out. It is believed that the Prince's arrival will be delayed a little by the question of the southern frontier, since he has stipulated that Albania shall be free from foreigners before his arrival. The delegates are, however, already chosen, and only await a favourable moment for departure.

The Control Commission

The members of the Control Commission are overwhelmed with work. It is to be regretted, however, that there are symptoms of slight friction among the members, since at this juncture perfect unanimity among the representatives of all the Powers is a *sine qua non* condition for the conclusion of their task of forming Albania.

The Near East, January 30th 1914
Albanian Affairs
from our own correspondent, M. Edith Durham

Valona, January 10th

The Valona Plot

Serious events have happened this week. Some little time ago it was known that Turkish emissaries were in the country. At first but little attention was paid to them, especially as the Provisional Government was quite unable to control their actions owing to the lack of unity in the country. Twenty days ago, however, Bekir Bey, of Grevena, arrived in Valona, where he represented that he had been sent from Constantinople with the object of forming bands of volunteers to fight against the Greeks in Epirus. While his mission was ridiculed, he himself was kept under observation, and the result justified the suspicions that were felt regarding him; for it was soon discovered that he had a vast and daring plan. Last Wednesday it was learned that 150 *soi-disant* Albanians were on board the Austrian steamer from Constantinople, intending to disembark at Valona. The Italian and Austrian gunboats that have been at that port for the past six months would not, however, allow any of these 150 volunteers to land; and Bekir Bey and six others, who called themselves officers of Albanian origin, were placed under arrest. Bekir Bey was the bearer of numerous important papers, despatches, cyphers, codes, etc. An investigation into the affair is proceeding, and it is reported that many persons are compromised by the discoveries already made. The same day martial law was proclaimed at Valona.

Disturbances in the North

Meanwhile there have been complications in the North also. It will be remembered that, in his proclamation of October 12 last, Essad Pasha aimed at making Central Albania (that is to say, the region between the Rivers Mati and Skumbi) a central State. Since that date Elbasan, Chermenika, and Koloborda, situated to the north of the Skumbi, have not been subject to Essad, but have continued under the Provisional Government at Valona. Things remained in this state in spite of certain demands made by Essad Pasha, when some fortnight ago some disturbances were reported from Koloborda, a district lying between Elbasan and the present Servian frontier. At first these disturbances attracted but little attention from the authorities, but the day before yesterday things took a more serious turn, and at the time of writing it is officially reported that fighting has taken place on the banks of the Skumbi, near the Hajji Begar bridge, between the Valona gendarmerie and Essad Pasha's forces.

This incident, occurring just when the country is expecting the arrival of the new Sovereign and the evacuation of Koritza and Argyrocastro, is regarded as singularly unfortunate. Pessimists go so far as to say that Essad is in communication with Greece and Servia, and that his action is not unconnected with Bekir Bey's plots at Valona, especially as certain documents seized on the latter lead to the belief that he was in communication with Essad.

Martial Law in Elbasan

These happenings have serious perturbed the Commission of Control and the Provisional Government. At the present moment martial law is proclaimed in Elbasan, and yesterday evening the Commission of Control, telegraphed to Essad, informing him that it would hold him personally responsible for affairs in the Elbasan region.

The fighting on the road to Koritza - for it is by way of the Skumbi that the best road to Koritza lies - seriously jeopardises the fate of that town. The gendarmerie organised by the Dutch officers, who had gone to Elbasan in order to proceed to Starova and Koritza, have been ordered to march against Essad Pasha's forces. Are we already embarked upon a civil war, or will the incident pass over without further complications? All depends upon the attitude of Essad and the energy shown by the Control Commission and the Provisional Government.

The Near East, February 6th 1914
Albanian Affairs
from our own correspondent, M. Edith Durham

Elbasan, January 19th

The situation here looked as if it might assume a very serious character. The partisans of Essad Pasha, led by a certain Dervish Bey, threatened the town of Elbasan, installing themselves in the surrounding villages. Dervish Bey had his own private grievances against the Governor of Elbasan; but in this matter there can be no doubt that he acted on the instigation of Essad Pasha, although they both denied that they had anything in common. The delegates of the Control Commission were in no wise imposed upon by this comedy, as they have given Essad Pasha plainly to understand.

For a week past, people in this town have been in a state of cruel suspense, living as if in a place besieged by a foreign foe. Yesterday, however, a reinforcement of gendarmerie arrived at Elbasan, and an attack was made on Dervish Bey and his followers, who were assembled at the village of Godolesh, about an hour's distance from here. As a result of the fighting, which lasted two hours, there were five killed and six wounded, and the insurgents took to flight in great disorder. The neighbouring villages hastened to make their submission, having only made common cause with the insurgents under compulsion. The incident may now be regarded as closed. Dervish Bey and his partisans have doubtless sought asylum with Essad Pasha. In yesterday's fight they appear to have numbered about 300.

The majority of Albanians regard Essad as their country's evil genius. It would seem certain that he is seeking to create difficulties. But whether he is anxious to achieve cheap notoriety or to make things unpleasant for the Provisional Government, or whether he is pursuing some deep-laid nefarious scheme, it would be hard to say. Some people suspect him of being secretly in touch with the Greeks and the Slavs. On the day that he handed Scutari over to the Montenegrins suspicion fell upon him; and ever since then he has maintained a sinister attitude at Durazzo, thwarting all the efforts of the patriots, and causing all sorts of rumours to be circulated regarding him and his intentions. It seems to be tolerably certain, however, that Essad maintained most cordial relations with the Greeks and Slavs, either through certain agents that he had abroad or through the Orthodox Patriarch of Durazzo and a doctor who went backwards and forwards between Athens and Durazzo. And this lends significance to the fact that the disturbance at Elbasan kept the gendarmerie from reaching Starovo to await the evacuation of Koritza; for the gendarmes are still at Elbasan. Perhaps it is also the reason of the delay in the evacuation of Southern Albania.

Everybody here will tell you that Essad and Ismail Kemal ought to be debarred permanently from meddling with Albanian affairs, and that as long as they remain in the country, no good can be expected from them, since they are both incorrigible plotters and schemers.

The Near East, February 13th 1914
Albanian Affairs
from our own correspondent, M. Edith Durham

Valona, January 25th

Ismail Kemal's Resignation

Ismail Kemal Bey, President of the Provisional Government, resigned the day before yesterday.

Valona has had a highly exciting week. On the one hand there has been the affaire Bekir Bey and the Turkish plot; on the other the grave difficulties caused by Essad. Bekir had some adherents here, whose names are whispered, but as yet nothing more precise is known regarding this point. The plot hardly appears to have had any definite form; for in order to avail himself of all possible help Bekir Bey represented his intentions variously to different interests, and very few people were initiated into the inner mysteries of the affair. However, the matter troubled Ismail Kemal, and, it is said, even compromised him to some extent, though personally I regard the latter statement as mere gossip.

On the other hand, Essad's conduct irritated the Albanians, who accused Ismail Kemal of letting things slide and, by his indifference, driving recruits into Essad's camp. Thus the President's position became critical, and his colleagues also were embarrassed. So, feeling that he could not remedy the existing state of affairs, Ismail Kemal had the courage to resign. A week before he had already notified the Commission of Control that if they desired to take over the direction of affairs until the Sovereign's arrival he was quite ready to hand over his authority to them. The delegates referred the matter to their respective Governments, and the result is as I have described it. The other members of the Cabinet remain in office, with the title of Directors-General. Ismail Kemal goes abroad to-day. His resignation has given rise to mixed feelings; for while one party is glad to be rid of him, another objects to seeing a foreign Commission vested with sole authority even for a short time.

The International Commission of Control will, it is thought, go to Durazzo in order to take charge of affairs, and thus put an end to Essad Pasha's dictatorate over Central Albania. It is also thought that the Commission will appoint an Albanian Governor of Scutari in place of Colonel Phillips, the present Governor, and thus unite the whole country under one authority pending the arrival of the Sovereign.

Preparations for the Greek Evacuation

Greece is preparing to evacuate the southern provinces of Albania, Koritza and Argyrocastro, and columns of the reorganised gendarmerie are in waiting to occupy the country as the Greeks withdraw. It is to be hoped that this evacuation will be accomplished without incident. The column destined for Starovo (north of Koritza), which was to set out from Elbasan, has been forced to take another route, the road between Elbasan and Starovo, which lies along the Shkumbi River, being still infested by partisans of Essad.

A Proclamation

The Commission of Control has had printed a proclamation for publication in the districts about to be evacuated. It is printed in four languages - Albanian, French, Turkish, and Greek - and it states that the Commission, representing the Powers responsible for the creation of the Albanian State, appeals to the evacuated districts. It refers to the rumours that have been put into circulation to stir up popular feeling against the Albanian Government, which, it states, are false and misleading; for the desire of the Powers is to create an independent State, prosperous and strong, based on the principle of equal treatment for all, and it is only by the co-operation of all the elements, without distinction, that this end can be achieved. At the head of the new State the Powers have placed a Prince chosen by them, and they have appointed the International Commission of Control, on which there is an Albanian delegate, and which will exist for some time. To the Prince and the Commission it will fall to establish an administration responding to all the needs and legitimate aspirations of the Albanian people.

Notes from Albania
from our own correspondent, M. Edith Durham

Durazzo, February 21st

Essad Pasha's Position

Many changes have taken place here since the departure of the delegation to offer the throne to Prince William of Wied.

Two days after the departure of Essad Pasha there was a demonstration against Greece, Turkey, and Essad himself. A crowd of young men, mostly Orthodox, assembled and shouted, *"Down with the Greek Metropolitan!"* *"Down with Turkey!"* *"Down with Essad!"* and, on the same day, two Orthodox citizens from Durazzo well-known for their Grecophile sympathies were mobbed.

The delegation should now be with the new Sovereign, who is expected here about March 5. The delegation consists of seventeen persons - Christians, Orthodox, Catholic, and Mussulman. Essad Pasha is held responsible for the fact that Scutari did not wish to send Mussulman delegates. He is accused of engaging in intrigues, during the last five months, with five leading men of the town, with the object of preventing the acceptance of other than a Mussulman Sovereign. These men, deserted by Essad, have now repented of their action, but rather late. It is rumoured that the Mussulmans of Scutari intend to make amends by sending a brilliant deputation to this town to receive the new Sovereign. They are greatly incensed against Essad.

It caused much astonishment that Essad, when consenting to leave Durazzo and to hand in his resignation, stipulated that no change should be made in the administration, and that its personnel, composed entirely of his own creatures, should remain unaltered. Nevertheless, six days ago, the Prefect of Durazzo, a cousin of Essad's, was dismissed and replaced by an Albanian Nationalist. It is hoped that in a few days there will be many changes, especially since the new posts of Directors of Police, of Justice, and of Finance have been created by the Commission of Control.

The Powers' Representations

Public opinion here would like to see greater unanimity among the representatives of the six Great Powers. It is impossible to realise how unfortunate intrigues and rivalries, often trifling and ridiculous, are in a country but recently granted independence as a State, which has yet been for a long period a free field for the ambitions of foreigners in consequence of the neglect of the superseded Ottoman Government.

The Gendarmerie

Much satisfaction is felt here with the dignity and sincerity shown by the officers of the Dutch Mission for reorganising the gendarmerie in carrying out their task. The results are already very obvious and important, and the impression produced is most favourable. This has raised the prestige of what is known here as *"Europe"*, i.e., Western civilisation and institutions.

This mission is still at Valona, but Commandant Thomson arrives to-morrow, and will apply himself to the necessary measures of organisation, after the model of Valona and other districts, where there are splendidly disciplined battalions of gendarmes fully equal to the work required of them.

Bands' Activities

The state of the country generally remains the same. A band still continues to infest the road between Starova and Elbasan; another band is at Chermenika, to the north of Elbasan; and a third in Lower Dibra. It is asserted that Essad, who is said to have organised them, has instructed them to maintain their position until his return. What will happen on the arrival of the Sovereign? And why has the International Commission of Control prevented the Prefect of Elbasan from conducting operations against these bands? What is the end in view? That is a question to which I dare not give an answer, and I refrain from guessing. In addition to the refugees from Dibra, two thousand Albanian fugitives have arrived at Berat from the sixteen villages in the neighbourhood of Koritza which the Greeks sacked when the Albanians approached the frontier. The Greeks have not scrupled to assert that their hands were forced by the arrival of bands of Albanians, which existed only in their imagination.

Later: Proclamation of the King

A despatch has just been received from the Albanian delegation to the effect that Prince William of Wied has been proclaimed King of Albania at Neuwied today. This news has been received here with acclamation by a large and enthusiastic crowd. Now, at last, Albania has officially a king.

The Near East, March 13th 1914
Notes from Albania
from our own correspondent, M. Edith Durham

Durazzo, March 8th

Reception of the Sovereign

Yesterday was certainly an historic day for Albania. No event could be more important than the arrival of a Sovereign in a country where he is so earnestly desired by the people and so urgently required by the political situation.

For the past two weeks - that is to say, ever since the date of Prince William's arrival was officially announced - there has been little talk of anything else. In this town, preparations have been pushed forward with feverish activity, and other places have been occupied in choosing representatives to come here in readiness to greet the Sovereign. Every town of importance was represented by a deputation, some even by too many delegates. Three days before the date fixed a deputation from the Albanian colonies in Calabria and Sicily arrived; the Albanian colonies in Roumania, the United States, Bulgaria, and even the little town of Borgo Erizzo in Dalmatia, were also represented.

The day before yesterday the news of Prince William's embarkation at Trieste became known, and there followed a time of tense suspense. Yesterday dawned calm and clear. According to programme, the *'Taurus'* arrived in the roadstead of Durazzo at about 2 p.m., accompanied by the men-of-war *'Gloucester'* (English), *'Quarto'* (Italian), and *'Bruix'* (French). The Austrian and Italian guardships here fired a salute. The mayor of the town, the councillors of Durazzo and Valona, and Essad Pasha went on board the *'Taurus'* to tender their homage.

After they had returned, at about three o'clock, the Prince and Princess landed amidst salutes from the warships and the batteries on shore, and as they set foot on land the Royal Standard was hoisted over the Palace. The Prefect of Durazzo met the Sovereigns at the point of disembarkation, and presented to them General de Veer, head of the Dutch Mission which is organising the Gendarmerie, the Consuls, and the leading dignitaries of the Mussulman and Christian communities. Next the Royal couple were greeted by the delegates of the International Commission of Control, in whose name Signor Leone, as President of the Commission for the time being, bade Prince William welcome. His speech, in which he remarked that the necessity of introducing law and order into the country had compelled the Commission to take the work in hand, has left a very bad impression on the Albanians, who are surprised at the lack of tact displayed in it. The Prince replied in French, in which language Signor Leone had also spoken. He remarked that he was acquainted with the services rendered by the Commission, and that he hoped it would continue its work in the future for the good of the country.

The Sovereigns were received at the entrance to the Royal Palace by a squadron of cavalry and the deputations from the towns. On their way their Majesties were greeted by the crowd with cries of *"Rrofte Mbreti!"* *("Long live the King!")* and *"Rrofte Mbreteresha!"* *("Long live the Queen!")*. In the garden of the Palace they were welcomed with enthusiasm by the scholars of the various Albanian schools. For about a quarter of an hour the King and Queen watched the excited and cheering crowd from the steps of the Palace, and afterwards from the balcony.

The night was spent in general rejoicings. At about eight o'clock in the evening a torchlight procession was admitted to the Palace gardens, and was received by the Sovereigns. The mosques and other chief buildings were decorated and illuminated.

Valona, February 27
The Schools Controversy

The question of the non-Albanian schools has been the subject of lively discussion during the last few days. It is necessary to remember that in Turkey the non-Mussulman communities enjoyed certain rights of self-government which made them, as it were, States within the State. It was these communities that controlled the schools, and ever since Mohammed II., at the time of the conquest of Constantinople, recognised the Orthodox Patriarch as *"Roum"*, i.e., as Greek, the Orthodox community has had only Greek schools throughout all Turkey, and consequently also in Albania. In vain the Albanians claimed the privilege of having Albanian schools; the Turkish authorities, strongly backed by the Orthodox Church, always opposed their claim vigorously. However, since the declaration of Albanian independence the first care of the Provisional Government has been to open national schools and discourage Greek schools.

Within the boundaries of the districts controlled by the Provisional Government of Valona not one Greek school has been opened; on the other hand, in every town and in some of the chief villages there are national schools attended by the Christian children. Only four buildings belonging to the Orthodox Church have been transformed into Albanian schools; for the remainder other premises have been erected. In the districts appertaining to Durazzo, however, Essad Pasha authorised the opening of Greek schools, ostensibly so as to maintain the status quo. Emboldened by this, and in obedience to instructions from the Œcumenical Patriarchate, the Metropolitan of Berat has just petitioned the International Commission of Control for permission to reopen the Greek schools which were in operation under the Turkish régime. The Russian and French delegates were inclined to support the Bishop's request, but the Albanian authorities vehemently opposed it, contending that the recognition of the right of the Patriarchate to set up Greek schools was tantamount to a refusal to the new Albanian State of the right to live. While the question was being warmly debated between the authorities and the Commission of Control several Orthodox communities protested against the anti-national tendencies of the Patriarchate, with the result that finally the Metropolitan of Berat showed a conciliatory spirit, and the Commission of Control determined to maintain the *status quo* pending a law *ad hoc*.

This question, however, is complicated by that of the schools of the Catholic communities, which is more important and difficult of solution. In the north of Albania there are several towns and villages with schools attached to the Catholic churches, and as Turkey recognised the protectorate of Austria-Hungary over the Catholics of Albania it has come about that these schools, in which the language is Albanian, are subsidised by that Power and maintained at her expense. Italy has no communal schools, but only schools in the towns on the littoral, where there are some communities of Italian subjects.

The general opinion is that the question of the non-Albanian schools will crop up again in the near future, and that then a definite settlement, both in the case of the Greek schools and in that of the schools maintained by Austria-Hungary, will be imperative.

The Question of Cables

Another question, which has caused less discussion, but is no less important, is that of the cables which connect Albania and Italy. There are two of these, one from Valona to Otranto, the other from San Giovanni di Medua to Bari. The former is about thirty years old; the latter was only laid down some five months back. Both belong to the Italian Government, who, not content with having one end of the cables, have just taken possession of the other, on Albanian soil. Quite unostentatiously, and without asking leave, the Italians intruded themselves into the Valona station. Italian employees were first graciously put at the disposal of the Provisional Government to help in certain repairs at the telegraphic station, and by this manœuvre they installed themselves there permanently.

The Italian Government allege that they are acting within their rights, in accordance with a contract between themselves and the Turkish Government. At the newly installed telegraph station at San Giovanni di Medua, the intruders proceeded with less compunction and circumspection. But the height of presumption was reached in the project which Italy had in view of connecting the San Giovanni di Medua cable with Scutari, and establishing an Italian station there; thereupon Austria-Hungary spoke of connecting her Bosnian telegraph line with Scutari, either across Montenegrin territory or by means of a submarine cable!

The situation is at present stationary, as Italy has not joined up her cable with Scutari, and Austria has for the moment surrendered her plan of laying a line.

The Near East, March 27th 1914
The Albanian Ministry
from our own correspondent, M. Edith Durham

Durazzo, March 18th

After days of delay, during which the Mpret rejected two proposed Ministries submitted to him by Turkhan Pasha, we at last have a Cabinet. In spite of the financial necessities of the country, two departments have been given chiefs of Cabinet rank, although they might perfectly well have been carried on in a less pretentious style - these are the Ministries of Mines and Forests and of Posts and Telegraphs. Apparently the appointment of their present incumbents, Aziz Pasha Vrioni and Hasan Bey Prishtina, was due to a desire to soothe certain susceptibilities and abate an inopportune rivalry.

Among the new Ministers three, in addition to Essad Pasha Toptani, have been members of the Ottoman Parliament. They are Mufid Bey, the Minister of Justice, who formerly represented Argyrokastro and, like the Prime Minister, was in the Ottoman Diplomatic Service; Aziz Pasha Vrioni and Hasan Bey Prishtina. The Ministers of Education and Finance, Turtulli Bey Koritza and George Adamides Bey Frachery, are both doctors of medicine.

The entire Ministry was received in audience by Prince William to-day, and each member took the following oath of office:- *"I swear before God and upon mine honour that I will well and truly serve the Mpret, the Mpreteresha, and the Realm."*

The Prince, who is officially styled here *'Madheri'* which is the equivalent of *'Majesty'* and *'Mpret'* which is *'King'* continues to receive deputations. The day before yesterday, he gave audience to the Latin prelates, yesterday the Mpretersha received a number of Christian and Moslem ladies, and to-day a very numerous deputation of chieftains from Skutari and the Malissor country - including both Latins and Mussulmans - waited upon the Sovereign.

The articles of the proposed Constitution, or *'Organic Statutes'* which have been drafted by the International Commission of Control, have now been submitted to the Mpret, who has been considering them to-day with the assistance of his Prime Minister, Turkhan Pasha.

As to the concession for the Bank of Albania, I understand that both of the interested Powers are exerting themselves in order to get it ratified by the present Government. In spite of the internationalisation of its capital, there is so much in the constitution of this bank which is considered contrary to Albanian interests that considerable feeling has been aroused against it here.

We understand that the correct English equivalent of the Albanian title Mpret has been decided - not by grammarians, but by diplomatists - to be Prince. The Powers have accepted Prince William of Wied as His Serene Highness the Prince of Albania - consequently the translation of Mpret should not be given as King. A diplomatist who had a great hand in the creation of the Albanian State has said that the idea was that the new ruler should remain a Prince until it was certain that he would not be compelled by force of circumstances to abdicate. He might become *'His Majesty the King'* when he was securely in the saddle, but not before, as, apparently, some of the more Conservative Courts of Europe object to the possibility of seeing another ex-King wandering about Europe.

This system of having a higher title for local use than that which has international recognition has a counterpart in Bulgaria, where the ruler is Tsar - that is to say Emperor - of the Bulgarians when in his own country, but is recognised abroad as enjoying the rank of King. Similarly his children are - according to the Almanach de Gotha - *'Altesses Royales'* and not *'Altesses Impériales'* no matter what their honorific designations may be in Bulgarians when at Sofia.

According to news from Durazzo published in the Jeune Turc, the Albanian flag was hoisted over the Castle of Scutari on March 19 in the presence of the Consular Body, the international Army of Occupation, the local authorities, and some 30,000 other spectators.

The Near East, May 29th 1914
Armistice in Albania
from our own correspondent, M. Edith Durham

Durazzo, May 10th [Delayed in Transmission].

Last Days of Strife

The last few days before the establishment of the armistice between the Albanians and the Greeks in arms against them were filled with sanguinary incidents. The efforts which the Greeks had been making for the past seven weeks to recover possession of Koritza culminated - after a period of repose lasting for twenty days - in a series of attacks from the direction of Liaskovik, which the Greeks had occupied with artillery since the Albanian gendarmes retired a fortnight ago from the Kolonia district. The first of these attacks began just a week ago when the Greeks moved northward, but were repulsed by the Albanians, who reoccupied several villages in the Kolonia district. In one of these, Stari, the partially burned corpses of a number of men and women were found, and those of three others who had been murdered. In all, twenty-three villages have been burned by the Greeks, either totally or in part, and I have myself visited several of these monuments to the vaunted superiority of Hellenic civilization and culture! Three days after this defeat a Greek force, estimated at some 3,000 men, attacked the Albanian positions at Nikolitza to the south-east of Koritza, and after ten hours' fighting was repulsed, leaving more than sixty dead on the field. Next day the armistice came into force.

The Orthodox in Albania

It is very greatly to be hoped that in any agreement come to as to the future status of the Epirotes no loophole will be afforded for the Greek Government to pose as the '*protector*' of Orthodox Christians in Albania. The attempt to give colour to such a pretension would lead to perpetual friction, and would permanently impair the national unity of this country and be a hardship to those Christian inhabitants who wish to remain Orthodox without becoming Greek.

Military Preparations

To-day orders have been received from Durazzo to call all the men fit for duty between the ages of twenty-five and thirty-five to the colours, and a good many have already presented themselves. The authorities have already sent a supply of the latest pattern Mauser rifles, and consignments of these are arriving daily from the capital. Advices have been received to the effect that two batteries of mountain guns are on their way. This will give the Albanians a chance of dealing with the insurgents on something like an equality in the matter of armament should recourse to fighting again become necessary.

A New Map: 'The Balkan Peninsula'

Scale 311/2 miles to an inch.
Size 28 by 22 inches.
Price in sheet, 3s.
Mounted to fold in case with complete index,
5s. (Bacon and Co.)

This is a praiseworthy attempt to wrestle with the difficulties of Balkan political geography as altered by the recent treaties and conventions, and with the intricacies of nomenclature, which has become worse confounded than ever since the transfer of territories has rendered Keupruli, Perlepe, Vodena, Eskeje, and Mustafa Pasha obsolete equivalents of Veles, Prilip, Edessa, Sketcha or Xanthi, and Svilengrad. In this connection we note that Messrs. Bacon have in many cases adopted the Croatian spelling of the Austrian staff maps, which gives values to certain consonants wholly different from those accepted in English. In the matter of frontiers the Serbo-Montenegrin is not quite right, and that given to Southern Albania is not in conformity with the most recent readjustments. We can appreciate the accuracy of leaving Mount Athos uncoloured, but why should Chios and the other Asiatic islands held by Greece be left white if Mitylene be coloured as Greek territory? In Europe, railways appear to be thoroughly up to date, but the Asiatic Soma-Panderma line opened in December, 1912, has been omitted. From a technical point of view the execution of the map is admirable.

The Near East, August 28th 1914
Albanian Letter
from our own correspondent, M. Edith Durham

Durazzo, August 14th

The Vanished Gendarmerie

Albania seems to have been entirely forgotten by the big world during the past two weeks. Since the outbreak of the general war no one has had time to give a thought to this country. Yet the situation is even more serious than before; insurrection is rampant throughout Central Albania; and it may be said that only two towns are left to the Government - Durazzo, the capital, and Valona, to the south.

Three weeks ago it was still hoped that a foreign nation would send troops to Albania for the purpose of introducing a little order while awaiting the organisation of the Gendarmerie. It is a fact that at the present time Albania has no armed force at all. It had, as your readers know, a small force of Gendarmerie, but this had to be employed against the Greeks in the South, and it has now become disorganised and reduced to nothing.

The journey of the Prime Minister, Turkhan Pasha, was undertaken solely with the view of enlisting the help of the Great Powers for this country. It was hoped that Roumania would receive the mandate of the six Great Powers and send a small contingent of troops here. The Albanian Government cited the case of Greece, pacified by 17,000 Bavarians of King Otho, and of Bulgaria, which was helped by the Russian army. But now that war has broken out there seems to be no hope at all.

Albania, therefore, finds herself compelled to rely upon her own resources. Here, at Durazzo, for instance, there are only 200 volunteers from Roumania, amongst whom, moreover, there are many members of the Albanian colonies at Bucharest and Constantza. The rest of the Albanian forces consist of irregulars, of men enrolled at hazard and without any military training. And the insurgents are at the door. Five hundred metres from Durazzo the Albanian trenches finish, and those of the enemy begin! Durazzo has been besieged for two months and a half, and only on the sea front is there any way open. Every night there are small skirmishes, and explosions are to be heard throughout the day.

The Insurgent's Attitude

All attempts to arrive at an understanding with the insurgents are unavailing for the immediate future. The insurgents are extraordinarily obstinate and infatuated, and it appears to be certain that Servian, Greek, and Young Turk agents are egging them on. There are only two courses open: to take the plunge and attacks the rebels, or to remain on the defensive and see what time will do. As for Durazzo, it has definitely decided to adopt the latter course, and rest strictly on the defensive; but Valona is animated by a different spirit.

It must be borne in mind that the people of South Albania are very faithful in their allegiance to the Mpret; and the districts now in the occupation of the insurgents only suffer that occupation of necessity, not from choice. Thus columns of irregulars have set out from Valona, and already Fier and a part of the plain of Muzeche have been cleared of the insurgents, and the town of Berat also has been retaken by the Government party, though stoutly defended by the insurgents. Should this enthusiasm not fade away, it may be hoped that peace and order may yet be established in Albania.

Italy's Attitude

I have said that Albania seems to have been forgotten; she has also been abandoned. One of the Powers which appears to be most directly interested in Albania's existence, namely, Austria, is engaged in the great war. The only other Power is Italy, who, only a short time ago, seemed to harbour anything but sympathy towards Albania; at present her Press is circumspect, and frankly states that in Italian diplomatic circles greater sympathy is being felt for the Prince of Wied. Evidently the tension created as a result of Essad's exile is dying a natural death. But what is Italy doing? She is taking advantage of the present situation to clamour for concessions, all of them burdensome to the country. They include fishery and forest rights, as well as the right to erect and exploit telegraph systems.

The Minister of Finance is in Rome, accompanied by the Italian Minister in Albania. The object is to raise the advance of one million francs promised to Albania by Italy and Austria. If they are not successful in their negotiations, this country will be in a sorry plight indeed, as it has absolutely no revenues whatsoever to fall back on.

The Refugees

To the above evils must be added the refugees, at least 100,000 men, women and children, who escaped from the Greek atrocities at Kortcha, Tepelen, Permeti, and Kurveleshi, leaving their burning villages behind them. In view of the financial situation, and given the rebellion in Central Albania, the problem of these refugees becomes very serious, the more so considering that the Epirus question is a long way from being settled.

Notes from Albania
from our own correspondent, M. Edith Durham

Durazzo, September 3rd

The Mpret's Departure

This morning, at seven o'clock, the Mpret Wilhelm left Durazzo and bade farewell to Albania - for the time being, at any rate. The sight was a depressing one, and I would not wish any nation - even an enemy nation - to have to witness the departure of its sovereign even *en congé*. For it is a compulsory holiday that King William of Albania has granted himself. It would be impossible to describe the feelings of the King's adherents. His Majesty, in spite of his customary calm, was obviously affected, and the Mpreteresha, who has a very sympathetic disposition, was profoundly moved.

Why has the Mpret had to leave Albania, where he had been such a short time? In three months the insurrectionary movement has spread through the greater part of the country. A few days ago Valona had to yield to the rebels, and with Valona in their hands the insurgents are masters of every town of importance in Albania except Durazzo and Scutari. In a few days more they would have concentrated all their forces against the capital. Nevertheless, the capture of Durazzo would have been very difficult, if not impossible, thanks to its defences and the fidelity of its garrison. Its defenders, almost all men of Kossovo and of South Albania, had sworn to remain absolutely faithful in all circumstances. Durazzo would therefore have been able to defend itself for a long time yet; and it would have been legitimate to expect the revolutionaries to become weaker, and the storm to blow over. The King might, then, have felt safe in the capital at least.

Financial Difficulties

For over a month Albania has been confronted by an insurmountable obstacle of quite a different nature - the lack of money. More than four months ago Austria and Italy jointly paid to Albania ten million francs, as a loan payable in instalments, and through the agency of the Bank of Milan and the Vienna Bank-verein. The interest on this loan was nominally $5^{1/2}$ per cent, but in reality 12 per cent.

This sum, so necessary for the development of the country's resources, was already expended, thanks to the expeditions against the Greeks and the insurgents; large quantities of war material, such as cannon, rifles, ammunition, and uniforms, had also been purchased; and it must not be forgotten that the receipts from the tithes had been practically nil, the country being either in a state of revolt or overrun by the Greeks.

Such a large loan was a heavy burden on the country's resources, but that fact did not prevent Essad Pasha and his associates from spending it with the greatest freedom in drawing up the budget. As a result the International Commission of Control, which is especially charged with the control of the country's finances, found a month ago, when it was investigating the financial situation, that of the ten millions 6,700,000 were already spent, and 3,000,000 francs was due for the payment of certain accounts owing to Italian and Austrian companies. Thus the Albanian Treasury had only 300,000 francs available; and this sum was in the banks which had advanced the loan; and as the International Commission of Control could not leave Albania without funds, it had decided to arrange for a further advance of one million francs by the two banks already mentioned, at the same nominal rate of interest. But the general war was on the point of breaking out, and there were difficulties in the way of placing the Albanian Government in possession of the sum intended for its use. The Minister of Finance himself went to Rome to see what could be done, in company with the Albanian Minister in Rome. But all their efforts were useless. Italy opposed her veto and refused to hand over to her banks not only 500,000 francs, the half of the new loan, but also the half of the 300,000 francs! And thus Albania found herself left in the lurch, without money, without means of carrying on.

Italy's Hostility
Italy has deliberately created all these difficulties. She has watched and waited for her right moment; and she has been rewarded. Austria-Hungary, desiring to humour an ally whose good faith seems rather doubtful, has not dared to cross her. Ever since Albania was made an autonomous State, Italy has shown but little sympathy towards her, and is quite unfavourable to national development, as witness her protection of Essad Pasha. This unfriendliness on the part of Italy was accentuated after the affair of Essad, which was regarded by the Italians as an attempt to undermine their prestige and to increase the influence of Austria-Hungary.

The Mpret's Manifesto
On his departure from Durazzo the Mpret issued a proclamation announcing to the Albanians that in consequence of the difficulties created by certain short-sighted spirits, by passion, and by the general war, having complicated the situation, he found himself forced to leave for the West, but that his thoughts would always be with Albania, and that he would hand over the Government to the Commission of Control during his absence. What the Commission will do, and what the insurgents will do, too, we shall see in a few days.

Pessimists say that Prince William will never be able to return to Albania, and that he must regard the pleasant dream of his reign as finished and done with. His return, they say, is out of the question; for he enjoys the good wishes of only part of the population, and the remainder is hostile to him. The optimists, on their side, consider that his return is possible, since the revolt must soon die out, and a reaction in the Mpret's favour must take place. I shall not attempt to prophesy.

As to the past, however, the mystery of the Albanian revolt, it is possible now to speak with some certainty. There can be very little doubt that the insurrection was fomented by Greece and Servia, and supported by the Powers that protect those two countries. Greeks and Servians both made use of Young Turk emissaries to stir up the religious sentiments of the Moslems, and to play upon their reactionary tendencies; and, in this direction, the ground may be said to have been well prepared by Essad Pasha and his adherents, who never hesitated to appeal to the lower instincts of the mob in order to achieve their selfish objects.

When the Mpret arrived, the country was in a quite abnormal condition. Essad and Ismail Kemal had let passions loose and stirred them up. Essad especially had been extraordinarily active in his endeavours to secure a Moslem Prince, and has roused fanaticism to a dangerous point. The treacherous policy of Greece and the crimes of the soi-disant Epirote Government further complicated the combined action of the Young Turks (real, or so-called, as the case may be), and of the reactionaries who represented the party of Essad. The Government found itself without any means of enforcing its authority - and without any real authority. On the other hand, Scutari, which had an international administration, was fertile soil for intrigues of all sorts.

At present the only districts openly loyal to the Mpret are the mountains of Hasi, Luma, Mat, and Dibra, all close to Servia. The danger across the border and the memory of recent foreign domination has taught them wisdom.

The Near East, October 2nd 1914
Notes from Albania
from our own correspondent, M. Edith Durham

Durazzo, September 223rd

From Bad to Worse

Things are going from bad to worse in Albania, and to-day the country is in a state of chaos. Since the departure of Prince Wilhelm, anarchy has reigned in this unhappy country.

When the Prince left, it was understood that the International Commission of Control would carry on the administration of affairs, the Prince himself having, in fact, announced in the proclamation he issued before his departure that he would provisionally hand over this duty to the Commission. But these anticipations and hopes have not been realized: for one thing, because there is no agreement either between the Ministers (and consequently between the Powers) or between the delegates of the Commission of Control; and for another because of the absolutely contradictory views and opinions held by the leaders of the insurrectionary movement. A few days later the foreign representatives in Albania left Durazzo as a measure of protest. The Commission of Control still remained, but rather in the character of mere spectators.

The Reactionaries

Meanwhile, the rebels lost no time in asserting themselves everywhere and endeavouring to organize their so-called Committee. For the time being their headquarters are at Shiak, a small village near Durazzo, and the cradle of the reactionary anti-dynastic movement. Up to the present Shkodra, Mati, Luma, and the Malissia of Dibra and of Hasi remain outside the jurisdiction of the revolutionary party; and as far as one can judge by the present state of affairs they will remain loyal to the Government and Prince William. It may be remarked that except for the majority of the inhabitants of the Shkodra district, who are Catholics, the population of these loyal districts is purely Moslem.

Insurgents' Divided Councils

What the insurgents will do remains to be seen. What is certain is that they are by no means agreed amongst themselves. Already misunderstandings and rivalries have broken out amongst them. They have not even got a single purpose. For whilst some of them desire to have the Ottoman Prince Burhan-ed-Din as their ruler, others want Prince Fuad, of the Khedivial family; others, again, want a foreign prince, but not Prince Wilhelm. A meeting will take place shortly at Durazzo, where all these parties will be represented and will choose their ruler. On the other hand, Essad Pasha Toptan is openly carrying on his intrigues with the Greeks on one side and the Serbs and Montenegrins on the other. It is even reported that Montenegro is working hard to get a Prince of its own Royal house elected.

Exodus of Royalists

In spite of all these various tendencies, the reactionary spirit is not strong in Albania itself. At Durazzo and Valona, wholesale arrests have been made, so that the number of Nationalists and Royalists now held as prisoners by the rebels in the various towns amounts to several hundreds. This persecution by the rebels has driven many Liberal-Nationalists to go into voluntary exile. A good many still remain in Albania, but only at Shkodra or in the Malissia. The others at first chose Brindisi and Bari as their places of refuge; but now Italy has just refused hospitality to them, having requested them to leave these towns. It is generally said here that Italy, being strongly in sympathy with the rebels, and opposed to Prince Wilhelm, could not bear to see these refugees, who still remained loyal. Now, therefore, a new centre is being formed at Lausanne, where a League for the Defence of the Independence and Integrity of Albania has just been founded. It is reported that several branches of the league have been established already. But what the near future has in store for the country, nobody can say.

The Near East, December 22nd 1916
Albania, Past and Present

X

The story of Albania was the theme of a lecture delivered by Miss M. Edith Durham before the Central Asian Society on December 14. She said that reports of the present condition of the country represented it as worse than that of Belgium. The men were being forced into the Austrian army, and the civil population were dying of starvation in many districts. An American missionary had recently stated that at least 150,000 people, largely women and children, had died of hunger and misery since the present war began.

The Albanians, said Miss Durham, are the direct descendants of the ancient inhabitants of Illyria and Epirus. They still cherish the tradition of Pyrrhus, *"who beat the Romans and everybody else."* They call him *'Burrus'*, and *"A je burra"* (*"How art thou, my brave?"*) is a common salutation among them to-day Plutarch tells us that the soldiers of Pyrrhus hailed him as the eagle. The modern Albanian calls himself Shkipetar and his country Shkiperia, words derived from shkip, an eagle. Christianity was introduced very early; the Albanians indeed claim to have been converted by St. Paul, who says, *"Round about Illyria have I preached the Gospel of Christ."* The Romans succeeded at last in subduing the country, but never in completely Romanising its inhabitants.

Afterwards came the Slavs. Stephen Dushan conquered Albania, and endeavoured to force its inhabitants to leave the Roman communion for that of the Greek Church. He punished by death those who obstinately refused to be converted. Thus was developed a hatred between the two peoples, which has lasted down to our own day; and, during the first Balkan war, hundreds of Albanians who refused to join the Orthodox Church were murdered or deprived of all they possessed and driven out of the country The Turks, said Miss Durham, had never treated the Balkan Christians as badly as they treated one another. After Kossovo, Albania maintained for centuries a fight against the Turks. Their great hero, Skanderbeg, made the country entirely independent while he lived, and, when the Turks at last conquered, they were content to exact only a military tribute.

The Albanians did not begin to embrace Islam until the seventeenth century, and their doing so was mainly the result of neglect by their own Church. They were put under bishops who were mostly foreigners, and who chiefly occupied themselves with squabbles about the frontiers of their dioceses. One unfortunate result of the change of faith was to lead other people to regard the Mohammedan half of the Albanian population, as Turks, though they were really as intensely national in spirit as their Christian compatriots, and joined in the efforts for Albanian freedom. Under Ali Pasha, Albania was for a time independent. At the time of the Berlin Treaty Great Britain was in favour of forming a large autonomous Albanian province, but the Powers were not unanimous, and all that was done was to recommend reforms.

The Sublime Porte responded to this by arresting the heads of the Albanian League and executing them or exiling them to Asia Minor. Afterwards it permitted Albanian schools to be opened, and allowed printing in the Albanian language. Then these privileges were withdrawn, and, when Miss Durham first visited Koritza, in 1904, its unfortunate schoolmaster was still serving a term of fifteen years' imprisonment. The Greeks helped the Turks in this work of repression. A Greek bishop excommunicated the Albanian language, and a Greek priest told the people it was useless to pray in that tongue because Christ did not understand it. The Young Turkish revolution was hailed with joy in Albania, newspapers sprouted up, and schools were opened. Then again came reaction, leading up to the revolt of 1910, since which time the country has been incessantly harried by foreign troops. Turkish, Montenegrin, Serbian, Greek, Bulgar, and Austrian armies have successively swept in, plundering and slaughtering the inhabitants.

The Near East, February 23rd 1917

Albanian Past and Present: The Language Question

by M. Edith Durham

It was in the year 1901 that I first visited Albania and was struck by the vigour and originality of the people. But it was not until a much longer visit in 1904 that I came in close touch with the national movement. The patriots of Koritza first inspired me with the interest for their heroic little nation which subsequent travels have ever increased.

The tale indeed of Albania's struggle for education and development is one of the most remarkable in the history of education, and deserves more detailed telling than we have space for here. The Turkish Government learnt by bitter experience that the result of permitting national schools to the Greeks, Bulgars, and Serbs was that they became centres of political propaganda, which was supported by money and teachers supplied by various Great Powers. And Greek, Bulgar, and Serb insurrections and independence followed. The Sultan resolved that no such thing should happen in the case of Albania. The Albanian tongue was prohibited; the printing of it and the teaching of it were made punishable by heavy terms of imprisonment. If an Albanian child was to learn to read, he or she must first learn a foreign tongue, and in that case the child was classed as belonging to the nationality of the school selected. This fact I found caused intense bitterness.

"When I was a little boy," said a Moslem Albanian, *"I was sent to school at Constantinople. They said that I was a Turk; I said that I was an Albanian. I would not say that I was a Turk. Then they turned on me, and called me a dog. I have hated them ever since." "I hate, hate, hate the Greeks,"* said a Koritza woman. *"When I was a child the Government would not permit any Albanian school. My parents wanted me to learn, so I had to go to the Greek one. There were Greek teachers. They used every day to tell me and my little friends that we were Greek. It was a lie. We did not know one word until we went to school. They used to tell us that Christ was Greek, and that it was useless for us to pray in Albanian because He did not understand it. Now they pretend that we are Greek! I will never again defile my tongue with their dirty language. Nor shall my children learn it. I hate, hate, hate it."*

Similarly, children attending Slav schools are denationalised, if possible. I had formed on previous journeys a very favourable opinion of certain Montenegrins, and afterwards found that they were not Slavs at all, but

Albanians, who spoke their mother tongue at home; but they had been educated in Serb, for Albanian schools are prohibited also in Montenegro.

England, in 1880, made a strong effort on Albania's behalf. Lord Goschen, then H.M. Ambassador at Constantinople, in his report on the subject, put Albania's case in a nutshell, when he said: *"Nor can it be denied that the Albanian movement is a perfectly natural one. As ancient and distinct a race as any by whom they are surrounded, they have seen the nationality of these neighbour races taken under the protection of various European Powers and gratified in their aspirations for more independent existence ... Meanwhile they have not received similar treatment. Their nationality is ignored, ... exchanges of territory are proposed, other difficulties arise, but it is still at the expense of Albania, and Albanians are handed over to Slavs and Greeks without reference to the claims of nationality."*

Lord Goschen then mapped out a large Albania with a view to its autonomy and future independence. Not all the Powers agreed to this scheme, unfortunately, and it was dropped. Had these frontiers been delimited, very many recent complications would have been avoided. It appears, indeed, that injustice to a small nation recoils sooner or later upon the Great Powers which inflict it. A tiny shell splinter will make a whole limb suppurate. So will a small race incorporated in a large one act as a perpetual sore which undermines the conqueror's strength. The result of the Sultan's attempts to crush Albanian development were the Albanian insurrections of 1910-11 and 1912. Similar results may be expected by any nation trying forcibly to annex Albanian territory.

To return to Koritza in 1904. An unhappy schoolmaster for a time had had permission to open an Albanian school, the permission had been suddenly withdrawn, and he was still working out his sentence of fifteen years' imprisonment.

Much talk did I hear of the difficulties and dangers of learning. Turkish spies and Greek propagandists were ever ready to denounce the readers and importers of Albanian books and papers. But I was furnished with the addresses in various lands where such could be obtained. And at great risk papers, published in London and Bucharest, were secretly circulated. A luckless zaptieh had just been given two years' imprisonment for being found with one in his pocket. And a poor restaurant keeper at Scutari, to whom one had been sent by post by some foolish foreigner, ignorant of the possible results, was condemned to fifteen years', and only released by the efforts of all the Consuls.

In Scutari, both Italy and Austria opened schools and protected them. In

Koritza, the American mission opened a girls' school. For a boys' school permission could not be obtained. Even under the protection of the Stars and Stripes, the heroic schoolmistress ran great risks. Turkish authorities spied on her continually. But she used English school books and translated her lessons, and so managed to teach her mother tongue. The girls taught their brothers to write at home. And though the school was essentially a Christian mission school, yet Moslems, too, sent their daughters, because it was Albanian. I visited with very great interest the homes of several of the parents of the school children, and was much impressed with the earnestness of their desire that their children should not be denationalized.

From Koritza I rode through Albania from south to north with one of the colporteurs of the British and Foreign Bible Society, himself an ardent patriot. It was a ride almost equal in incident and excitement to Borrow's well-known journey with the Bible in Spain. The Turkish authorities had not the smallest objection to the sale of the Scriptures. It was to the sale of them in Albanian that they objected. But the society had leave to sell all its publications, and the Albanians seized upon this as a means for circulating books in their mother tongue. We had a stock of the Gospels and of the Book of Genesis. We were stopped and searched in all places except those where the local Governor happened to be an Albanian. There we were warmly welcomed. One Turkish Kaimakam seized all our stock, but we picked up more at a depot further on. Everywhere folk flocked to buy, secretly in some places, publicly in others. I realised the strength of the national feeling when a Moslem schoolmaster brought all his boys, and they bought a book apiece.

At Liaskovik, a deputation waited on me and begged that I would make a school under English protection. And at Permeti we were received with such enthusiasm that the Turkish Kaimakam would not allow us to speak to anyone without a soldier as witness. As some of our visitors spoke French the soldier's presence did not incommode us much. More than one officer in the Turkish army bought books, and even begged us to come again with a greater variety. That journey I shall never forget. What a people, indeed. They have survived five empires, and successfully resisted every effort to denationalize them. Brave, intelligent, and receptive - the artists of the Balkan peninsula - they have retained their language, their national customs and traditions through all the centuries. But Mr. Asquith has declared that the present war is waged for the purpose of defending the rights of little nationalities, and we may therefore hope, together with the Albanians, that their day, too, is about to dawn.

The story of their epic struggle for existence we may tell in another article.

The Near East, March 2nd 1917

Albania Past and present: The Race Instinct

by M. Edith Durham

Let us now consider the Albanian's centuries of struggle for existence. Save the Balkans themselves, Albania is about the oldest thing in the Balkan peninsula. We first hear of the land as Illyria, a very strong kingdom, which fought with the Romans as early as 230 B.C., so strong, indeed, that the Romans did not succeed in subduing and conquering it till A.D. 169. Scodra, now called Scutari by us, was then already its capital. And the Albanians call it by its old name very slightly modified - Shkodra - to this day. It is one of Europe's oldest capitals. Berlin, Petrograd, Sofia, and Belgrade are but modern in comparison.

The native population seems to have flourished under Rome. Many even rose to be Emperors, among them Diocletian and Constantine the Great, and others of less note. Christianity was early introduced. Scutari became a bishopric as early as 307 A.D. Judging by the things found in the numerous ancient graves there was a considerable native civilization before the advent of the Romans. Illyria manufactured and probably exported iron at a very early date.

Roman-Illyrian civilization was overwhelmed and largely destroyed by the inrush of great numbers of savage Slavonic tribes from across the Danube. They were pagan, and drove the Latins to the coast, where Roman influence has never yet quite died out, and settled on the plains of the interior. They were the ancestors of the modern Serbs, Bosniaks, and Montenegrins. Though they spread over wide land, they were a tribal people, and therefore weak. They were, therefore, in their turn speedily overwhelmed by the Bulgars who founded the first Bulgar Empire, which flourished in the Tenth Century and included the greater part of the Balkan peninsula. The Illyrian population, it would appear, had taken to the mountains of the West, just as did the Welsh in England. Here they maintained their language, traditions, and customs, and a certain amount of independence.

Two Bulgar Empires successively rose and fell. Finally the Serbs united under the Kings of the Nemanya line, and for about two hundred years were the dominant race in the Balkans. During the twenty years, indeed, of Tsar Stefan Dushan's reign the Serbian Empire included almost all the peninsula. But all Balkan Empires have been one-man empires: have gone up like rockets and down like sticks. Ambitious Serb nobles tore up

Dushan's empire shortly after his death. Albania was one of the first to break loose, and we hear of local native chieftains.

It is highly probable that the inclusion in these fleeting mediæval Empires of a large and vigorous Albanian population was one of the sources of their weakness.

The Slav invaders, who did not become Christian till the Ninth Century - that is some five centuries after the Albanians - threw in their lot with Byzantium. Illyria, on the other hand, formed part of the Patriarchate of Rome. The efforts of the Serbs, however, to Slavize the Albanians failed completely. The Serb occupation was but brief, and ran off the Albanian as does water from a duck's back. All that remains is the hatred of the invaded for the invader. The Albanian has never forgotten that he is the aboriginal and the Slav a comparative newcomer.

The next great Balkan catastrophe - for we must be brief - was the advent of the Turk. The peninsula was at this time in a wholly incoherent state, and no one race was supreme. The Balkan peoples have in fact owed all their troubles to the fact that they hate each other more than they hate any outsider, and so fail to combine. Even when faced with the Turkish danger this rule held good. The son-in-law of the Serb Tsar deserted to the Turks with all his men. Christian, not for the first nor the last time, betrayed Christian.

The Albanians were the last of all the Balkan peoples to succumb. Under the leadership of their celebrated champion, Skenderbeg, they successfully resisted one Turkish invasion after another. But he died in 1468, leaving no one capable of replacing him. Venice had for some time been creeping down the coast, occupying several towns and trading with the interior. The Albanians and Venetians united against the Turk. But Scutari fell after a long and fierce siege in 1479, and Albania was soon completely overrun. True to their traditions, the mountain tribesmen managed to retain their autonomy, and for over a century sent repeated appeals to Venice for help. But none came. The Albanians then, in the Seventeenth Century, began to go over to Islam. The Slavs had already done so in numbers, especially in Bosnia.

Gaining power as Moslems, the Albanians rapidly spread down on to the plains from which their ancestors had been evicted by the Serbs. The mountain tribes founded villages as far north as Mitrovitza, and spread towards Monastir. They reconquered, in fact, a large portion of their ancient Illyria. The Serbs of Kossovo vilayet accepted Austria's invitation, and migrated in a body into Austria.

The Albanians now began to struggle for independence. The Pashas of Scutari and the celebrated Ali Pasha, whose capital was Janina, were indeed for a time almost wholly independent. Crushed by the Turks at the beginning of the Nineteenth Century, they have never wholly yielded nor given up their national aspirations. They have survived Rome and Byzantium, two Bulgar Empires, one Serb Empire, and the Turkish Empire without losing their identity or their strong race instinct. Today they look forward eagerly to the fulfilment of the promise that this war is one for the rights of small nationalities.

They look forward to the fulfilment of the promise made by Europe in 1913. Their hopes were cruelly disappointed when, in response to their appeal, Europe sent them a wholly incompetent and incapable German Prince - the Prince von Wied. They expected him as a Messiah. He did not even deign to visit his lands and people, but sat in a very comfortable palace, pastured off diet provided by a very excellent chef, and played at trying to form a little German Court, leaving the unfortunate Albanians to be made at once the prey of numerous and most unscrupulous European intriguers.

That story is too recent to tell.

Let us hope, though, that Albania's day is about to dawn, and that the oldest and in many ways the most capable of the Balkan peoples will soon have their *"place in the sun"*. Given a fair chance, no one who knows the Albanian doubts that he will ultimately succeed. But in order that the chance should be fair it would be advisable that some one strong protector should guard Albania's interests. And that she should not a second time be left to the 'too many cooks' of many Powers.

History and racial sympathies seem to indicate Italy as the most suitable protector. But in this, as on other national questions, let us hope the people themselves will be consulted. Above all, if even partially permanent peace is to be made, let us hope that no Albanian territory will be included in any other State. History shows that this results always in the break up of the State that is so constituted.

The Saturday Review June 2nd, 1917
Albania and the Albanians

by M.E. Durham

Of the smaller nations of Europe who are looking forward anxiously for the results of this war, which is being waged on behalf of their right to exist and develop, none awaits more eagerly than Albania. And of all small nations none has fought a longer battle for liberty. The Albanian is the oldest thing in the Balkan Peninsula, and from the early days when the Romans fought his Illyrian ancestors and their proud queen, Teuta, his history has been a series of epic struggles against one invader after the other. He has outlived four empires and retained his individuality. Scutari, as we call it (Shkodra in Albanian), was Illyria's capital before the coming of the Romans. Berlin, Petrograd, Belgrade, even Vienna, are modern in comparison with Scutari.

Roman civilisation seems to have spread swiftly in Illyria. Judging by ornaments and implements found in pre-Roman graves, indeed, the Illyrians had a considerable civilisation of their own, and were among the earliest manufacturers and users of iron. The Albanians claim that they were converted to Christianity by St. Paul himself. At any rate, they were early converted, for we find Scutari an Archbishopric as early as 307. And Albania has formed part of the Patriarchate of Rome ever since. Nor were the Illyrians a conquered people. More than one Roman Emperor - Diocletian and Constantine the Great among them - was of native blood.

Roman-Illyrian civilisation was rudely broken into and largely destroyed by the invasion of huge hordes of a pagan people - the Slavs. By the seventh century they had seized large tracts of the plain lands and driven Roman civilisation to the coast, where it has never entirely died out. Of the Illyrian population part, no doubt, was absorbed, though it has left traces. The bulk of the people, who sheltered in the mountainous districts of modern Albania, retained its language, its individuality, and its customs with remarkable tenacity. Every effort made to Slavise them failed completely, and when, on the death of Tsar Stefan Dushan, in 1356, his great but short-lived Serbian Empire fell to pieces, the Albanians were among the first to break loose.

Albania's first catastrophe was the coming of the Slavs, whom she was wont to consider her foe. Her second was the coming of the Turks. To these the Albanians were the last of all the Balkan peoples to succumb. Their chieftain, Skenderbeg, kept the Turks at bay for twenty-four victorious years, and extended his territories. It was not till his death in 1467 that the Turks overran the land. But the old Illyrian spirit remained unbroken. The tribesmen retained local autonomy, and in the mountains no doubt much independence. Again and again they sent appeals to Venice to help them fight for freedom. But in vain. Finally, in the 17th century they began going over to Islam in considerable numbers. The Greeks and the Slavs had done so as early as the 15th century Again it was the Albanian who was the last to succumb to environment.

Favoured by the Turkish Government, Albanian chiefs rapidly gained power, and soon reconquered a large part of the ancestral lands which had been torn from their forebears by the previous invaders. So strong did they become that they again struck for freedom. For many years Ali Pasha, of South Albania, whose capital was Janina, was quite independent and almost succeeded in getting English support. And the Pasha of Scutari was almost as powerful. The Turks then made a very determined effort to crush the Albanians once for all. South Albania fell entirely into Turkish hands. The north was badly beaten, but not wholly subdued. Nor did the nation as a whole forget its traditions.

When other peoples of the Balkans obtained favour at the Congress of Berlin, the Albanians too, asked for recognition. England favoured the formation of a large Albanian province, with a view to its future independence. It is obvious that, had this been effected and the frontiers delimited, very many recent evils and difficulties would have been avoided. But the Powers were not agreed. And the Turks punished the chieftains who had risen for freedom by death or by exile. Turkish governors and often garrisons were put in the Albanian towns, and Albania was in hard plight, worse than that of any other Balkan race. Each of the others had a 'big brother' outside, who, for more or less selfish reasons, saw that she had churches, priests, books and schools of her own, through which to develop her nationality.

No outside Power protected Albania, and the Turks, knowing the result of national development, had early forbidden the use of Albanian in schools and in print. No race in Europe has had to struggle against such dangers and difficulties as the Albanians in order to learn. Koritza was the centre of nationalism in the south. When I first visited it in 1904, the schoolmaster was still serving out his term of fifteen years' imprisonment for teaching the language, and the same penalty was inflicted on anyone found with an Albanian book or paper in his possession. But I found the work at Koritza going bravely and steadily on. Papers were printed in London, Brussels, and Bucharest, and secretly circulated. The British and Foreign Bible Society had the right to sell its publications in the Turkish Empire, and quantities of Albanian copies of the Book of Genesis and the Gospel of St. Mark were bought up greedily by Moslem and Christian alike to serve as means of learning to read. For religion has made no difference to the Albanjians' sense of nationality.

I shall never forget the enthusiasm with which the Young Turks proclamation of the freedom of the Press was hailed in Albania. Mushroom newspapers sprang up almost in a night, Albanian clubs and schools were opened and overfilled. *"Liria! Lliria!" (Liberty! Liberty!)* was on every lip.

Down came the Turk, more fierce than ever. Printing presses were closed, schoolmasters, editors, printers imprisoned. Albanian, if printed at all, was to be printed in Arabic characters - totally unfit for a European language. The Government printed thousands of alphabets and sent them to Albania. The people collected them and burnt them at Berat. The immediate results of these oppressions were the Albanian insurrections of 1910-11 and 1912. They were the precursors of the Balkan War of 1912-13. In these wars, the Albanians as a whole remained neutral, defending themselves only when attacked. But they were invaded and devastated in parts by more than one army.

It is perhaps not desirable here to enter into criticism of the recent actions of allies and foes in that war. I will say only that throughout its horrors the Albanians never lost hope in the ultimate justice of Europe, and that these hopes were most cruelly blighted when, in response to their earnest prayer, the Powers sent them a wholly incapable and incompetent German, the Prince von Wied. He did not even deign to visit his country and people, but sat in a very comfortable palace on the coast and tried to make a little German court And the people who had looked towards him as to a Messiah saw, to their helpless dismay, their land made the prey of most unscrupulous and disgraceful European intrigues.

But it is darkest before dawn. Albania hopes that the day for which she has struggled so long is coming at last. Sixty thousand refugees who have found shelter in America are awaiting the day when peace is proclaimed, and they may take up the work - with new-found knowledge - of reorganising their fatherland.

No one who knows the Albanian, his quick intelligence, his industry and energy, can doubt his ultimate success if given a fair chance. He is the artist of the Balkans, and his aptitude for trade is greater than that of any Balkan race, except perhaps the Greeks, while as a skilled craftsman he excels all other Balkan peoples. His silverwork, wood carving, and gold embroideries are to be found in the museums of Europe. But to do himself justice he must be able to call his soul his own. Each of the other Balkan peoples, on being given independence, has been given also the help and protection of some strong Power till able to stand alone. Let us hope that this time Albania will not be left to the mercies of an '*International Control*', which means that each nation concerned plays for its own hand, and the wretched protégé suffers. But may there be one strong protector to whose interest it will be to warn off all trespassers and see that Albania shall belong to the Albanians.

Her vital interests in the Adriatic point to Italy as best fitted to be that protector.

Autonomy under a European Prince as a protectorate would be gladly accepted by the Albanians, who of all things dread to see their country dismembered and themselves subjected to the rule of races whom they regard only as foes.

The Near East, August 31st 1917
The Fallen Idol

To the Editor of The Near East

Sir,

The revelations of the Greek White Book prove to all the world how little reliance can be placed on any of the statements of the Greek Government made when Constantine was on the throne. Among them was the denial that the Greek Government had any part in the infamous attempt in the spring and summer of 1914 to seize South Albania. That this was the work of Greek regulars was proved by all the evidence. Greek soldiers who gave their names, regiments, and the names of their officers were taken prisoner. All the refugees - and they were from many different districts - told of soldiers, and in many places of artillery.

But, as first-hand evidence is the very best, I went myself to the mountains to try to spy out the position of the Greek troops. Creeping along the mountain side in the neighbourhood of Tepeleni, which had already been captured by them, I saw with field glasses their military outposts and men in khaki, on the other side of the valley. That they were military posts and not a native encampment was obvious. I returned in haste to Valona, meaning to try to arouse Europe on the subject But I arrived there to find that the present great war had broken out. England had, in fact, declared war forty-eight hours before I had news that we were likely to be drawn into it.

In the whirlpool of excitement which I found when I reached England at the end of August, 1914, any attempts to draw attention to the miseries of South Albania were hopeless.

That the seizure of South Albania was part of the German scheme is fairly obvious. The Kaiser himself, some time before, had visited that land from his *pied à terre* at Corfu, and his visit had aroused great distrust in the minds of the Albanians. Many persons at the time were surprised that the Prince of Wied, feeble stick though he was, made no effort to claim those districts which formed part of his realm. The patriots of Koritza hoped and longed for his coming.

It would appear, however, from papers which Wied left when he fled, that he had been instructed from Germany not to move in the matter, as his realm would later be extended in the direction of Serbia and Montenegro. In the light of recent revelations this report seems highly probable.

During the few months that Wied was at Durazzo, so multitudinous and conflicting were European political interests that we can best describe it by saying that diamonds busily strove to cut diamonds, while wheels ran within wheels, troubled waters were fished in, and everyone tried to make a catspaw of the other. A nice *'confusion of epitaphs'* for confusion worse confounded. We may add another, and say Constantine's finger was in the pie.

Yours, etc.,

M. E. Durham,
71, Belsize Park Gardens.
August 24

The Contemporary Review, October 1917
The Albanian Question
by M. E. Durham

Of the many after-war questions which will have to be solved, few are more important than the Albanian question, for few, if any, involve so many conflicting interests; and in none is there more danger that the wishes of the people may be ignored and the seeds of future trouble sown. Alsace-Lorraine is coveted by but two Powers, and the facts connected with it have been publicly discussed for the past forty years. But Albania, or a strong position in Albania, is coveted by four Powers - Austria, Italy, Serbia, and Greece. Truly we may say five, and add Bulgaria. And the Albanians themselves greatly desire independence, and have, moreover, been promised it.

The man in the street knows nothing about Albania. He often asks if all the people really have white hair and pink eyes. Or he heard of the Balkan peoples for the first time with any interest, during the Balkan wars of 1912-13, espoused warmly the cause of either Serb, Greek, or Montenegrin, and, through his friends of the race in question, learnt to regard Albania merely as a Tom Tiddler's ground, at whose expense *"victors"* were to be *"recompensed."* The Balkan War, which began with the noble object of freeing the Balkan peoples, quickly degenerated into an attempt to dismember and destroy the oldest of them. It began with a hymn to *"Liberty!"* and ended with a howl for *"Loot!"* Let us strive that the present war may not end thus disgracefully, but that an Allied victory may bring the freedom and justice it promised.

The Albanians are among the very oldest inhabitants of the Balkan peninsula. Classical authors give the names of very many tribes which dwelt in those lands when history dawns. The Greeks classed them as *"barbarians"* and they spoke a non-Greek tongue. They were united in groups under native kings, and of these groups some of the most important were the Macedonians, the Illyrians, and the Epirotes. According to Strabo, all three spoke the same language. And it is from the Illyrians and the Epirotes that the Albanians of to-day descend. Modern Albania, in all probability, derives from the language of Alexander the Great and King Pyrrhus. Illyria and Epirus, in old days, extended from Trieste along the whole of the Adriatic coast, comprising at one time all Bosnia and the Herzegovina, a large part of modern Serbia, and all Montenegro, as well as modern Albania. And though since then Albania has been invaded and the population modified by contact with the invaders, as often as have the British Isles, yet the race remains to-day distinct, speaking a language which differs in important respects from the tongues of its Slav and Greek neighbours, having distinct traditions, and with marked physical types which we recognise at once as Albanian in a mixed Balkan crowd.

I entered South Albania for the first time in the spring of 1904. The carriage, in which we had driven nearly all night from Monastir, rattled down from the mountains. We left behind us the thickset, Slav-speaking peasants of Macedonia, and, as we came out on the Koritza plain and I saw the lean, long-necked Albanians, with their aquiline features, swinging along with the easy stride which I knew so well in the North, I felt that I was once again in a familiar land, and that though the Northerner has been subjected to Slav influence and the Southerner to Greek, yet an Albanian is an Albanian *"for a' that."* Rome, Byzantium, the fleeting mediæval Empires of the Bulgar and the Serb, and the great Ottoman Empire have, in turn, risen and fallen.

The Albanian has emerged from each wave of invasion, shaken off the drops, and gone his way. Many Powers have spent much effort and much money upon trying to turn the Albanian into something else. He has entered their schools, and has often learnt things that he was not intended to, but *"in spite of all temptations to belong to other nations"* he remains Albanian. Diplomatic *'Mrs. Bonds'* have toddled industriously round and round the Albanian pond with their pockets full of *'onions and sage'* in the shape of schools, hospitals, and charitable institutions. The Albanian wild-duck has feasted freely, but has so far resolutely refused to come and be annexed, and fill the pockets of the would-be exploiters of forests, mines, and strategical positions who greedily watch diplomatic efforts. The object of each Power was so obvious that it drew from my dear, old dragoman the shrewd remark *"Lady, these so-called Great Powers are no better than a band of brigands. By day they quarrel with one another. But when it is dark they all go out robbing together."*

And still the Albanian struggles for independence, for the right to develop on his own lines, and for the freedom of his language. This has been denied him by every conqueror. The printing and teaching of Albanian was forbidden, under heavy penalties, by the Turkish Government, and was carried on only with great difficulties, under the protection of various foreign Powers, who themselves so dreaded the formation of a united and strong Albania that they each insisted in their schools upon using a different alphabet and system of orthography in order to hamper national development. In the instances where large Albanian-inhabited districts were annexed by Serbia, Montenegro, and Greece, things were even worse. Not one single Albanian school was permitted; not one single Albanian newspaper. In some instances, large masses of the population were forcibly expelled, and efforts were made to Slavise or Grecise the remainder.

Christianity arrived in Illyria as early as the first century. Scodra (Scutari), Durazzo, and Antivari were bishoprics dependent on Rome, some three centuries before the pagan Slavs poured into the Balkan peninsula in the seventh century. And ever since that great inrush has the struggle of the Albanian against Slavism gone on. During the two centuries (1180-1356) when the Serb Empire flourished, and by degrees encroached further and further on Albanian territory, the Northern Albanians strenuously resisted the efforts made to Slavise them and force them to join the Orthodox Eastern Church, and when the Serb Empire fell to pieces on the death of the great Tsar Dushan in 1356, they were among the first to break loose and begin their long struggle to regain the lands from which the Serbs had driven their forefathers. When the Slavs of the peninsula fell under Turkish dominion after the Battle of Kosovo in 1389, the Albanians successfully resisted, and under their celebrated leader, Skenderbeg, the whole of the North, including Dibra and Ochrida,. was independent till his death in 1478. Under the Turk, they yet retained considerable local autonomy. In the seventeenth century Islam began to make progress among them. They grew in power, and harried their secular enemies, the Serbs, so effectually that in 1690 the bulk of the Serb population of the Kosovo and Metoya plains accepted the invitation of Austria and withdrew across the Danube, whence their ancestors had originally come. The Albanians then rapidly resettled the district, and reoccupied the lands of their Illyrian forefathers in great numbers as far north as Nish and eastward towards Monastir.

Then, in the eighteenth century, they began their struggle for complete independence. Ali Pasha (born 1740) subdued the local Albanian Pashas and Beys, and ruled over all South Albania as far as Parga, holding his own successfully against the Turks. He had representatives in foreign lands, and entered into negotiations with England. And in the North there arose to power the Bushatlis, hereditary Pashas of Scutari. Mehmed Bushatli extended his Pashalik to Ochrida. His son, Kara Mahmoud, became so independent that the Sultan sent a large army against him, which he routed completely on the plain of Kosovo. Had he and Ali joined forces they could have freed all Albania from the Turks. But Ali could bear no rival, and hoped to extend his rule northward. He, therefore, sent troops to assist the Sultan, which shared in the Turkish defeat. No reconciliation was then possible between Ali and the Bushatlis. Albania was torn in half by its two Pashas. Ali was attacked and overwhelmed in his old age by a large Turkish force, and he and his sons were beheaded in 1822.

South Albania then fell completely under the Turks, who, the better to check the development of national feeling, permitted, and even encouraged, Greek propaganda. The Greek language, then, was spoken, it would appear, only by Greek immigrants. Edward Brerewood, writing in 1625, says of the Greek language: *'But at this day the Greek tongue is very much decayed, not only as touching the largeness and vulgarness of it, but also in elegance of language. For as touching the former, the Natural languages of the Countries have usurped upon it so that the parts in which Greek is spoken at this day are, in a few words, but these. First, Greece itself - excepting Epirus and the west part of Macedon ... likewise in the isles west of Candie and along the coast of Epirus and Corfu.'* This shows clearly the thoroughly non-Greek character of Epirus - the coast places being merely Greek trading centres. Just as Greece has tried to acquire wide tracts of Slavonic lands by classing all members of the Orthodox Church as *'Greek'*, so has she striven to lay claim to South Albania. Rome, with equal justice, might claim all English and French Catholics as Italians. Kara Mahmoud meanwhile further extended his power, and might have shaken off Turkish rule in time. But he was killed by the Montenegrins in 1799, who thus rendered a great service to their secular foe, the Sultan.

About this time, the Toptani Beys of Kroya took Tirana and began to gain power in Central Albania. Mustafa Pasha Bushatli, Kara Mahmoud's nephew, made a bid for independence by marching against the Turks at the moment when Diebitch was leading a Russian Army to Constantinople. Unluckily for him, the Russians unexpectedly made peace, leaving the Turks free to send a punitive expedition, under Reshid Pasha, to Scutari. Mustafa was forced to capitulate. He and his family were exiled to Asia, and the dynasty was extinct in Scutari. Reshid's Army then over-ran all North Albania, attacking Djakova, Ipek, and Pristina, and killing or exiling the local chiefs. Albania, both North and South, was now hard hit, and the Porte further weakened it in 1865 by dividing it into vilayets (Scutari, Janina, Kosovo, and part of Monastir), and appointing Turkish governors in the larger towns, and garrisons, too, in some of them. Meanwhile, helped by more than one great Power, Serbia and Greece had obtained recognition and autonomy. Albania did much to aid the Greeks, but no Power assisted her to rise in her turn.

After the Russo-Turkish War of 1877, when Turkish territory was being divided among the Balkan peoples, the Albanians saw, with dismay, much of their best land torn from them and given to the Greeks, Serbs, and Montenegrins. They resisted fiercely, saved some of it, and formed the Albanian League. Its centres were at Prizren and Argyrocastro, and its objects the defence of Albanian rights.

As Lord Goschen, then H.B.M. Ambassador at Constantinople, put it in a despatch to Earl Granville: *'As ancient and distinct a race as any by whom they are surrounded, they have seen the nationality of these neighbour races taken under the protection of various European Powers and gratified in their aspirations. ... Meanwhile, they see that they have not received similar treatment. ... Exchanges of territory are proposed, difficulties arise, but it is still at the expense of the Albanians, and Albanians are handed over to Greeks and Slavs without reference to the principles of nationality.'*

Great Britain then (1880) strove to create a strong Albania (Kosovo, Scutari, Janina and part of Monastir vilayets), which should eventually become independent. Lord Goschen and Lord E. Fitzmaurice, both foreseeing the importance of the Albanian question, worked hard for this end. Had they succeeded, many recent complications and much misery would have been obviated. But the Powers who met in council were not unanimous, and all that was done was to recommend certain reforms to the Turks, who responded by arresting the heads of the Albanian League, and executing or exiling them. Albanians were forcibly expelled in thousands from the districts given to Serbia and Montenegro, and the hatred between the races was still further embittered. The Albanian League was shattered, but its spirit lived. Albanian papers were published in London, Brussels, and Bucarest, and smuggled into the country, though the possession of one rendered a man liable to fifteen years' imprisonment. Albanian gospels, circulated by the British and Foreign Bible Society, were used as reading-books by Christians and Moslems alike. Christians and Moslems, too, took advantage of the Austrian and Italian and American Mission Schools. Koritza, in the south, and Scutari, in the north, were centres of patriotic movements.

No subject race hailed with greater joy the promises of the Young Turks than did the Albanians. National equality and freedom of the Press were at last accorded them. Fifty-eight schools, sixty-six national clubs, four printing presses, and eleven Albanian newspapers were promptly started. The girls' school at Koritza, called *'The Beacon Light'* was overcrowded with pupils. People sang *"Liria! Liria!" ("Freedom! Freedom!")*, and dreamed of Utopia. But free Albania was the last thing the Turks wanted. They fell upon the national enterprises, closed schools and printing presses, and exiled or imprisoned editors and teachers. The result was a series of Albanian insurrections, which began in 1910, and were at first suppressed by the Turks with much severity. Large tracts of land were devastated. This only aroused fury, and, finally, the Albanians of Kosovo vilayet forced their way to Uskub and compelled the Turkish Authorities to listen to them. It was the beginning of the end. The other Balkan States, seeing the Turk yield, thought the time for attacking him had come and, uniting for once in their history, fell upon him. Montenegro fired the first shot without declaring war. Followed the Balkan wars of 1912-13.

The Albanians, as a whole, remained neutral, except when attacked, and expected their neutrality to be respected. Those who were in the Turkish Army, notably Essad Pasha and his men, sided with the Turk. The surrounding tribesmen, who wished to have no truck with the Young Turks, fell upon Essad as he was on his way to Scutari, and tried to drive him back. Unluckily for them, he fought his way through, and, on the death of the Turkish General, Hussein Riza (in which popular opinion believed him to be implicated), he took over the command of the town. Then, though the ships of all the Powers were off the coast and another day would have saved the town, he handed it over to the Montenegrins, who, in return for this favour, supplied him with arms and ammunition and food, and let him march his force to Tirana, of which town his family, the Toptanis, are hereditary Beys.

Albania then asked and obtained recognition of the Powers, but was again most unjustly shorn of some of its best land, largely by the influence of Tsarist Russia, which aimed at Balkan Power. While the Powers were discussing whom to name as Prince of Albania, admirable order was kept by the local authorities. One of my most interesting journeys was a ride at that time through the length and breadth of the land. One thing only was feared, and that was Essad Pasha and his armed force. It was currently believed that he was in treaty with one or more of Albania's foes, and that, in return for relinquishing part of the land, he would obtain recognition and a small principality of his own. And to this all Albania was, and is, opposed. From Scutari to Koritza all longed for the foreign prince, who had been promised them, as for a Messiah. I was begged to sit on the doorstep of Prince Arthur of Connaught, and not to leave till he had promised to accept the throne. My protests, that I could not hope to influence His Royal Highness were met with *"God will help you to do what is right."*

And in response to all these hopes, to their eternal shame, the Powers sent them the Prince of Wied - a wholly incompetent person and a coward to boot. Had he had the sense to establish himself at Scutari, where General G. F. Phillips, at the head of the international forces, had done very much to win the esteem and confidence of the population, even he might have done well. Wied, however, would take no advice. He fell into the hands of Essad, and, under his guidance, went to Durazzo, where he tried ridiculously to make a little German Court, and kept an excellent chef-de-cuisine.

Durazzo at once became a seething mass of intrigue between the representatives of rival Powers, into the sordid details of which it is perhaps not yet advisable to enter. The Albanians of the South, who expected that the Prince would come to Koritza and, by claiming the territory as part of his realm, make them safe against Greek intrigue, were bitterly disappointed. He made no move. The recently published White Book, showing King Constantine's complete complicity with Germany, make it only too probable that the Greek invasion of South Albania and its accompanying atrocities, which took place in the early summer of 1914, were all part of the German plan to obtain control over the Balkan peninsula. It is, indeed, reported that when Wied finally left Durazzo in a hurry, German instructions were found in his desk, promising him additional territory in the North, at the expense of Serbia, if he took no action in the South. The whole of the west of the peninsula would thus have come under German control. King Constantine at the time loudly denied all responsibility for the attack on South Albania. But plenty of witnesses, including myself, saw his khaki-clad soldiers - and we all know now what his word is worth. His explanation, that if soldiers were there they were deserters over whom he had no control, was ludicrous, unless we may believe that, for the first time in history, a quantity of artillery deserted also.

France and Italy have now reclaimed those districts for Albania, France has declared Koritza an Albanian republic and has again hoisted the Albanian flag there. The reason why Albania's foes are so anxious to deprive her of Koritza is that there are large deposits of brown coal and copper in the neighbourhood. And they hope by depriving the Albanians of all their cultivable land and mineral resources to make independent existence impossible for them.

Albania's future must be now considered. It has been amply proved that a mixed Commission of control is useless, as the Commissioners work each for his own country and not for Albania. Greece and Bulgaria, when first liberated, were given strong Protectors, and financed till able to stand alone. Albania should receive similar protection. And of the many Powers, Italy seems the best qualified for the post. It is very much to her interest to have a strong Albania and a friendly one on the Adriatic coast. Albania has traded amicably with Italy since the early days of the Venetian Republic, and, as we have seen, Venice and Albania together resisted the Turkish invasion.

Another proven point is that Albania's worst troubles have been caused by her rival Beys. Old Prenk Bib Doda, head of the Mirdites, remarked cheerily one day to the Prince of Wied: *"If you want to make a united Albania, you must kill Ismail Kémal, Essad Pasha, and me - don't forget me!"* It is not necessary to take such drastic measures, but nations on all sides are throwing off their hereditary despots, and the Albanians are well aware that the Beys, who have torn Albania to pieces in the past, must not be allowed to do so in the future. There is not one hereditary Bey whom the nation as a whole would now accept as ruler. They ask for a foreign Prince, but a better one this time - and protection.

Italy, if she will see that Albania's frontiers are so rectified that all Albanian districts are included within it, and will say, *"Hands off!"* to would-be intruders, would give such satisfaction to the whole nation that no objection is likely to be made to her holding Valona with a small garrison. But it must be clearly understood that no attempts at Italianising are made and that Albania is free to develop on her own lines and save her own soul. Such an arrangement would make for future peace. Albania divided between the Serbs and Greeks would be only a future Poland and a source of great weakness to those who annexed her. The Albanians are second to none in the Balkans for energy and intelligence, apt both at trade and handicraft. Other Balkan peoples have been given their chance. The Albanian has struggled for freedom as much as any of them. Let us hope that his day, too, will now dawn.

M. E. Durham

Journal of the Central Asian Society, Vol. IV, 1917*

Albania Past and Present

by M. Edith Durham

Colonel Sir Francis Younghusband presided at a meeting of the Society on December 13, 1916, when Miss M. Edith Durham read a paper on *'Albania Past and Present'*, illustrated by lantern views. He said that Miss Durham was well known to them by name, and they were certain to learn a great deal pertinent to the position in the Balkans from her paper Albania might be described as the bedrock of the Balkans. Miss Durham said Albania has a very long past, and a present that is heavy with pain and anxiety.

Of her present, the latest reports are that it is worse even than that of Belgium, that her men are being forced into the Austrian Army, and that the civil population is dying of starvation in many districts. Mr. Howard, an American missionary, whose report is the latest that I have, states that at least 150,000, largely women and children, have died of hunger and misery since this war began.

Other nations in Europe have now suffered for over two years. But it was in the summer of 1910 that the Albanians first made their bold rising and tried to win freedom from Young Turkish rule, and ever since then Albania has been almost incessantly plundered, harried, and devastated by foreign troops.

She has been the victim of the greed of many Powers. Turkish, Montenegrin, Serb, Greek, Bulgar, and Austrian armies have successively swept and plundered and slaughtered in Albania during the past five years Of all war's victims, not even Poland is more to be pitied or is in greater need of help.

So much for the present. We will now turn to Albania's past. It is a very long past; Albania is, in fact, the bedrock of the Balkans. We can only here touch very briefly on the main points of her history.

In prehistoric times the Balkans were inhabited by a number of tribes, which appear to have been closely related as to blood. We first hear of them as Illyrians, Macedonians, Molossi, and so forth. Illyria, whence sprang the modern Albania, was a large territory, comprising all that is now known as Bosnia and the Herzegovina, Dalmatia (as far even as

* This article has been reprinted by the Centre for Albanian Studies from the Journal of the Central Asian society, volume IV, part 1, 1917 by permission of the Royal Society for Asian Affairs, successor body to the Central Asian Society.

Trieste), Montenegro, a large part of modern Serbia, and the larger part of modern Albania. Farther south, a closely related group of similar tribes formed a separate kingdom of Epirus. The ancient Illyrians had evidently a fairly high civilization. Masses of implements and ornaments have been found in the extensive cemeteries of Bosnia and Serbia, in graves that lie beneath those of the Romans, who afterwards invaded the country. And these implements show that the Illyrians were among the first to manufacture and use iron. It was probably carried thence to other places.

When we first hear of Illyria in history, it was strong enough to insult the Romans. The seafaring population of the coast harried and plundered Roman shipping, and Illyria's proud Queen, Teuta, returned a rude answer to Roman remonstrances. Possibly the fine seafaring qualities of the modern Dalmatian are in part due to his Illyrian pirate ancestry. A Roman punitive expedition resulted in 230 B.C. At this time, as now, Scodra, which you probably know better as Scutari, was the capital. It, indeed, is one of the oldest capitals of Europe. And the people still call it by its old name, very slightly modified, Shkodra.

Of the difficulties the Romans had with the kingdom of Epirus, and of the exploits of King Pyrrhus, we have all heard at school. The Albanians still cherish his memory, and say that his name was Burrus, which means the warrior, or brave man. *"A je burre?"* (*"How art thou, my brave?"*) is to-day the common greeting when one mountain-man meets another. I well remember the pride with which a Moslem Albanian gendarme, who was guiding me from Permeti to Tepelen, pointed up to the clouded mountain-top, and said that *"Up there were the ruins of the castle of our great Kind Burrus, who beat the Romans and everyone else."* And at the carnival masquerade at Scutari, I saw Pyrrhuses in marvellous tin helmets fashioned by the local smith - the most admired of any of the masquers.

Plutarch tells us that the soldiers of Pyrrhus hailed him as the *"eagle."* Which is of great interest, for the Albanian does not call himself an Albanian, but Shkipetar (from shkip, an eagle), the people of the eagle. And his land is Shkiperia. The term *'Albania'* has been given by foreigners, and its origin is somewhat disputed. It probably derives from the name of a tribe in Central Albania - Arberia or Arbonia.

The word *'liria'* in modern Albania means 'free' and the Albanian of to-day translates' *Illyria'* to mean *'the land of the free'*. Certainly no race has made a more continuous struggle for freedom throughout the ages than has the Albanian. Albanian history is one long tale of epic struggles against one invader after the other.

We have no time to detail the various invasions. But let us note that, though each invader in turn has striven to crush the Albanian's individuality, none has as yet succeeded. He has clung with such tenacity to his national customs, his idea of race, and his language, that no Power has as yet assimilated him All efforts to Slavize, Grecicize, or Ottomanize him have failed. The Romans did not succeed in subduing Illyria till A.D. 169, when they took Scodra, and forced the Illyrian King, Gentius, to march as prisoner in a Roman triumph.

Judging by the length of time which the Romans took to conquer Illyria, and also by the great amount of pre-Roman graves, the country must have been pretty thickly populated. And this aboriginal population has left its mark, for the ornaments found in quantities in these graves are in many cases almost precisely like those which are still worn by Balkan peasants. And in most parts the silversmith turns out usually to be either an Albanian or a Vlah, which points to a long and unbroken tradition.

Under the Romans, Illyria seems to have prospered. Rome found some of her best soldiers among the tribesmen, and more than one Emperor - Diocletian, Constantine the Great, and others of lesser note - were of native blood.

Christianity reached the Dalmatian coast as early as the first century, and had penetrated far inland by the fourth. The Albanians, in fact, claim to have been converted by St. Paul himself, who says: *"Round about Illyria I have fully preached the Gospel of Christ."* Be this as it may, Illyria early formed, and still forms, part of the patriarchate of Rome. And the Christians of the north, which includes almost the whole of the mountain tribes, have remained faithful to Rome ever since.

Scutari became an archbishopric as early as A.D. 307. The archbishopric was, however, transferred later to Antivari. But Scutari was continuously the seat of a Bishop till the nineteenth century, when it again became an archbishopric.

Under Rome, Illyria was dotted with Roman colonies, joined by roads, which were probably better than any that have since existed. Roman coins are still found in plenty in many places. Apollonia, on the coast rather to the north of Avlona, was a celebrated university, and was joined to Salonika by the Via Egnatia. The name Avlona, or Valona, is, in fact, merely a corruption of Apollonia.

We now come to the second period of Albanian history, the Slav period. The Roman Illyrian civilization was rudely broken into and largely destroyed by the irruption into the peninsula, in the seventh century, of huge savage hordes, the ancestors of the modern Serbians. They were a tribal people and were pagans. Coming in overpowering numbers, they drove the Roman civilization to the coasts, where Roman influence is not yet dead, and possessed themselves of the fertile plains inland; for they were a nation of herdsmen.

The Albanians, as we may as well now call them, maintained their freedom and language in the mountains of the Albania of to-day. In the north - modern Bosnia, that is - the language died out; but it is very possible that we may still find traces of the old Illyrian population. In certain districts of Bosnia all the Roman Catholics are tattooed with strange devices. Now, tattooing has never been recorded as a Slavonic custom, whereas we are told by classical authors that tattooing was one of the peculiarities of the ancient Balkan tribes. The fact, therefore, that these people are tattooed, and are also members of the Church of Rome, looks like a direct tradition from very ancient times. It is strengthened by the fact that tattooing in similar designs is found also in many parts of Albania. Some of the tattoo patterns, moreover, resemble some of the ornaments found in the ancient graves.

Nor, indeed, is all trace of the Roman colonists gone. We find groups of what are known as Kutzo-Vlahs dotted about all through these lands. They speak a Latin dialect which resembles, but is not the same as, the Roumanian language. And in physical types they bear a strong resemblance to the darker type of Albanians. There is a particularly large group of them at Elbasan and at Ochrida, both of which were important points on the Roman Via Egnatia. They, in all probability, derive from the intermarriage of Romans with the native population. The Albanians seem to me to have an instinctive feeling of relationship with them. For I have been repeatedly told that *"Vlahs have sweet blood"* and that a *"man need not mind giving a daughter in marriage to a Vlah,"* and also that *"Vlah"* is Albanian for *"a brother"*.

The invading Slavs were pagan, and were not converted to Christianity till the ninth century - that is, some five hundred years after the Illyrians - and then by missionaries from Salonika. The differences which were later to make the two Christian Churches hate one another more than they did the Turk were already beginning to make themselves felt, and when the final split came the Serbs threw in their lot with Byzantium. Thus, as Serb power grew and spread over Illyria, or Albania, as we may as well call it now, the Roman Catholic Albanians suffered not only the woe of being invaded, but were also subjected to religious persecution. To race hatred was added religious hatred.

The Christians of the south, we may here mention, later, under the influence of Byzantium, went over to the Orthodox faith. But they have not forgotten the ties of blood, and remain in racial sympathy with their Catholic brethren. The north never wavered in its allegiance to Rome. Not one Orthodox is to be found among the Christian tribes of the north. The Serbians formed their stronghold and centre on the fertile plains of Kosovo and the Metoya, for they were a nation of herdsmen. And they called this kingdom, not Serbia, but Rashia. This is a fact of great interest, for *'rashia'* is an Albanian word meaning *'a plain'* - the kingdom, therefore, of the plain, possibly the name by which the original inhabitants called it.

The Nemanya Kings, who made Serbia, ruled from 1180 to 1356, and pushed farther and farther into Albania. They took and fortified Scutari, and strove, it would appear, to Slavize the people, but unsuccessfully.

In 1321 we find the Catholic Albanians appealing to Charles of Anjou and to Prince Filippo of Taranto to force King Milutin to recognize and respect their religious rights. And in 1332 a certain French friar, Frère Brocardus or Brochart, gives us an interesting contemporary account of the state of the country. He says: *"There is, among other things, one which would make it easier to take this kingdom of Rashia ... There are two peoples, the Abbanois and the Latins, who both belong to the Church of Rome. The Latins have six cities, and as many Bishops - Anthibaire (Antivari), Cathare (Cattaro), Dulcedine (Dulcigno), Suacinense (?), Scutari, and Drivaste (now ruined completely). In these the Latins live. Outside the walls the Abbanois have four cities - Polat Major, Polat Minor (these are the modern tribal districts of Upper and Lower Pulati), Sabbate (Sappa), and Albanie (Elbassan and Durazzo district). They are all under the Archbishop of Anthibaire. These Abbanois have a language which is quite other than Latin, but use in their books the Latin letters."* (What would we not give now for a book of that date!) *Both of these people are oppressed under the very hard servitude of the most hateful and abominable lordship of the Slavs. If they saw a Prince of France coming towards them, they would make him their leader against the accursed Slavs, the enemies of the truth and our faith."* That the worthy Frère did not exaggerate is proved by the severity of the celebrated Canon of Laws enacted by the Serb Tsar, Stefan Dushan, in 1349.

During the twenty years of Dushan's reign - that is, from 1336 to 1356 - all Albania formed part of the Serbian Empire. Dushan made special laws against the Catholics. For example, Law 6: *" As to the Latin heresy and those that draw Orthodox believers to its faith, the Ecclesiastical Authorities must strive to convert all such to the true faith. If such a one will not be converted, he shall be punished with death. The Orthodox Tsar* must eradicate all heresy from his State. The property of all such as refuse conversion shall be confiscated. Heretical churches will be consecrated and opened for priests of the Orthodox faith." Law 8: "If a Latin priest be found trying to convert a Christian to the Latin faith, he shall be punished with death." And so forth. In truth, the Turk, with all his faults, has not treated the Christians so badly as one Christian sect has treated another.

I have dwelt at some length on this period because it has so much bearing on recent events. The Albanian since that time has never ceased to regard the Slav as his bitterest and cruellest foe, and the Slav, in turn, has preserved his mediæval way of dealing with the Albanian. During and after the first Balkan War, the old laws of Stefan Dushan were pitilessly enforced. Hundreds of persons who refused to join the Orthodox Church were martyred, hundreds more were expelled and deprived of all they possessed.

Modern Balkan troubles are all built on early mediæval and pre-Turkish hatreds. And it is failure to recognize this important fact that has led us into some of the painful positions in which we now find ourselves.

We now come to the third period, the Turkish. Great Serbia was torn to pieces very shortly after Tsar Dushan's death by his nobles, who struggled for supremacy. It had lasted, indeed, barely two hundred years. Albania broke loose at once, and the names of many local chieftains have come down to us; but we have no time now to dwell on details, for we must pass on to the next great Balkan catastrophe - the coming of the Turks. Till this time the Balkan peoples had been wholly occupied fighting each other. The Greeks, in fact, invited the Turks to help them against the Slavs.

In view of present-day events, it is of interest to note that ever since the Turk was first established in Europe, the Balkan peoples have taken turns in aiding him against each other, instead of uniting to expel him. Not till the Turks were settled in the eastern part of the Balkan Peninsula and were marching westward in force did the Balkan peoples realize their danger. Then Lazar, who was Tsar of a very much reduced Serbia, collected together Bosniaks, Serbs, and Albanians, and led them against Sultan Murad's army on the plains of Kosovo. A long and fierce fight ensued, and the issue was doubtful till a Serb noble - the son-in-law, in fact, of Tsar Lazar himself - deserted to the enemy with his twelve thousand men - bribed, it is said, by offers of power. This act of Serb treachery established the Turk in Europe.

The Serbs accepted the son of the traitor as King under Turkish suzerainty. The Albanians, however, were far from submitting. They joined with the Venetians, who had been for some time past settling on the Adriatic coast and trading with the interior. Albano-Venetian relations seem to have been good. The names of many powerful Albanian chiefs are found in Venetian records. Scutari and all the north was free from the Turks, but they penetrated South and Central Albania.

Then there arose an Albanian chieftain who has gained world-wide fame, George Castrioti, known as Skenderbeg, called in his day the '*Champion of Christendom*'. This remarkable man is one of the great warriors of history. Taken as a child from his father by the Turks as a hostage, he was brought up a soldier and a Moslem. He, however, threw over the Turks and their religion, and returned to his fatherland to Kroya, and was hailed by the Albanians as their leader. For twenty-four years he was continuously victorious. Two Sultans successively hurled larger and larger troops against him in vain. Murad II came himself at the head of 40,000 men, and attempted to storm Kroya, but was repulsed, and had to retire discomfited.

Skenderbeg not only freed the land, but kept it free. His realm extended as far as Ochrida, and Dibra was one of his towns. I shall not forget the grief of the Albanians when they heard that Dibra, one of Skenderbeg's towns, had been given by the Powers of Europe to their secular enemy the Serbs. So long as Skenderbeg lived Albania was free. He died of fever in 1478, aged sixty-four, leaving no one who was great enough to take his place.

Skenderbeg dead, Venice could not hold out much longer. The Turks violently attacked Scutari, which was defended by combined Venetian and Albanian forces. Scutari fell in 1479, after a most bloody struggle. When the new road was being built along the foot of the old citadel in 1911-12, I saw hundreds of old stone shot and cannon-balls dug out of the ground, the relics doubtless of that last great fight. And old Venetian bronze cannons stood in the citadel till 1913, when unfortunately they were looted by the Montenegrins.

Previous to the fall of Scutari, it is said that angels came and carried away the picture of the Madonna from the Church of Our Lady at the foot of the hill, and deposited it safely at Genzano, in Italy. Many a time have I assisted at the celebration of this festival, the greatest feast-day of Scutari, when the poor people - who are now starving - came joyfully from every mountain and village, glad and good-natured, in their best attire - a happy crowd, so orderly and so friendly. I think now sadly of the huge admiration they had for the Great Powers of Europe, their infinite faith in the goodwill of those Powers. And now they have been dragged into the hell created by those same Powers, and are dying as innocent victims.

When the Turks overpowered Albania, many Albanians fled into Italy, where some eighty Albanian villages are still in existence, and the Albanian language, customs, and costume are to a large extent preserved. For many years the Albanians hoped and hoped in vain for the help of their former friends and allies, the Venetians, against the Turks. But Venetian power, too, was on the wane. Venice lost successively Durazzo, Dulcigno, and Antivari. The Albanians of the Mirdite and Dukagin mountains sent appeals for help in 1570, 1571, 1580, 1596, 1601, and 1616. Then they gave up hope.

From the beginning of the Turkish invasion they had succeeded in obtaining recognition of their tribal autonomy from the Turks. They now began in the seventeenth century to adopt Islam. Many Greeks and a very large number of Slavs had become Madommedan as early as the fifteenth century In the case of Albania, one reason seems to have been the fact that the Christian Bishops of Albania were foreigners, and were mainly occupied in quarrelling with one another about the frontiers of their dioceses instead of looking after their flocks. *"The hungry sheep looked up and were not fed."* And a Moslem manger was no doubt ready for them. Thus in 1638 we find a violent dissension between the Bishop of Alessio and the Archbishop of Durazzo. And again, in 1703, no less than three Bishops were contending for the district of Postripa, and allowing no priest to officiate in it, till the quarrel was settled by Pope Clement XI, who sent a special legate for the purpose. Clement XI was Albanian on his mother's side, and made a strong effort to aid the Catholic Albanians; but on his death, Rome seems to have lost interest. Albania was largely served by foreign priests who had no understanding of the people.

The conversion to Islam of a large portion of the Albanians has had a disastrous effect on Albania. Though the Moslem Albanian is as tenaciously Albanian as ever, the fact that he is Moslem has caused ignorant outsiders to consider him a Turk. Islam has also had a retarding influence on education. But far from Islamism making the Albanian into a Turk, no sooner did the Moslem Albanian chiefs begin to gain power than they again began to assert themselves and make efforts for freedom. The Albanians had, indeed, been increasing in strength and flowing back on to the plains from which the Serbs had expelled or held in subjugation their ancestors.

The town of Djakova (of St. Giacomo, that is) was founded by an offshoot of the Christian tribe of Merturi. And when, in 1690, the Serb population elected to emigrate to Austria, where they were given assistance and wide lands in the Banat, the mountain Albanian tribes resettled almost the whole of the district as far north as Mitrovitza and north-east to Nish and Uskub, and made scattered Albanian villages as far even as Monastir. They regained, in truth, a large part of their ancient Illyria. Nor did they submit to Turkish interference. Christian and Moslem alike united to preserve their ancient laws and customs. Much liberty was allowed them, and they gave, in return, military service.

So powerful, then, did the Albanian chiefs become that they struck out for complete independence. Ali Pasha, the ruler of the south, whose capital was Janina, was, in fact, for years quite independent, and tried, and almost succeeded, in persuading England to support him. The Pasha of Scutari was almost as powerful. It was then that the Turks made a determined effort to subdue Albania once more. After stern fighting, they conquered Ali Pasha, now an old man, and slaughtered him and his family. South Albania then fell entirely under the Turk, and entered on a difficult period.

In order to kill national sentiment, the Turks then permitted the Greeks to open schools and work at propaganda. The Greeks in those days always worked with the Turks to destroy the racial and national spirit of the other subject races. The Pasha of Scutari was also badly beaten, though not wholly subdued. But the nation as a whole never forgot its traditions.

At the time of the Congress of Berlin - that fatal Congress at which the seeds of so many troubles were sown - the Albanians saw the other Balkan races obtaining European support and recognition, and formed the well-known Albanian League to protect their land and their rights and to beg also for recognition. Great Britain, it is interesting to find, was strongly in favour of forming a large Albanian province, to include the whole of the vilayets of Scutari and Janina and the larger part of Kosovo vilayet, with a portion of Monastir vilayet, too, and to grant it considerable autonomy with a view to future independence. Both Lord Goschen, then our Ambassador at Constantinople, and Sir Edmund Fitzmaurice worked hard for this end. Its formation would have obviated very many recent misfortunes. But the Powers were not unanimous on the subject, and all that was done was to recommend some such reforms to the Turks.

The Turks responded by arresting most of the heads of the League and executing or exiling them into Asia. Albania was in worse plight than ever. Turkish governors, and sometimes garrisons too, were put in the Albanian towns. But the Sultan did not wish for another national rising, and to propitiate the Albanians gave permission for Albanian schools, and consented to allow the language to be printed. A huge impetus was at once given to the national spirit. Especially in Koritza, in South

Albania, was an active centre formed, to the anger of the Greek priests and propagandists. The Sultan then, seeing that national education would soon produce an Albania stronger than ever, and influenced, no doubt, too, by the Greeks, suddenly withdrew his consent, prohibited the printing of the language, and threw the unfortunate schoolmasters into prison.

When I first visited Koritza in 1904, its schoolmaster was still serving out his term of fifteen years' imprisonment. A similar term was the penalty for being found in possession of newspapers printed in Albanian. Newspapers were nevertheless printed abroad and secretly circulated, and the Koritza patriots, at great risk to themselves, continued working. The Turkish Government had already given permission to the British and Foreign Bible Society to sell its publications in the Turkish Empire. The Albanians, therefore, made a translation of the Gospels and some of the books of the Old Testament. Albanian colporteurs carried stocks of these around along with other publications. And the demand for twopenny copies of the Book of Genesis was amazing. I once assisted at the selling of seventy-four such books in one day. Almost all were bought by Mahommedans, some even by Albanian officers in the Turkish Army.

Thus, under shelter of Great Britain, Albania struggled towards national development, greatly hampered by the Greeks, who lost no opportunity of denouncing the secret readers and teachers of Albanian to the Turkish authorities. A Greek Bishop even went so far as excommunicating the language, and Greek priests told the people that it was useless to pray in Albanian, as Christ did not understand it.

At Koritza, however, under protection of America, the American Mission opened a girls' school. Its Albanian headmistress, one of the bravest women I know, ran the school successfully. The Turkish authorities searched vainly for Albanian books. She used English ones, and translated her lessons orally. Writing was destroyed as soon as finished when danger was suspected. The girls taught their brothers, and the school was a centre of culture and national feeling. I am very sorry to tell you that in the summer of 1914, just before the outbreak of the present war, this school, which had done splendid work for fifteen years, was pillaged and burnt by Greek invaders, who devastated and pillaged all the surrounding country. The schoolmistress, after many adventures, is now safe in America, together with some sixty thousand Albanian refugees, whose centre is in Boston, and who are working earnestly with a view to reorganizing their country when peace is once more proclaimed. They publish a paper called Illyria, and are all engaged in various trades and manufactures. I hear that they are reckoned in America as very good and industrious citizens.

Nor was national education confined to the south. In Scrutari also, schools were opened both by the Austrians and the Italians and protected by them, and Scutari thus became the educational centre of the north.

To return to Albania's story. The Albanians, like many other people, hoped great things from the Young Turk revolution, and especially grasped at the promise of national equality and the freedom of the press. I was in Albania when that revolution took place. Never, perhaps, in the world's history has there been a greater outburst of national feeling than when freedom of the press was announced in Albania. Almost in a night crops of little newspapers sprouted up. Albanian clubs were opened, Albanian schools formed. The nation at once collected money and opened the Normal school at Elbassan, which was to train teachers for all, and books were written and translated. The restrictions on the use of the Latin alphabet were cast aside. A national conference was held. The rush of children to the schools was such that there was not room for them. The Koritza schoolmistress wrote to me that Mahommedan girls were being sent to her from distant parts as boarders, and that she did not know where to stow them all.

It was a bright dream while it lasted, but all too soon shattered. The Turkish Government again intervened and forbade the use of the Latin alphabet, and began at once arresting and imprisoning editors and schoolmasters and closing the printing-presses, and ordered that Albanian, if printed, should be printed in Arabic characters - characters totally unsuited to a European language. Thousands of Arabic alphabets were printed and sent into Albania by the Turkish Government. The people collected them and burnt them in public at Berat.

The results of these and other oppressions were the Albanian revolutions of 1910-11-12 - revolutions which the Young Turks put down with great severity, but which finally shook Young Turk rule to its foundations. And they paved the way for the Balkan wars of 1912-13.

Into quite recent politics it is, perhaps, better not to enter. We are too near the events for criticisms of our Allies or our foes to be desirable here. I will therefore only say that Albania as a whole remained neutral during those wars, and fought only in self-defence when attacked; that she was invaded and spoiled by three armies; that terrible atrocities were committed on Albanians; and that in the end her hopes were cruelly disappointed when, in response to her appeal for recognition, the Powers sent her a wholly incapable and incompetent German Prince, the Prince of Wied, who did not deign even to visit his land and subjects, but preferred to sit in his comfortable palace at Durazzo and tried to form a little imitation of a German Court. It is a disgrace to all who were concerned in the choice that such a man should have been appointed. And the unfortunate Albanians were at once made the prey of numerous and unscrupulous European intriguers.

We may be, however, allowed to hope, with the Albanians, that as the present war is being waged for the rights of small nationalities, Albania's day, too, will dawn, and that once again this oldest of European peoples will have her place in the sun. And all of us who know the Albanians' great possibilities, their intelligence, industry, and vigour, have no doubt that, if given a chance, they will ultimately succeed.

We will now look at a few views of the people and country.

The CHAIRMAN: Miss Durham has given us an exceedingly interesting and very instructive paper; but it contained one statement with which, I am sure, not one single person here will agree. She said that the very curious man-lady or lady-man she showed us on the screen *"treated her with the contempt she deserved."* You will all say, I know, that it is not contempt Miss Durham deserves, but very different feelings. She has nobly set herself to see and understand something of the trials this little state has had to go through in the past and what it is suffering at the present time. She finished her lecture by saying that she hoped a better day was dawning for Albania, and in this hope we earnestly join. In this war we are fighting for the freedom of smaller nationalities, and we certainly shall not fail in interest in and sympathy for Albania, after what Miss Durham has told us. We must admire from the bottom of our hearts the sturdiness with which the Albanians through all these centuries of oppression have stuck to their own individuality; and we may hope that in the years to come they may have that opportunity for which they are evidently panting to express that individuality to the full. There is one Albanian gentleman here this afternoon. He is rather modest in regard to his knowledge of English; but I am sure we would be only too lenient with him if he would very kindly speak to us.

The Albanian gentleman referred to said that Miss Durham had done more for his country than anyone he could think of. Her work had earned for her among the people the title of the *"Queen of Albania"*. He trusted she would be able to continue to help them and, as in the past, do everything she could for Albanian nationality.

Mr. H. W. Nevinson said that, intensely interesting as the address had been to everyone there, it was, he thought, of most interest to himself, because he had had the privilege and honour of going through Albania with Miss Durham and under her auspices. Whenever her name was mentioned she was respectfully termed their Queen. He was interested in the slides of the most beautiful country he had ever seen, especially Northern Albania; and he was interested to see in one picture so fine a photograph of his own back, this being the first time he had seen it. He could not describe with what respect and honour Miss Durham had for many years now been regarded in Albania. He was charmed and overwhelmed by the welcome he always received when he mentioned her name. From her reflected glory, he was sometimes called the King of Albania, because they all believed that Miss Durham and he had been sent out by King George to take over the government of the country. He would like to mention another thing which even Miss Durham did not know. When he was in Salonika last winter a large party of English nurses arrived, having fought their way with great difficulty through the Albanian frontiers from the north of Serbia, accompanied by a small body of guides. They told him that as they journeyed they were received by the people (though they were in a state of semi-starvation) with the greatest enthusiasm and hospitality, simply because they belonged to the same nation as Miss Durham. That seemed to him a very fine tribute for any Englishwoman to receive, showing as it did how great her influence had been over a nation of tribes which were supposed to be so savage in the past.

We were engaged in this war for the protection and freedom of small nationalities. Our late Prime Minister announced at the very beginning of the war that that was one of our objects. What a disaster, what a crime it would be to Europe, if we allowed a small nationality like Albania, which had held together since the time of the Roman Empire, to be divided, as had been proposed, between its most intense enemies, the Serbians and the Greeks! Let us at all events resolve that whatever might be the protection or management Albania might require, it should be protected mainly as an independent State.

Dr. Gaster said that he had an Albanian nurse in his infancy at Bucharest, and ever since he had retained a love and admiration for the Albanians - the Scots of the Balkan Peninsula. He wished Miss Durham had told them a little more of her own achievements, not only to tell what she had done, but to bring out more clearly the character of these Albanians. The story would show their gratitude, simplicity, chivalry, and undaunted courage. It was his privilege to be a member of the Albanian Committee after the Balkan War, and he joined in trying to urge their claims upon the diplomatists of the British Government. They did not succeed to the extent they desired. He did not wish to enter upon politics; but he would say that if the concessions to the Albanians pressed at the time by people who knew the country had been made, they were convinced that a much better outlook would have been opened up for the Albanians. Perhaps even the situation in the Balkans would have been somewhat different to what it was now. The Albanians had suffered both in the north and the south by the oppressions of two implacable foes, the Serbians and the Greeks. It was the first necessity for them to have an independent status when the war was over. Most of the sailors of the Greek fleet were Albanians and most of the traders were Albanians, and the Greeks had a great dread and dislike of them. In the past they used the Turkish Power to destroy the Albanians, and now they were using other Powers for a similar purpose, and we had to see to it that they were not successful.

It was most interesting to watch the resource and determination of the Albanians in trying to develop a literature of their own. He was the possessor of some very good specimens of their efforts in this direction during the last century. One of the oldest was a translation of the Gospels in parallel columns, one in Greek and the other in the Albanian language, but Greek characters. There were also translations in which the Latin alphabet was used, and there was a society in Bucharest which had invested another alphabet for use in Albania. Both Turkish and Italian were used in their books; so that altogether the Albanians had to relearn their written speech five times over. Yet in a marvellous way they persevered in trying to develop their literature and their language. It was to be hoped that in the future the impediments arbitrarily imposed on their aspirations would never be renewed, and they would have free scope to develop their literature and their country as they wished. Alexander the Great was reputed to have been an Albanian. They hoped that another Alexander might soon arise to be the instrument of giving these people the freedom they had so amply earned by their fidelity and their sufferings.

The meeting closed with a vote of thanks to Miss Durham.

The Near East, February 1st 1918
The Antiquity of Albania
by M. E. Durham

Nations come and nations go. Race after race has swept Europe. Some that were mighty have disappeared completely. Others, pouring in from unknown and uncharted regions, have supplanted them. And among all the ebb and flow few have shown themselves more tenacious of their ancestral lands than the Albanians. If ancient tenure gives right, few have better claims. Strabo gives us a curiously detailed account of Albania, made the more interesting by the fact that he himself was of mixed Greek and Asiatic blood, and wrote in Greek. For he states emphatically that the early inhabitants of the land were non-Greek. Writing at the very beginning of the Christian era, he tells us that the Adriatic coast was inhabited by the Illyrians in the north and the Epirotes in the south.

Illyria begins, he says, in the recesses of the Adriatic. It approaches the Alps which lie between Italy and Germany. Tergestum, now Trieste, was a city of the Illyrians. Its name may tell of them, for the modern Albanian word for commerce is *'tregtim'*; *'tregtue'* is to trade. The Illyrians then, as their descendants now, were divided into tribes, some of whom have given their names to the lands of to-day - the Carni and the Istri. *"The present Government,"* says Strabo, *"has advanced the limits of Italy to Pola, a city of Istria."* The Iapodes, who dwelt on a termination of the Alps, were a warlike people, poor - for the land was barren - and living largely on millet. Maize, now one of the staple foods of the Balkans, was then still undiscovered on the plains of America, along with potatoes and tobacco, now considered necessaries of existence. Nevertheless, though tobacco-less, the Ispodes were a warlike people *"wearing armour after the Keltic fashion and puncturing their bodies after the fashion of the other Illyrian and Thracian peoples."* A passage, this, of the highest interest.

For the tattooed people of Bosnia, the Herzegovina, and Albania are, doubtless, direct descendants of these tribes. No Slav people are recorded as tattooing; but here we find whole districts of Roman Catholic peasants marked with the sun and the crescent moon, signs, it may be, of some early form of nature-worship. Catholic too they are, and not Orthodox. The Illyrians received Christianity from the Romans, and the coincidence is of interest.

From Istria all down the coast Strabo enumerates the various tribes, and their lands, he states, extend inland to Pannonia. Then, as now among the Albanians, the land was common to the tribe. *"The Dalmatae,"* says our historian, *"redivided their land every eighth year."* Those who have witnessed such a scene will call to mind the tribal meetings of the head-men in the Albanian mountains, and the heated debates over the periodical redistribution of grazing and wood-cutting rights. Seafaring folk, too, were the Illyrians, and famed for piracy. The many islands and harbours were, in fact, greatly apt for the purpose, and the rich vessels of Roman merchandise were robbed and harassed especially by the Ardaei, who dwelt in and around the Bocche di Cattaro. This brought down upon them Roman vengeance, and, says Strabo, they were driven inland *"and compelled to cultivate the land. But so rugged and barren was it that the nation was completely ruined and nearly extinguished. Other once powerful tribes were similarly reduced, and are now in the lowest condition."*

What remains of the pirate tribes now? Probably the Morlachs, or Sea Vlachs, are their direct descendants, Slav-speaking now, it is true. But it is only of recent years that an old Roman dialect died out on the coast. The Morlachs have throughout their history been Roman Catholic, faithful to the Church which first converted their Illyrian ancestors. And it is possibly to the fact that these were pirates that the Austrian navy owes its best seamen.

From the Rhizonic Gulf (Bocche di Cattaro) Strabo takes us on to the mouth of the Drin, near which is Lissus (Alessio). The river is navigable inland as far as the district of the Dardanii, he tells us, *"which country is close to the Macedonia and the land of the Pœonians."* The name may mean the land of pear-trees; *'Dardhe'* is Albanian for a pear, and in this region we find Slav names denoting pear-tree land - Krushevo and Krushevatz.

Off the coast he tells of the many islands, especially Black Corcyra (now Curzola), *"on which is a town founded by the Cnidians."* Further south he comes to Dyrrachium (Durazzo), and describes minutely the Egnatian Way passing by Scampis (? Elbassan) to the lake of Lychnidus (Ochrida). 'Licheni' is modern Albanian for 'a lake' be it noted. Of Macedonia Strabo tells us that 'it was formerly called Emathia', another interesting name, for 'e madhe' is Albania for 'the great'.

But we must pass on to South Albania, the land of the Epirotae. These also, he tells us, are divided into numerous tribes which extend as far south as the Gulf of Arta (Ambracia). 'On sailing in on the right hand are the Acarnanians, who are Greeks ... on the left are the Cassiopoei, a tribe of Epirotae extending as far as the recesses of the gulf.' 'The greatest part of Greece is, however, at present uninhabited, and the cities especially have been destroyed. Thracians, Illyrians, and Epirotae are settled even at present on the sides of Greece.' ... "The country above Aetolia and Acarnania is occupied by Thesproti, Molotti, etc., Epirote tribes ... Theopompus says that there are fourteen Epirotic nations, the most celebrated of which are the Chaones and the Molotti (or Molossi), because the whole of Epirus was once subject to them.' 'Mol' may indeed be the same word as 'mal' (a mountain), and 'Molossi' a form of the modern 'Maltsori' meaning mountain men. Of Epirote coast towns he mentions Onchesmus - on the site of the modern Santa Quaranta - Posidium, Buthrotum, and Panormus. In the Gulf of Valone is the port of Oricum; and inland in the territory of Apollonia he describes 'what is called a nymphaeum, a rock which emits fire; below it are springs flowing with hot water and asphalte. Asphaltum is dug out of the neighbouring hill.' This is evidently the Selenitza mine, worked until the war broke out by a French company. The long strings of donkeys, each with a couple of cakes of asphalte slung on its packsaddle, were a familiar sight to all visitors to Valona.

Finally, Strabo tells us of the famous oracle of Dodona, founded, he says, by the Pelasgi. 'Homer clearly intimates that the people who lived about the mountain were barbarians ... persons who do not wash their feet and who sleep on the ground ... Dodona was formerly subject to the Thesproti and in later times, it is said, to the Molossi. The first prophets were men. Afterwards three old women were appointed ... The oracular answers were conveyed not by words, but by certain signs. Probably the doves made a peculiar flight which suggested the answer to the priestesses. Some say that in the language of the Molotti and Thesproti old women are called 'pellaei' and old men 'pelii', so that the celebrated doves were not birds, but old women who passed an idle time in the temple.' He adds, 'Persons who hold office are called peligones as among the Macedonians.' Albanian for 'old' is 'pelak' or 'plak,' and the members of the council of headmen are the 'peleknit' or 'pleknit.'.

To the aged wisdom is attributed, and many an old man to this day is a famed reader of the future in the breastbones of birds. Grimly truthful, too, are some of these prophecies. The writer vividly remembers a hot day on the quay at Durazzo in the early summer of 1914, when a ragged Maltsor held a fowl's breastbone against the sun's glare and said gravely that he saw nothing but blood. His comrade jeered at him, and said he did not understand the bones; but the seer stared hard again, and said, sadly and earnestly, "It is true, I tell you; blood, blood, and blood everywhere, and nothing but blood." Did the oracle of Dodona ever foresee so truly?

Thus we see in Strabo's day the Albanians' ancestors occupying the whole of the western side of the Balkan peninsula. For these tribes of Illyrians and Epirotae in 'the mode of cutting the hair, their language, and their use of the chlamys resembled also the Macedonians.' The mountain men of to-day - and women, too - all shave their heads in patches, each locality having its own head-shave. And the big sheeps' wool cloak, or talagan, is a characteristic dress of the land. The Slavs had not in Strabo's time been even heard of. The Greeks, though they had made trading colonies along the coast in earlier days, had long ago retired. Nor did they ever again firmly establish themselves, though they have tried peaceful, and other, penetration since.

In the heyday of Byzantium, Greek influence probably spread northwards, but only to ebb again. Brerewood in 1625 tells us that 'at this day the Greeke language is very much decayed, not only as touching the largnesse and vulgarity of it, but also in purenesses and elegance. For the naturall languages of the Countries have usurped upon it so that the parts in which the Greeke language is spoken at this daye are but these ... Greece itself, excepting Epirus and West Macedon.' Turk, Greek, and Slav alike have striven to kill that language spoken of the Macedonians, Illyrians, and Epirotes, but so far striven in vain. In recent years it in fact extended and re-took a large part of Macedonia. And its speakers to day are printing newspapers in it in far away America - a land unknown in Strabo's time. And as in Strabo's time, they still regard, and with considerable justice, the Gulf of Arta as their southern frontier. Northwards, where recently much of their land has fallen into the hands of the Slavs, their true frontier needs redrawing. But not all the efforts of King Nikola, who forbade the teaching, printing, and selling of Albanian in Montenegro, could prevent a large number of his land's inhabitants speaking it.

One thing seems certain, and that is that a people that has shown in the past such endurance and such a capacity for surviving all foreign influence must have a future, although Mr. Lloyd George has omitted them from his last war aim speech. Somewhat unkindly, too, for he is a man of a little mountain land himself. And it is even yet possible that in the future an Albanian Lloyd George may sway the Balkans.

The Near East, November 8th 1918
An Albanian Protest

To the Editor of The Near East

Sir,

May I say a few words in answer to Mr. Kessary's letter in your issue of November 1? He says he *'knows something about Turco-Albanian Beys,'* and is *'painfully surprised to see Mehmed Bey Konitza posing as Albanian delegate and protesting on behalf of Epirus'*. Mehmed Bey is the official representative of at least 60,000 Albanians at present refugees in America. They are well organised; publish a paper expressing their views regarding their country, and their representatives have been received by President Wilson and by Mr. Roosevelt, both of whom have promised the Albanians to support them in their claim for independence. Mehmed Bey is thus fully justified in describing himself as Albanian delegate. The Albanians he represents include Orthodox, Moslems and Catholics. The very large majority are from South Albania - called by Mr. Kessary *'Epirus'*. That there are certain inhabitants of that district who are renegades and wish their native land handed over to alien rule is true. We, too, have our Mr. Houston Chamberlain. But the mass of the people do not. Rather more than half of the inhabitants are Moslem. None of these want Greek rule. And of the Christians, the bulk are patriotically Albanian.

When I travelled through the country in 1904, I was visited by deputations of people begging me to establish Albanian schools under British protection and to help the establishment of an Albanian Church. Albanian was a forbidden language under Turkish rule, and the penalties for printing and teaching it were very severe. Not once was I asked to support Greek claims. When the French arrived in Koritza, in 1916, they freed it from King Constantine's troops, who were actively in co-operation with Germany and Austria. M. Vaucher, the correspondent of *l'Illustration*, says: *'The town having been occupied by our troops and the Germanophile Greeks expelled, the National Government at Salonika sent soon a Venezelist prefect. But that was not what the Albanians wanted. Mussulman and Orthodox, they often speak Greek, but are none the less Albanian.'*

The Orthodox Albanians then came forward, and said that if *'France will proclaim our independence and give us military protection she may be sure that tranquillity will rein'*. Having ascertained that this was the wish of the immense majority of the population, and that he would thus obtain the calm necessary for his operations, General Sarrail proclaimed the independence of the *kaza*. The Albanian flag was hoisted on December 10 before an enthusiastic crowd. Some fifty Albanian schools were shortly opened and at once filled with pupils.

I have also in my possession letters written to me by Koritza Christians during the Greek occupation of Koritza in 1912-13, which entirely contradict Mr. Kessary's statements. In 1913 I went to Koritza myself, and during my stay a similar mass meeting was got up, soldiers visiting all the houses and commanding the attendance of the inhabitants.

Mr. Kessary further states that Kemal Bey of Valona '*always looked to Athens*'. On the contrary, Kemal Bey hoisted the Albanian flag at Valona and proclaimed Albania's independence.

Let the Albanians be allowed independence within their own ethnographic frontiers. Strabo in the first century tells us that the Greek frontier was at Arta and that on the north of the bay were Epirote tribes who were not Greek but spoke the same tongue as the Illyrians and Macedonians. Brerewood, in 1625, tells us that Greek is not spoken in Epirus and west Macedon; that it had spread there, but that '*the natural language of the country*' had driven it out again. All that Albania asks is that a census of opinion should be taken, supervised by some impartial power, such as America or England, so as to prevent fraud or terrorism. She has then no doubts as to what would be the result.

I am, etc.,

M. E. Durham.

[In a portion of his letter for which we could not find space, Mr. Kessary referred to Mehmed Konitza Bey's connection with the Albanians in the United States, but refused to recognise the Bey's '*right to speak as Albanian delegate*.' - Ed.]

The Near East, November 15th 1918
The Future of Albania

To the Editor of The Near East

Sir,

At a meeting held by the Anglo-Albanian Society on November 12, at which Lord Lamington presided, the following resolution was passed:-

'That inasmuch as the right of self-determination for the smaller nations of Europe has been solemnly agreed to by the United Kingdom and the United States, this meeting of the Anglo-Albanian Society trusts that those Governments and the Governments of the Allied Powers will secure the integrity of Albanian territory and will assure to the Albanian people the right to choose their own form of Government. It hopes that by these means the independence of Albania, accorded by Treaty in 1913, shall be firmly established.'

As the solution of the Albanian question must inevitably have an important bearing on future peace, the Society hopes that you will give space for the publication of this resolution.

I am, etc.,

M. E. Durham

The Near East, November 22nd 1918
An Albanian Protest

To the Editor of The Near East

Sir,

May I beg a few lines to correct some errors in the letter of Mr. Kessary? I do not confuse Konitza and Koritza. They are two quite distinct places. Konitza is mainly inhabited not by Greeks but by Vlahs. Koritza is Albanian in population.

The Vlahs largely speak Greek. So do some of the Albanians. But, as Mr. Kessary himself points out, language is not a clear test of nationality. The people are none the less Vlahs and Albanians. He is mistaken also in supposing that Mehmed Bey represents '*only a few Moslems*'. The President of the Pan-Albanian Society, which he represents, is an Orthodox priest, and a large number of the Federation are Christian - both Catholic and Orthodox. The number, 60,000, is, I believe, correct, as I have taken much trouble, from American as well as Albanian sources, to make certain.

Mr. Kessary is, however, correct in saying: '*It is not surprising that Miss Durham was not asked for Greek schools in North Epirus*' - no, it is not. I was, on the contrary, asked to help get rid of them and get national schools established, and especially to free the country of Greek priests. Just as Alsace-Lorraine had German schools forced on it, so has Albania been afflicted with Greek ones. So strong is the feeling that Orthodox Albanians have told me that they will not allow their children to learn "that accursed tongue, Greek."

I am, etc.,

M. E. Durham

The Contemporary Review, July 1919
Albania and the Powers
by M. E. Durham

Of the evils of secret diplomacy we have heard much of late. Yet probably few people realise the way in which a small nation which possesses petroleum, or forests, or a '*strategical position*' is marked down, ringed round, and deliberately hunted to death by a Great Power or a Group of Great Powers, who prate hypocritically the while of self-determination, honour, and justice. The tale of Albania's doom is typical. For over a thousand years the Albanians, the original inhabitants of the land, continuously resisted all invaders and preserved their language, customs, and a portion of territory. But though every other Balkan race in turn was helped to independence, Albania alone was in each case sacrificed. Why? Because her preservation suited neither the plans of Russia nor Austria. The former would not permit the existence of any non-Slav or non-Orthodox State. Austria intended the '*absorption*' of the whole Adriatic coast.

Meanwhile, the Albanian nationalists struggled, with a courage and persistence which should have aroused general sympathy, for the right to call their land and their souls their own. Albania's demand for a Constitution overthrew Abdul Hamid. Albania's revolt against the Young Turks' attempts at forcible Ottomanisation overthrew the Young Turks in 1912. Albania was on the eve of recognition when the Balkan War of 1912-13 was precipitated by Serbia, Greece, Montenegro, and Bulgaria, because the erection of an independent Albania would have ruined their schemes of land-grabbing. The Great Powers did not fight in that war. But they sat behind it and pulled the strings. Behind Serbia and Greece was the Russo-French combine. France meant both her protégés to be in a position to pay the interest on her loans. Moreover, she was building up Greece as a naval make-weight to Italy in the Mediterranean. So early as 1906 she had raked in Serbia as junior member of the Russo-French combine, and had supplied her with Creusot guns. Italy manœuvred her puppets too. She had an age-long hatred of the Slav. But she had a foothold in Montenegro (her *"father-in-law"*), and by fanning Serb and Montenegrin jealousy hoped for good results. And, above all, she desired influence in Albania.

In the winter of 1912-13, Scutari, the capital of North Albania, had been vainly besieged for months by the Montenegrin Army. Hussein Riza, the Turkish commander (of partly Albanian origin), when he saw that relief from Turkey was impossible, determined to declare the town Albanian and call up the Albanian clans to its defence. This plan would have, no doubt, succeeded, but the evil genius of Albania, Essad Pasha Toptani, thwarted it. This man, a notorious turncoat to be bought by the highest bidder, was first an Old Turk, servant of Abdul Hamid and hated everywhere for his robberies and extortions. Only among his own retainers at Tirana had he a following. When the revolution of 1908 took place he waited to see which way the cat hopped, and then proclaimed himself a Young Turk, and leapt to power.

When Scutari was attacked, he hastened thither with the troops of which he was commander, but was regarded by the local clansmen as a Turk and an enemy, and they did their best to drive him back. Unluckily for Albania, he fought his way through, reached Scutari, and was second in command. Power for himself was his aim. He could not, therefore, suffer Hassan Riza to be the saviour of Scutari, and had him assassinated by two of his retainers. Then, by means of the Italian Consulate, through the hands of whose dragoman the correspondence passed, he entered into negotiations with Montenegro and arranged the sale of the town. Italy appears to have been head engineer in this affair for she preferred Scutari to be Montenegrin to its falling into the hands either of Austrian or Serb. Her policy was to split Serbia and Montenegro, and thwart Austria. Russia and France, playing for Slav at any price, supported her game and purposely delayed the landing of the naval force which was feebly demonstrating off the Montenegrin coast.

England, Austria, and Germany were thus all out-witted, Scutari fell, and the ladies of the Italian Legation at Cettinje naively declared they had danced round and round the table for joy. Italy believed she had bought Essad, and that forward steps in Albania would be easy. He was to be recognised as Prince of his own district of Tirana, and even went so far as to have postage stamps printed. But Italy and many others have had to learn that a man you can buy, can also sell you! England, Germany, and Austria would not allow the dirty trick to succeed. Russia's army was not yet ready for the field. She, too, brought pressure to bear. *"We shall be quite ready for our Balkan war in 1914,"* said one of the Russian military attachés to me; *"now it is impossible."*

Albania's independence was recognised and guaranteed by all the Great Powers, and a work of justice was at last accomplished. The next step of the Great Powers was, however, one of almost unparalleled cynicism and brutality. Albania prayed very earnestly for an English Prince. The Russo-French combine, with Serbia and Greece as their jackals, had, however, planned Albania's destruction from the beginning. Italy, who did not foresee the speedy rise of the hated Jugo-Slav, and dreaded only Austria, entered into the game and acquiesced in the election of a German prince, with the prior intention of evicting him. Wied, it is true, was a fool;

but a well-meaning one, and had he been given a chance, would have succeeded as well as many another ruler.

In the summer of 1913, when no Prince had as yet been chosen, I found all through Albania that the one dread of the people was Essad Pasha. He was already in constant communication with the Greek Bishop of Durazzo from whom he was reported to be receiving large sums. And he was the only man in the country with a well-equipped army. The Serbs and Montenegrins had supplied him fully. At Ochrida, in June, 1913, the Serb officers in command boasted freely to me that their plans were laid, and that in six months they would be back in Durazzo.

The snares were set, Essad, a born intriguer, managed to be one of the party of Albanians sent to invite Wied to accept the throne. And he wormed his way into the unfortunate man's favour. Wied was persuaded by Essad to go to Durazzo, in every way unfitted to be a capital, instead of to Scutari, where he would have had British support. He was thus in Essad's territory and helpless. The Powers who planned his destruction chose fit agents. Italy was represented by Allioti, of Smyrna Levantine extraction, it was said, and France by Krajewsky, a Pole, born in Bosnia, and also of Levantine antecedents. He boasted to me immediately after the fall of Scutari that France would not allow Albania to exist, and was raised from a Vice-Consulate to represent France on the International Commission.

Against all this, Wied and Albania were helpless.The Dutch Gendarmerie, who were loyal, soon saw Essad's game and arrested him. Italy intervened, and demanded his release He went to Rome and was decorated. A relative of the King of Montenegro - Gjurashkovitch - was also suspect and was arrested. Russia came forward and insisted on his release. In both cases 'the capitulations', which had died with the Turks, were pleaded in order to make trial for treason impossible. Italy and the Serbs then started the so-called revolution against Wied. Dibra, a mainly Albanian town had been allotted to Serbia in 1913. A large number of the inhabitants had spent the winter in Albania as refugees, fed by the American mission. Essad and the Serbs got hold of these Dibrans and promised them that, as a reward for evicting Wied, they should have Dibra restored to them.

In vain did Albania's friends tell them this was false. Dibra was their one hope and desire. Together with Essad's men, they attacked Durazzo. Red lights were flashed to them from a house in the town. It was entered by the gendarmerie and - an Italian Colonel was found in it. Capitulations were pleaded again, and there was no trial. The English, Austrians, and Germans of the International Control, strove honestly to keep the treaty guaranteeing Albania's independence. The Russo-French combine had planned war in the Balkans, and meant to have it. Italy, too, still believed in her Essad. So soon as the attack on Durazzo had begun, and Albania's small gendarmerie was occupied with it, the results of Essad's colloquies with the Greek bishop were apparent. The so-called wounded Greeks who had been allowed to remain in the hospital at Koritza, telephoned for medical comforts, which arrived in the shape of Greek troops (largely Cretans, but also of other regiments; many were taken prisoner, and photographed, and gave details of whence they came) and machine guns. Albania was thus attacked at two places at once, by the Russo-French combine. The Albanians were dazed with the falsity of the Powers and confused by counter-orders. One of the Russian representatives went about telling them to take no part in the fighting against the Greeks or the Powers would be angry with them. Albania was to be destroyed. Nevertheless, the Albanians put up a brave fight, and though they possessed no artillery, kept the Greeks at bay till a further influx of Greek troops overwhelmed them.

Meanwhile, in Durazzo, the Italians most naively demonstrated the large part they were playing in the game by striving to create panics, building a senseless sort of a barricade (just in front of the hotel) which I partly pulled down, and even going so far as to write and print in the Italian papers a most gory account of the fall of the town and the slaughter which ensued; so sure were they of the success of their plans and their Essad. But the town did not fall.

While Durazzo still held out, and the Greeks were flooding South Albania, burning and massacring as they went, came the news of the assassination of the Archduke Franz Ferdinand. War seemed then certain. The struggle in Albania was not Albanian at all. It was the beginning of the fight between Slav and Teuton for the Near East and the route to the Far East. Like a flash I remembered how, in May of the previous year, I had been told in triumph at Podgoritza in Montenegro: *"We, the Serb people, are now a danger to Europe. We have beaten the Turk. We shall fight Austria next. The Serbs will march to Vienna. We (the Montenegrins) shall march to Sarajevo. We have the whole of the Russian Army with us. We shall take what we please. We shall begin in Bosnia."*

Nevertheless, it seemed incredible that the neutrality of Albania, guaranteed by every Power in Europe, would be so shamelessly violated. The Albanians themselves fondly hoped that a war in Europe would withdraw their tormentors and they would then be able to arrange their own affairs. We all had yet to learn that all treaties are potential waste paper.

Seventy thousand starving refugees crowded in and around Valona, victims of the Greek invasion. I went up into the mountains and in the fatal early days of August was spying the position of the Greek troops near Tepeleni unaware of what was going on in Europe. Nor, till I went over to Brindisi to learn if further relief work were possible, did I hear that Great Britain had already declared war.

After this, Albania was marked down as a prey. Wied fled on September 3rd. Essad then entered Durazzo, having come direct from Serbia, and was publicly embraced by Allioti, the Italian. Italy had not yet learnt that a paid agent can be bought up by others. No sooner had Italy entered the war than she was up against her old Slav foe. But Essad was already in the employ solely of the Russo-French combine. All Italy's intrigues with him were lost time and money. He was now pledged against her and settled comfortably in Salonika. Owing to his unpopularity in Albania he was, however, unable to raise the large Albanian force his employers doubtless hoped for. And it was soon apparent that France was building up steadily against Italy. Wherever Italy appeared Adriaticwards her path was blocked by Serb or Greek, backed by France or Russia. Russia's disappearance from the scene of action in no way mended matters. Italy, it is true, landed at Valona in 1914, and took it in spite of the treaty signed in 1913, but elsewhere she met with difficulties.

France worked systematically. Throughout the war she was advanced in Balkan lands only to retire in favour of either Greek or Serb, while Italy has panted after her. For example, in December, 1916, the French gained entrance to Koritza by promising the inhabitants that it should be recognised as an Albanian town and have local self-government. M. Vaucher, the correspondent of *'L'Illustration'* has given a detailed account of the enthusiasm with which the Albanian flag was greeted and the extraordinary rapidity with which Albanian schools, previously forbidden under heavy penalties, were opened and crowded with pupils. The Albanians cried *"Vive la France!"* only to be cruelly disappointed. When once firmly established, Colonel Descouins summoned Greek gendarmes, took down Albania's flag, and suppressed the Albanian Government. Temistokle Germenli, a much beloved nationalist, was arrested and executed, to the dismay of his compatriots, who knew that his only crime was love of his motherland.

The American mission also, it may be observed, regarded him as wholly innocent of the charges brought against him. Greek officials now replaced Albanian ones, and threatened Albanian parents with court martial, says the report, if they refused to send their children to Greek schools. The land has copper and lignite in it, which may help Greece to pay her debts to France. Italy made a counter-march. She proclaimed at

Argyrokastro, in June, 1917, that she would protect all Albania. She even penetrated Greek territory and roused wild hopes that she meant to restore Albania to her ethnographical frontiers. For a brief moment France, Greece, and Italy bared their teeth. Then Italy retired, and the luckless Albanians who had risen to her call, paid the penalty. Hard on this came the publication of the Secret Treaty of 1915, and a thrill of horror ran through Albania. How could Italy, who had all through professed to be Albania's friend, have signed away three-quarters of it? *"Russia clapped a pistol to her head"* was the reply. People clung to the hope that the collapse of Russia had made it void. The treaties then revealed were all strenuously denied by the parties who had signed them. They were said to be *"inaccurate and incomplete"* by Lloyd George. They were buried. But they rose again, in much the same form, and are the cause of much unholy squabble in Paris.

The *débâcle* of the Central Powers was followed by a neck and neck race through the coveted lands by Italy and France. France trying to be first to occupy all that she desires to bestow on her Serb and Greek protégés, Italy striving to get there first and occupy the land for Albania - and herself. Since the growth to power of the South Slavs, Italy has struggled fiercely to form a make-weight.

Italy arrived first at Elbassan. France was first in Kossovo Vilayet. Here she was welcomed by the Albanian population. She, however, having once entered, withdrew in favour of the Serbs, who, so far as recent information goes, have massacred or expelled the bulk of the Albanians in order to prove a Serb majority there. Gusinje, Plava, Jakova, and Ipek have all during the past months of *'armistice'* been bombarded and bombed. And Italy, the friend who promised to protect Albania, has stirred no finger to help.

Up till last January, the Albanians were willing to accept Italian protection, though they looked askance upon the wide lands Italy has seized around Valona. But now they ask themselves, *"What good is a protector who does not protect?"* Moreover, Italy, though she held the trump cards in Albania, has played badly and lost. She has estranged Albanian sympathies by her reckless attempts at Italianisation. Italian colonists are poured into the land, and settled on the sites of the villages burnt in 1914. Italian schools are opened in numbers, and, worst of all, the Albanians are not permitted to open schools of their own. It was for their national schools that they fought the Turk. They say the Italian is as bad as he. They have now appealed urgently and earnestly to America to take over the mandate and give them shelter till they can stand alone. If given this chance those who know them believe that in fifty years they would be second to none in the Balkans. They are more intelligent than the Bulgar; they are far more industrious than the Serb, and they have all the Greek's aptitude for commerce. Will they be given this chance? If not, they say that there is nothing to choose between denationalisation by Italy, Greece, or Serbia. If one is to be made the unwilling subject of another race, it does not much matter which.

The Franco-Greco-Serb group now holds out offers. *"The Balkans for the Balkan people, and no Italian need intrude"* is their catchword. Albania looks on all as equally unreliable. Italy, she says, will fight Jugoslavia at no distant date. Albania would then be a battleground. Italy's attention would all be riveted on Trieste and Fiume. Thither would go all her troops. Of what value would her 'protection' then be to Albania?

As my dear old dragoman said when he saw the coil of intrigue which threatened to throttle his land: *"The Great Powers, lady, are like a band of brigands. By day they quarrel with one another. At night they all go out robbing together."* It is a perfect definition of foreign policy.

But Albania knows also that 'When thieves fall out honest men come by their own' and awaits what the future may bring.

M. E. Durham

Since writing the above a Central News telegram informs us (June 13th) that the remains of the Serajevo murderers have been exhumed with great solemnity and are to be sent to their native country. The Serbs thus publicly acknowledge them as national heroes, and prove indisputably that the assassination of the Archduke was part of a well-laid plan to achieve Slav hegemony in the Near East.

The New Europe Vol. XIV, No. 177, March 4th 1920

Albania's Fate in the Balance

[In our opinion, the only solution to the Albanian problem which can avert renewed war in the Balkans is the recognition of Albania as an Independent State, in accordance with the London decisions of 1913. We trust that President Wilson will uphold the view that the immoral secret Treaty of 1915 does not wipe out the solemn pledges given in the face of Europe two short years before, and will oppose any renewal of the fatal Bosnian blunder of 1878, for which Europe has had to pay so dearly. We also rely confidently upon the Jugoslavs maintaining their refusal to be fobbed off with Albanian territory. But it is obvious that whatever decision be reached, a special régime is likely to be secured to Italy at Valona. - Ed.]

Unless, now in the eleventh hour, hands are stretched out to save Albania, the war, which was said to be for the freeing of small nations - for conferring the right of self-determination upon the peoples of Europe - will have ended by the martyrdom of a small and brave nation; martyrdom indeed, for it is proposed not only to deny her the liberty for which she has struggled for a thousand years, but to dismember and tear up the land and place it under the rule of Albania's secular enemies.

All England was filled with wrath when the neutrality of Belgium was violated. But England, as well as the other Powers signed the Treaty of London in 1913, which guaranteed independence to Albania. Albania asks bitterly whether our outcry over Belgium was mere hypocrisy, and whether we, too, are ready to tear up *'scraps of paper'* when we wish to make gifts at someone else's expense?

The excuse for the destruction of Albania is the Secret Pact of 1915. According to this pact, which was signed but two years after the Treaty guaranteeing Albania's independence, Italy, on acquiring certain parts of the Adriatic coast, shall not oppose the possible desire of France, Russia and Great Britain to divide North and South Albania between the Serbs, Montenegrins and Greeks. It does not bind the said Powers to divide Albania. When the Bolsheviks first published the Treaty, many of us could not believe that such an iniquitous proposal could have been signed by Great Britain. An appeal was made direct to the Prime Minister on behalf of Albania. He replied that the version of the Treaty quoted was *"incomplete and inaccurate"*. Yet he now proposes to carry out its worst clauses to the bitter end. Even though Tsarist Russia, who was party to the scheme, is now non-existent. What has Albania done that she should thus be hanged, drawn, and quartered? For the sentence amounts to no less.

The oldest of the Balkan peoples, the Albanians, have striven throughout the centuries to preserve their nationality. The Roman, the Byzantine Empires - the fleeting mediæval Empires of the Bulgars and Serbs - the mighty Empire of the Ottoman - all in turn rose and fell, and as they ebbed the Albanian emerged as a rock against which each flood had beaten in vain. When each Empire fell, the Albanians again made efforts to expand. Time after time we see them spreading back again into the lands from which invaders had driven their forefathers. An archæologist, who managed to do a little digging in the Balkans during military operations in the Great War, spoke with enthusiasm to the writer of the wealth of interesting material underground awaiting the investigator. *"Greek?"* we asked. *"Oh, dear, no! The Hellene is a comparatively recent comer!"*

People who have not lived in the land often say that the Albanians have not a sense of nationality. The mere fact that they have preserved their language and customs and certain parts of their lands against all comers for so many centuries, is alone enough to disprove this statement. But all who have lived with the people have been struck, not only by their love for Shkyperia - their land - but also by the heroic efforts they have made not only to defend it but also to develop themselves.

It was in Koritza in 1904 that the writer first realised the magnitude of that courage. How many people in England would send their children to school, or even teach them to read at home, if by so doing they risked excommunication by the Church and fifteen years' imprisonment? Under the Turkish Government the Albanian language was prohibited. Even to be found in possession of an Albanian newspaper was a crime. In one case, of which the writer has personal knowledge, an unhappy man was sent such a paper by a rash friend abroad. As it had not been confiscated in the post, he foolishly though it was all right and put it on his restaurant table. He was condemned to fifteen years in prison. The case was such an iniquitous one that the Consulates took it up and after a year obtained his release, but on condition only that he was never to open another shop or restaurant. Only in schools under the protection of a Foreign Power could an Albanian have his children taught in his own language Scutari alone was rich in schools; for here Austria and Italy competed one against the other and endeavoured to gain influence by providing schools. Even here the Albanian laboured under difficulties, for neither Austria nor Italy really wished to aid Albanian nationality, and so each, in their schools, used a different alphabet and orthography. It is often thrown against the Albanians in scorn that they *"do not even agree about the alphabet."* They were not allowed to. No sooner had a system been agreed to than Italy called in the school books and started a fresh set with the 'e's printed upside down!

But, in 1908, so soon as freedom of the press was announced by the Young Turk, representatives of all Albania flocked to a Congress at Monastir and at once settled the question. Settled it so effectually that the Young Turk was terrified at the rapid rise of Albanian nationality, and rushed to repress it and to try to forcibly Ottomanise the land. The Turks cried aloud to Europe that the Albanians of Kosovo, who rose against them, were opposed to civilisation. But these same chieftains who were fighting the Turk had sent their children to the newly-opened Albanian schools and were fighting for their language and their fatherland. Through all the dark years of struggle the Albanians managed to send their sons to Robert College, to France, to Vienna, to Italy, even to America; and among Albania's sons are to be found men second in culture to none of their Balkan *confrères*.

It has been asserted by those who wish Albania's destruction that the Albanians are a military race who are not capable of developing their land. In truth the Albanian has a very great aptitude for industry and commerce. The Swiss in the Middle Ages went as mercenary soldiers to many lands. It was a trade open to a poor mountaineer; but the Swiss have shown that their true bent is towards peaceful development. Similarly the Albanian has fought for a living abroad and to defend his land at home. But when allowed a chance of peaceful life he shows very great enterprise and capacity. The handicrafts, the silver-work, the magnificent embroideries of Albania all show the invention, patience and perseverance of the race; the gay, gold-embroidered garments of King Nikola's court were not the work of his Montenegrins, but the creation of the artist mind of the Scutarene.

It has again been objected that the Albanian is not capable of forming a Government. Any who will take the trouble to do so will find in contemporary records precisely similar criticism of the early efforts of Greece. The first steps are always difficult. The early history of the Serbs after their emancipation is such a complicated tale of internal differences, changes of Government, of dynasty, that it is amazing that the nation pulled through. Greece and Serbia, both rent by parties within, and hustled by foes without, have nevertheless developed. And in all probability developed more strongly and surely by working out their own salvation, than they would have done if cut up and handed over as 'mandatories' to, say, Russia, Austria, and France. We know what would have happened; each of these Powers would have intrigued against the other, and the Serbs and Greeks would have had their development delayed probably for a century.

The present proposal to give Greece, Italy, and Jugoslavia mandates over Albania is about the most unfortunate that could possibly have been devised. Albania in the first place has already been promised independence, and begs not to be put under a mandate at all. If put under a mandate, however, it should certainly be given to a neutral Power or to one who has *"no axe to grind"* in that part of Europe. It is a quite open secret to all interested in the Near East that the relations between the three proposed Powers - Italy, Greece, and Jugoslavia - are bad. Here we need not enter into the rights and wrongs of their differences. It is enough that those differences exist and are acute. The Albanians dread that their land, thus divided, will be made a battlefield for the rivals. In which case it is Albania which will bear the brunt of the loss and suffering, and may even be blamed for the quarrel. It is rank folly to put the spark near the powder magazine. Italian, Jugoslav, and Greek troops cheek by jowl in Albania cannot be expected to lead to peace. Nor can they be expected to assist the Albanians to develop on their own lines, and only by so doing can a nation arrive at its best.

Italy, Greece, and Jugoslavia, all, as a result of the war, receive wide lands, wider far than many had dared hope; Albania prays that in the name of humanity and justice they will content themselves with these lands, and will not rob a poor nation of its 'one ewe lamb'. They have all, in fact, problems in plenty to solve under their new conditions. They have their own houses to set in order. The Albanians have recently elected a Government, in spite of many difficulties thrown in their way by interested Powers; they ask to be allowed to govern themselves within at least the frontiers of 1913. They maintain with truth that if they have different political parties in their land, so have other nations, and that their internal affairs are their own concern. They believe in the Balkans for the Balkan peoples, and wish to take their place among the Balkan peoples as a free nation.

Europe on previous occasions has been faced by a similar problem and has failed lamentably. We all know the results of the partition of Poland and of giving Austria what was indeed 'a mandate' over Bosnia. Peace never has resulted, and never can result from forcing upon a nation a form of Government against its will. Hundreds of years have not reconciled Ireland to English rule; reason as well as justice demands that Albania shall be given independence, free from all foreign control.

M. Edith Durham

Contemporary Review, August 1920
The Story of Essad Pasha
by M. E. Durham

Essad Pasha, who fell by the hand of an assassin on June 13th, in a Paris street, was such a strange relic of the Middle Ages that his story seems worth the telling. He is one with the handsome swashbucklers who sold themselves and their services to the rival monarchs, princelings and dukes in the fifteenth and sixteenth centuries, and cheerfully transferred themselves to the enemy if he offered better pay - men in whom the sense of nationality was not developed at all, and whose sense of honour was, to put it mildly, deficient.

Essad Bey Toptani, of Tirana, was the head of the Toptani family, who claim descent, though with little proof, from the Chieftain Topias, and are believed to have been exterminated by the Turks when they overthrew Albania. According to the Toptanis, one infant was spared by a merciful soldier who brought him up as his own child; he subsequently returned to his home, Croia, and was there identified by his resemblance to the Topias and by a tattoo mark on his arm.

Be this as it may, the Toptanis became powerful semi-independent chiefs and ruled in the Croia district. Tirana was not founded till early in the seventeenth century. Its founder, Suleiman Bey, was an officer in the conquering Turkish army which invaded Persia. On his return from the campaign he built a mosque on the fertile plain, and after fighting for the land with a neighbouring Bey, took possession of it and named his new town after the Persian town Teheran. Suleiman returned to the Persian war and was mortally wounded. He died at Bagdad, where it is said those curious in inscriptions may read in a *'turba'*: *'Here lies the heart of the brave and generous Barkin Zadé Suleiman Pasha.'* His body was brought to Tirana and is buried near the Esky Djamia, one of the beautiful old mosques which adorn the town. His descendants held Tirana, though it was much coveted by neighbour chieftains, till in 1798 but four daughters were left to carry on the line. These four married the four sons of the then head of the Toptani family, which thus became possessed of Tirana.

In 1904, I first went to Tirana and heard of Essad. It was in the spring when all was at its loveliest. Tirana was a bower of blossoming fruit trees. Above the tender pink and white masses rose the dark spires of huge cypresses, for which Tirana is famous, and the slim white minarets of the mosques. A sparkling rivulet refreshed and cleaned the gutters; little irrigation channels kept green the gardens. The streets were gay with varied costumes and busy happy life. Under one of Turkey's futile 'reform' schemes, a Greek from Smyrna had just been appointed as Judge. He invited me to *"fifeocloque tea"* at six in the morning, and gave me a humorous forecast which is fast coming true. *"It is a waste of time for me to stay here,"* he said; *"the Albanians do not want the Turks. What can I do, I ask you, with a people each of whom is as shrewd as Bismarck? Some day they will arise and tell Europe what they want. And Europe will have to listen. In other countries, when a peasant is arrested and is brought before a court he is intimidated. He hands his head. He cannot speak. These people - I have one arrested. I am sure he is guilty. He is fearless. Instead of my putting questions to him it is he who speaks. His friends come. They argue. What can I do? I cannot prove them guilty. I am helpless. I thought to visit them in the mountains and explain the situation to them and the reform scheme of the Government. I rode out a long way. They received me and asked if I came as a friend or as an official of the Turks. 'If as a friend,' they said, 'we are delighted to see you and will roast a sheep. If as a Turkish official, run away as fast as you can and don't come here again.' I was very hungry. I ate roast sheep with them, which was excellent. Enfin, I think it will be best for me to return to Smyrna."* Sixteen years have passed. The Albanians have spoken. It remains to be seen whether the Powers will be as sensible as was the little Smyrniote.

Round about Tirana stand the big country houses of the Toptanis. Essad's house was pointed out to me. I was curious to visit a Bey's house. My Albanian guide and dragoman would not hear of it. *"Essad,"* he told me, *"is a bad man. He is very ambitious. He wants to be the Prince of Albania. And he never will be."* The Toptanis, according to him, were all tarred with the same brush. I was not to visit them. This was, however, not just. Some have turned out to be true patriots. In 1908 I first met Essad. He was gendarmerie commander at Scutari and came along with the Vali to the consular lawn tennis ground, where both were filled with amazement that anyone should take such violent exercise unless forced to.

Essad was not the eldest born of his family. His elder brother, Gani Bey, had been murdered in Constantinople some fifteen years before by the son of the then Grand Vizier, and by the order, it was said, of Abdul Hamid. Abdul, like my guide, believed the Toptanis to be aspiring too high. Essad seems not to have greatly deplored the loss of his brother, for it left him head of the family. Gani's death was avenged by one of his retainers, Gujo-i-Fais, of Croia, whose deed is celebrated in a much sung and very vivid ballad, which tells how Essad briefly remarked, *"Per Ganim mos dhimet shpirt."* *"Don't vex thy soul about Gani."* And how Gujo, rejecting this advice, entrusting his wife and children to his comrades, bought two altipatlars (revolvers) and went straight to Stamboul, where he waited on the Galata bridge till the carriage of the murderer came up, and he -

"Seized the horses by the head,
'I've a word with you,' he said,
'I've a word that I must say -
To give you salaam from Gani Bey!"

He fired pointblank at the Vizier's son, killed him at once, and threw his second revolver into the river, saying he had no use for it. The song tells how all the monarchs of Europe met expressly to forbid the Sultan from slaying Gujo. He was in fact condemned to a very long imprisonment, and Essad promised that if ever he were released he would give him lands and cattle, but, it would appear, did not expect ever to have to fulfil the promise.

In 1908, Essad had but recently arrived in Scutari, and was already detested. He had been moved from Janina, where he had held a similar post, and where he had made himself so hated by his extortions and quarrels that the place became too hot to hold him. He realised then that South Albania could never form part of his projected realm, and was therefore ready to arrange for the Greeks to have it for a *"consideration"*. The place rang with tales of the unscrupulous methods by which he added to his domains. Most of the mountain Albanians bring their flocks to graze on the plains in winter, and have certain districts and grazing rights, and much of this common land had been filched, it was said, by Essad both by fraud and by force. There was much excitement, too, over Essad's second wife.

Tirana for many years was celebrated for its troop of gypsy dancers. Foreign consuls used to make a visit to Tirana and be treated to an exhibition. To the sound of a tambourine the dancers would swirl, whirl and bend and sway while their draperies and hair plaits, set with coins, flew around them, till breathless and exhausted, and streaming with perspiration, they came to the audience for reward and clapped the coins on their moist foreheads and necks, where they adhered. Essad's gypsies were notorious. So much so that his wife, when he was absent from home, complained of them to the Vali of Scutari, who, to oblige her, evicted them from the neighbourhood. Alas, poor lady! she did not benefit; for Essad promptly took a second wife and deserted her. Scutari fondly hoped that she or her relatives would be avenged on him.

One of his duties in Scutari was to prevent any foreigners from travelling up country, for the Government was just then terrified that foreigners would help the Albanians to revolt. I crawled out of Scutari in the grey before the dawn, and waded through wet asphodel, dodging Essad's outposts till far enough for safety, when I mounted the horse that had been sent out overnight and was soon away to the mountains. Essad enquired my whereabouts, in vain, of the foreign consulates; and I should probably have been ignominiously brought back by his gendarmes had not the Young Turk revolution broken out and upset his plans - and those of all the Powers. Essad knew that trouble was brewing. But he did not know which side would win, and until the 13th of June, 1920, he has always been an adept in falling '*butterside uppermost*'. He applied to the Government for leave to take a cure in a foreign watering place, which was granted him, though he appeared to be enjoying rude health, and remained abroad till the victory of the Young Turk was certain. Scutari naively hoped for a reign of justice, and foretold that the first reform of the new régime would be the execution of Essad and the restoration of the goods he had filched. But Essad returned in triumph as a member of the Committee of Union and Progress. And Scutari's faith in the Young Turks was hopelessly shattered.

He had formerly taken the pay of Abdul Hamid and carried out his orders. He now contrived to be one of the two who were sent to command Abdul to abdicate, thus avenging very completely the death of Gani Bey. Essad, now a Pasha, was hand-in-glove with the Young Turks, and the Young Turks started upon his foolish policy of forcible Ottomanisation. All Albania had supported the revolution with enthusiasm.The long-forbidden Albanian language was printed, newspapers were published, schools were opened. Albanian congresses met and fixed the orthography.

Freed from Turkish prohibition, and Austrian, Greek and Italian influence, the cult of the national language became almost a religion to the Albanians. Up till 1908 the foreign schools, where alone Albanian could be taught as a written language, had for political purposes frequently changed the spelling of their school books, and Italy and Austria each adopted different systems for the express purpose of preventing the nationalist development.The Young Turks, alarmed by Albanian enthusiasm, began again the persecution of the national language, made Turkish compulsory in the schools, and closed the national printing presses. Essad was a Young Turk. *"The Young Turks,"* said the Scutarenes, *"are the sons of the old ones."* Essad had sided with the enemy. He further called down contempt upon himself by his treatment of Gujo-i-Fais. All prisoners were released on the proclamation of the Young Turk victory, and among them Gujo-i-Fais, the avenger of Gani Bey, returned to his home. Essad had never expected to be called on to fulfil his promises of land and oxen, made no attempt to do so, and it was said was only forced to assist Gujo by the pressure of public opinion.

The power of the Toptanis, however, was great in and around Tirana, and Essad contrived to be elected as deputy for that region, to the Young Turk Parliament. Rumour had it that Essad now aspired to be head of Albania under the Young Turks. Albania, however, speedily revolted against Young Turk despotism. In 1910-1912, fierce fighting took place between the Albanians and the Turkish forces. Essad perceived that his chance of ruling Albania under the Young Turk was nil; that other leaders, for example the gallant Issa Boletin and Hussein Bey of Prishtina, were popular heroes, and that Prenk Bibdoda of Mirdita and Ismail Kemal were dangerous rivals. He quarrelled with the Young Turks, but did not '*burn his boats*' and withdrew to Tirana to play his favourite pastime of waiting to see '*which way the cat hopped*'. When the victory of the Albanians seemed certain, Essad went to the British consul at Scutari and asked if it were possible to obtain British protection for Albania.

About this time I happened to be at the house of a priest in one of the most outlying tribes of the mountains. At night there came a man and asked, as is customary, for hospitality. A parley at the door ensued. The man was a Greek, a wandering carpenter noted for good craftsmanship. In he came and supped with us, a swarthy sinewy creature with black eyes. He told his tale. On a point of honour he had stabbed a man in Greece a year or two before. Dramatically he told of his escape, hunted by the Greek police, lurking by day and travelling by night till he crossed the Turkish frontier. Since then he had earned a living by taking on building jobs. Essad had taken him as headman in the rebuilding of the bazaar at Tirana. This bazaar was Essad's boast. Strangers were always told of the generous Essad who had thus benefited his native town. But by common report, when the bazaar was finished, it was only by threatening violence that the workmen got their pay. The Greek, snarling like a wild cat, told how he had got none. Essad told him to be off quickly or he would extradite him to the Greek Government and would at once report his presence to the nearest Greek consul. The company was thrilled. *"This is Essad! The tyrant of Tirana."* And the Greek, in a frenzy of rage, showed his white teeth and swore that Essad should not live long. But the pitcher goes oft to the well before it breaks.

The Balkan States declared war against the Turks. Essad thought the cat would hop Turkwards, and hastened towards Scutari with the troops of which he was still in command. The Maltsori tribesmen regarded him as a Turk and fiercely opposed his approach. But he fought his way through and reached Scutari, where he was second in command under General Hussein Riza Bey, who conducted the defence of the town with great ability. Hussein Riza was Albanian on his mother's side. When he perceived that no relief was possible from Turkey, he decided to declare Scutari Albanian and to call in the help of the tribesmen. He therefore consulted a well-known Scutarene Christian and arranged that he and some others should go through the lines at night and call up the clansmen who were fiercely angered against both Serb and Montenegrin. When the Albanian flag was hoisted on the citadel the tribesmen were to attack the besiegers in the rear while Hussein Riza's forces made a sortie. Hussein Riza left the Scutarene, having charged him to find two other messengers and promising to settle things next day. That night he dined with Essad and, as he left after dinner, was shot close to Essad's door and mortally wounded by two men disguised as women. Essad who took over the command of the town sent round a public crier next day to say that the episode was closed and no enquiry was to be held. Later, Osman Bali, Essad's right-hand man boasted freely that he had done the deed. The second man was said to be Mehmed Kavaia, also a retainer of Essad's.

Essad withdrew to the citadel. No more sorties were made, and parleys with Montenegro began. Essad knew that Scutari hated him as badly as did Janina. He knew, too, that he would never rule Albania under the Young Turks. Italy was extremely anxious to block Austria's influence in Albania and connived at Essad's plans. He could only understand Turkish and Albanian. While his compatriots were striving hard for education, and French, German and Italian were widely learnt and spoken, Essad remained ignorant, and his communications with Montenegro passed through the Italian consulate for translation - so said Scutari. At the very last moment when the International force was off the coast and its landing was merely a matter of a few days, Essad sold Scutari. He was given in return plenty of ammunition, was allowed to withdraw his force fully armed, and was later to be recognised as ruler of a small central Albania - viz., Tirana and his own retainers.

In the summer of 1913, in a long ride through Albania, the same tale was told me everywhere. Local men were keeping excellent order, but Essad and his army, the one armed force in the land, were dreaded. The arrival of a European Prince who should suppress and disarm him was the hope of all. Already in June, 1913, he was known to be in constant communication with the Greek Bishop at Durazzo and with the Serbs. Neither Scutari nor South Albania would accept Essad. Very well, then, he would throw both overboard to Greek and Serb, and, as the well-paid ally of both, would reign at Tirana. He even had postage stamps printed with his head on them - but they have never been circulated. He began by opposing the provisional government set up at Valona by Ismail Kemal, who proclaimed Albania's independence there in November, 1912, thereby making Valona a sacred spot for all Albanian patriots. All sensible Albanians agreed that though that government was but an embryo, any dissension must be avoided and the decision of the Powers quietly awaited. Essad's task, however, was to destroy Albania. All he could do to disrupt the land he did. Nor did the arrival of the International Commission of Control aid matters, for Essad in fact was working for some of the Powers represented upon it, and tried to set up a government of his own at Durazzo. He insisted on going as head of the delegation to Neuwied to invite the Prince, and there he managed so to insinuate himself into the Prince's favour that he induced him to go, not to Scutari, but to Durazzo, where Essad had him, so to speak, trapped; surrounded, moreover, by a gang of foreign ministers and advisers, many of whom were actively working to overthrow Albania with Essad's aid. When I spoke with the Prince in June, 1914, he seemed dazed and helpless as a netted creature, finding himself caught by cunning intrigue through blindly following Essad's advice, and not knowing which way to turn.

Essad, as War Minister, had been conveying arms and ammunition to Tirana in readiness for a rising. He was arrested; but Italy, whose man he then was, intervened and forbade his trial, fearing possibly awkward revelations. Essad was expelled from Albania, went to Rome, and was decorated. The rising, nevertheless, ensued. It had been skilfully engineered by telling the ignorant Moslem peasants that Wied was the sworn foe of Islam, and by promising them that the town of Dibra, which had been given to the Serbs, should be restored to Albania if they expelled Wied. The Russian Vice-Consul at Valona went so far as to tell folk that the Great Powers would be very angry if they fought on Wied's side. So, to please the greed of certain Powers, Albanian peasants were tricked to their own destruction. Simultaneously with the rising, the Greeks attacked South Albania. The Albanians defended themselves with great bravery, but owing to the trouble at Durazzo were short of ammunition, and also, as the Dutch gendarmerie officers stated, could not hope to oppose the Greek army, which had artillery.

Then came the Great War. The Albanians hoped at first that they would be left to themselves by the Powers who had declared them a neutral and independent State. But they were invaded on all sides. Greeks, Italians, Montenegrins and Serbs, all came to 'peg out claims'. Essad, after Wied's departure, tried to proclaim himself as Prince, but no one heeded him. The Italian representative, however, welcomed him ostentatiously in public. Essad was still one of Italy's hopes. Had not Essad been chosen by the Entente as their man, a very large Albanian force might have been recruited by means of which the frontier could have been held and the Serbian débâcle avoided. But to do this would have been to spoil the plan of Essad for an Albania of his own, and of the Greeks and Serbs for the South and North of Albania, the plan of the Secret Pact of April, 1915. The chance was thrown away. Essad has

The house at 71, Belsize Park Gardens, London NW3 in which Edith Durham lived from 1918 to 1921. It also served as the administrative base of the Anglo-Albanian Society.

A woman from North Albania (Photo by Marubi)

A woman from Scutari (Photo by Marubi)

A woman from Milësia (Photo by Marubi)

A woman from Prizren in Kosova (Photo by Marubi)

A man from North Albania (Photo by Marubi, reproduced by kind permission of Mr. Alexander Duma)

An Albanian refugee family from Kosova (Photo by Ruth Pennington, reproduced by kind permission of the Somerset Record Office, Taunton)

An Albanian family from Zadrima (Photo by Marubi, reproduced by kind permission of Mr. Alexander Duma)

An Albanian family from the North of Albania, gathered for a meal, divided into three groups, the men, the women and the children (Photo from the Chatin P. Sarachi Collection in the Centre for Albanian Studies archive, reproduced by kind permission of Mrs Elizabeth Milburn)

Two Albanians greet each other. (Photo from the Chatin P. Sarachi Collection in the Centre for Albanian Studies archive, reproduced by kind permission of Mrs Elizabeth Milburn)

A street scene from Skutari at the turn of the century (Photo reproduced by kind permission of Alexander Duma)

Churchgoers gathered outside the Albanian Catholic Church in Mirdita (Photo by Margaret Haslock, reproduced by kind permission of Mr. Alexander Duma)

A gathering of the Albanian aristocracy in the 1930s

Tribesmen from Northern Albania

A marketplace in Tirana at the turn of the century
(Photo reproduced by kind permission of Alexander Duma)

Gani Bey Toptani (centre), with his retainers
(Photo by Marubi in the CAS archive)

The house at Valona where Albanian independence was proclaimed. This photograph taken by Edith Durham in July 1913 and has been reproduced by kind permission of Mr. Alexander Duma.

Ismail Kemal Bey

Prince Wilhelm von Wied

Prenk Bib Doda

Essad Pasha

Hasan Bey Prishtina, Kosova leader

Rt. Hon. Colonel Aubrey Herbert

King Zog of the Albanians

Faik Bey Konitza

The house at 36, Glenoch Road, London NW3 on the top floor of which Edith Durham resided from 1921 to her death in 1944.

posed as the man who saved the Serbian troops when they crossed the Albanian mountains. The fact that the Albanians relied on the word of England and knew that both General Phillips and Admiral Troubridge were with the Serbs had much more to do with it. General Phillips throughout has stood up for Albania's rights and is widely respected. As an officer, Essad, in fact, showed no bravery. One who was with him gave me a ludicrous account of his abject terror when sheltering from an air raid under the ancient citadel of Durazzo. Nor did he in any way distinguish himself in Salonika where his main employment was to pose as a dethroned monarch. Albania never recognised him. Only upon his visiting cards was the President of the Albanian Government! Italy found that her interests clashed with those of France and the Slavs. Essad, forgetting Rome and his decoration, now played Slav and anti-Italian. The Franco-Slav group was the stronger, and therefore the more attractive.

When the armistice came, he did not hurry to claim his throne, being well aware of the reception he would meet. The Albanians hastened to send delegates to the Peace Conference, but he was not one of them. Who paid him, and how much he was paid, is not known, but he was able in Paris to have sets of apartments at the '*Continental*', a villa, and a house in the Avenue Marceau, plenty of servants, three motor cars, and horses, and was described by a compatriot to be *"living like an American Croesus"*.

In January, 1920, the Albanians elected a Government representative of all districts and all religions. It set to work and was remarkably successful. But in spite of its appeals the Powers refused to recognise it. The plan of a little central Albania for Essad, and division of the rest of the land between Greek, Serb, and Italian still had their support; and Essad, to hasten matters, sent Osman Bali, the man who boasted of killing Hussein Riza, to Tirana to attempt to overthrow the Albanian Government. He failed completely. So long as Essad lived it was obvious that he would be the tool of any enemy, and would never cease to misrepresent his compatriots. They looked on him as a traitor and a dangerous one; Albanian students have been studying and working in America, in France, in England. Neither they nor the two great nationalist centres of Albania, Scutari and Koritza, would recognise the ignorant and unscrupulous man, a relic of the dark ages of the old Turk, who was luxuriating in a foreign capital, and growing fat on the wealth for which he had betrayed his fatherland.

Small wonder that a passing student, angered by his swagger, fired the shot which ended his unclean life on June 13th, 1920. The only wonder is that Great Powers should have stooped to use such a tool, and to use it moreover in order to destroy a small and brave nation. Their tool failed them. Some even cut their own fingers. The Albanians have lost belief in the Powers' methods, and cry to all lovers of justice to be allowed to manage their land in their own way. They have risen to evict the Italians who have occupied Valona, the place where Albania's independence was proclaimed. They wish for no small central State, but for an Albania which shall include all the territories awarded them by the Powers in 1920. As a nation they have never consented to the partition of their land. And the one man who signed it away is now dead. The Great War was fought, said the Powers, for the freedom of small nations. Let them now show that this was indeed the case.

M. E. Durham

Man, February 1923

Head Hunting in the Balkans
by M. E. Durham

Head-hunting, studied usually in distant lands, flourished in Europe well into the middle of the 19th century and is not yet quite extinct. When I travelled in Montenegro at the beginning of the present century all the elderly men could, and did, tell tales of the heads that they or their friends had taken. My guide confessed, with shame and humiliation, that he had not taken a single one in the war of 1877, pleading that he was only seventeen, and was severely told that others, even younger, had done better. Every man in earlier days went to war or to a border fray intending to take as many heads as he could. The short heavy 'hanzhar' was used for the purpose. Never for stabbing. An expert severed the head at one blow. If two Montenegrins both wounded the same man, the head 'legally' belonged to the man who took first blood. I was told of cases in which a dispute followed about the head and that the rival claimants have been known to fight each other for it to the death. The reasons for head-taking were given as *"to show how brave you are"* and *"to shame the enemy"*. I gathered that it was also supposed to affect the future life of the enemy. But whether it would prevent it altogether I could not learn. That it was formerly believed to do so seems probable, as I heard grisly tales of heroic women who crawled over the border at night and, with danger and difficulty, brought back their husbands' heads in order to bury them with the bodies.

Blood vengeance raged between Montenegrin, Turk and Albanian, and for one head many would be taken. The heads were tied by the lock of hair left on them to the neck or belt of the warrior. A Ragusan lady gave me her grandfather's vivid account of the horror produced there when the Russians enlisted Montenegrins to fight the French troops during the Napoleonic wars, and how the wild inrush of yelling Montenegrins, with decapitated French heads dripping and dangling from belt and neck, struck terror into Napoleon's hardened troops. Till recently, the heads of all Serbs, Montenegrins and Albanians were shaven and a long lock, plait, or two side tufts only left. The reason popularly given for this custom was that if the head was completely shaven the only way to carry it was by hooking your finger in its mouth. If you were a Christian you would not like a Moslem finger stuck in. Nor would a Moslem like an unclean Christian finger. Hence a handle was left. The reason is improbable, but the tale is of interest as showing that a large proportion of the people were accustomed to the idea of having their heads carried away. The medieval ballads of the Serbs give plenty of examples of head-cutting and narrate mainly the slaying of chieftains by chieftains. To realise the wholesale head-taking of recent times we must refer to the ballads of Grand Voyvoda Mirko, father of the late King of Montenegro, who gives very precise details. Thus, in *'The Slaying of Chulek Beg'*, 1852, after the fight they *'counted out three hundred Turkish heads. Among them that of Chulek Beg . . . . . Off went the Serbs singing and carrying Turkish turbans and glittering clothing and the Turkish heads on oaken stakes and Chulek's head among them.'* In *'The Fight at Drobnjak'*, 1855, *'As the Turks rushed from the burning tower the young Montenegrins seized them and cut off the head of each. And lo and behold the three Mladitches, carrying dead Turkish heads . . . . and they said to Serdar Bogdan of the frontier, "Here, O Serdar, have we cut off for thee fifty Turkish heads and taken all their clothing."*

In *'The Slaying of Betchko Agimanitch'* to avenge one Montenegrin, twelve Turks are killed. *'Then with the Turks' clothes and weapons and the heads upon oaken stakes they marched back to the village of Markovitch and set up eleven heads before the white tower of the Serdar and Betchko's head they carried to Cetinje to the tower above the Monastery where up till now many Turkish heads have been impaled and many more shall be, God willing, heads of Pashas and Vezirs, of Agas and Begs. A fine booty was this of Serdar Scepan and great honour did he gain. God grant him long life!'*

Sir Gardner Wilkinson, who went as British Envoy to Montenegro in 1848, broke it gently to Prince Nikola (as he then was) that the sight of so many heads on a tower in the capital was unpleasant to British envoys. But the practice continued and a dried head was kept in the Monastery after public exhibition had ceased.

In *'The Avenging of Pope Radisav'* we find thirty-three heads taken to avenge one man. *'They cut off thirty-three heads. Not the devil a one did they let live . . . And they went to Bijelopavlitch, above the bloody town of Spuzh [then in Turkish possession], carrying the heads on stakes, and stuck them up that the Turkish wives and women of the town might see them and. know they were a monument to Pope Radisav. May the ravens and crows claw the heads and the foxes tear them!'*

These were border frays. More serious work was put in at Kolashin in 1858. Here, 1,000 heads were cut off. *'I was on Kum mountain and I saw it myself,'* adds the poet proudly. In *'The Slaying of Selim Pasha'* in 1862, 1,600 heads are taken, including those of the Pasha and his two sons, and carried in triumph. In the fight at Nikshitch the same year the score is 3,700. It is noteworthy that a share of the booty, some fine swords or horses,were usually sent to the Prince (the late King of Montenegro) after every big affair. That the heads were cut from dead bodies and from the wounded is shown by *'The Fight at Martinitch, 1862'*. *'By the time they had driven the Turks back on Spuzh they had cut off 600 heads, and mortally wounded 1,000 men whom the Turks carried away that the Serbs might not cut off their heads too.'*

The last heads that I heard of as being cut off were those of three Montenegrins killed in a border fight just preparatory to the first Balkan war in August, 1912. I spoke with a nephew of one of the decapitated. He took it very calmly and seemed to think it might happen to anybody's uncle. During the war which followed, nosetaking was substituted by the Montenegrins for head-taking and a great deal went on. I saw nine of the victims. The nasal bone was hacked right through and the whole upper lip removed as well as the nose. The trophy was carried by the moustache. It is only fair to the Turks to say that I did not see or hear of a single case of a mutilated Montenegrin. The practice was to go round the battle-field and cut the nose, and in some cases also castrate, the wounded, who usually died of the additional shock and haemorrhage.

The desire to take a trophy was so great that a wounded Montenegrin whose hands were disabled would sometimes seize his enemy's nose with his teeth and try to bite it off. A Montenegrin gendarme told me how, in the war of 1877, he had thus made a supreme effort, had been cut down, and on recovering consciousness in a Russian field hospital found, to his intense joy, the nose in his breeches pocket, a friend having generously cut it off for him!

I once stopped a terrible fight on the road between Cattaro and Njegus, in which one man had his teeth firmly fixed in the other's nose and was hanging on like a bulldog, while the blood dripped freely from the ends of his enemy's long moustache.

Turning to the best collection of old Montenegrin ballads, Ogledalo Srpsko, we find many more examples of head-taking, and further confirmation of the fact that the dead heads were worn by the triumphant victors. Thus in *'The Slaying of Bechir Beg Bushatli'*: *'the Krajitchnitzi, those grey falcons, charged down on the rest of the Turks and cut off fifty heads... They then turned back towards home decked out with Turkish heads and many Turkish weapons ... and they carried the heads to Cetinje and ornamented Cetinje with them.'* This in 1839. In the case of mighty Pashas, I was told it was sometimes customary to salt the head to make it keep the longer.

I could multiply instances, but have given sufficient to show the ardour with which head-hunting was pursued in Europe, within five days of London, during the lifetime of many of us.

M. Edith Durham.

Man, April 1923
A Bird Tradition in the West of the Balkan Peninsula
by M. E. Durham

The fact that a considerable proportion of the people of the Western side of the Balkan peninsula even to-day identify themselves with birds, and that a mass of traditional songs shows that the belief is ancient, has not, so far as I know, received the notice it deserves. Briefly the facts are as follows.

The Albanians in their own language call themselves Shkypetars, their language Shkyp, and their land Shkyperia or Shkypnia. They derive this from ' *Shkype'.* an eagle, and say, *"We are the sons of the eagle, our land is the land of eagles."* Beyond a vague idea that to kill an eagle is unlucky I have learnt no particulars. But in Plutarch's *'Life of Pyrrhus, King of Epirus',* who is still a popular hero in Albania, it is of interest to find that after his great victory over the Macedonians his Epirots hailed him as the *"Eagle".* The medieval chieftain Skenderbeg adopted an eagle for his banner, and the eagle has been chosen as the crest of the newly-formed Albanian State.

Passing from Albania into Montenegro (now merged in Jugoslavia) I found a very strongly marked tradition. As all maps up to the end of the elghteenth century, and indeed into the nineteenth, merely mark Montenegro as a part of North Albania, and as much of the tribal law and custom was the same in both lands till 1865, it is not surprising to find that all Montenegrins also are birds. But, in this case, *falcons (soko,* plural, *sokolovi).* This word is used in common parlance. When I tramped the country my guide hailed everyone we met on the way with *"Whither will ye, my falcons ?"* or, *"Forward, my falcons!"* (*Napried sokolovi!)*, and so forth. Every officer addressed his men as *"moji sokolovi"* (*my falcons).* I have heard this again and again. There is also a verb derived from *'soko', 'sokoliti', (to urge on, or incite). Soko, Sokol,* and the derivatives *Sokolitch and Sokolovitch* are common enough names among the South Slavs.

The Montenegrins have a dance which seems to be unknown in Serbia. A pair or two pair of dancers stand opposite each other and dance at each other, retiring, advancing and performing various steps and finally leaping as high as possible into the air, flapping their arms and uttering wild yells. The leaping, flapping, yelling dancer is said to represent a falcon or eagle. When danced at night by a big bonfire, it is extraordinarily picturesque. I once saw this danced by a North Albanian tribesman, and was told it was Albanian. But the Albanian tribesmen very rarely dance, whereas the Montenegrins seldom lost a chance of doing so.

The custom of death wailing was universal when I was in Montenegro. In these wails a large number of stock phrases are used, interspersed with howls and shrieks of *"Lé! Lé! Lé! Lé'!"* The men of the tribe when approaching the house of the deceased cried: *"Zhao mi za tebe. Moj krilati brate."* (Woe is me for thee, oh my winged brother!) I could get no explanation of the word *"winged"* except that *" We always say it."* or *" It is our custom."* and at first supposed it meant an angel. But taken along with the other facts it probably indicates that the man was a *" soko"* and also, as we shall see later, a brave man entitled to wear plumes.

The use of the word 'soko' for a fighting man is so common in Montenegrin songs that I could easily fill a page with quotations. Grand Voyvoda Mirko, father of the late King Nikola of Montenegro, a wild man of the mountains. whose life was occupied alternately with border fighting and composing ballads on his frays, supplies any number of examples in his *'Junacki Spomenik'* (Heroes' Monument), dealing with the fights between 1852 and 1862. *'Voyvoda Jovo was drinking wine in his tower at Banyani. With the Voyvoda were three hundred f alcons ... Among them, two grey falcons, both heroes, Sirdar Stepan Radoyev and Sirdar Djoko of Banyani.'* In *'The Avenging of Pope Radosav'*, the Kapetan cries that he has news from Biyelopavlitch that the Turks have *'broken faith and killed that grey falcon Pope Radosav... Now up with ye, my falcons, let us go and avenge him!'* etc. Briefly, almost everyone is a falcon, and the leaders urge on *(sokoliti)* their men. The thing becomes comical when we are told *'three grey falcons sat drinking wine before the inn'*. The names of three chieftains are then given. I have heard a love song yelled: *'Thou art the swallow bird. I am the grey falcon who will swoop and carry you off.'* Whether this song was old or new I do not know.

The use of the term 'soko' to denote a warrior is very much more frequent in the ballads of Montenegro than in those of Serbia (in the pre-War sense). Thus in those concerning the Serb rising led by Karageorge at the beginning of the nineteenth century, I have found scarcely an example.

Turning to the old ballads, of which large numbers have been collected and published, we find many curious facts about falcons. Falcons carry special messages to Serb chieftains. Want of space prevents quoting these tales in entirety, though many well deserve it. In *'The Sons of Ivan Beg'* (about 1510), given in Ogledalo Srpsko, the chief Montenegrin collection of traditional ballads, Ivan Tsrnoievitch, Prince of Montenegro, drinks wine at Cattaro with some comrades. A grey falcon hovers over the market place. The Montenegrins try to hunt it into a corner and catch it, but it soars aloft. Ivan then wraps his cloak around his shoulders and calls to the falcon, which settles on his shoulder and gives him a letter from under its wing which it has brought him from Stamboul. Ivan addresses it as *"My falcon, thou black news carrier"*. And they have a long talk about Ivan's renegade son Stanisha.

The falcon as influencing the fate of the Serb nation appears in one of the Kosovo cycle songs (see collection of Vuk Karadjitch) thus: '*A falcon, that grey bird, flew from Holy Jerusalem and carried a little swallow. This was not a grey falcon, but holy St. Elijah. He did not carry a swallow, but a letter from the Holy Mother of God.*' This letter tells King Lazar how, by losing the coming battle of Kosovo (1389), he may save his own soul. Which he accordingly does! Among the songs about that most popular hero, Marko Kralyevitch, are some references of much interest. Marko, of course, is often referred to as a falcon. He is described as winning a shooting competition against the Turks by using an arrow fledged with six falcon feathers. Two songs describe the love that exists between him and falcons, '*Kralyevitch Marko fell sorely ill by the wayside. He thrust his spear in the ground and tied his horse Sharatz to it. And Marko cried aloud : Who will bring me water to drink? Who will make shade for me? Down there came a grey falcon, and brought water in its beak, and spread its wings over him. . . . And Marko said : "Oh falcon, my grey bird, what good have I done thee that thou shouldst bring water and make shade for me?" And the falcon said : "Don't be silly, Marko! When we were in the fight at Kosovo the four Turks took me and cut off both my wings. Then didst thou take me and set me up on a green fir tree that the Turkish horses might not trample me, and fed'st me with the flesh of heroes, and gave me blood to drink. Thus hast thou done me a good deed."* In a longer version the bird is an eagle. Marko rescues it from the battle, and also saves its nestlings from a burning tower, and feeds them '*for a month and one week more*'. In a third song, Marko goes a-hunting with the Turks, and his falcon when flying at a duck is shot by a Turk with an arrow, and falls with a broken wing. In barbarous times, bloody vengeance for a favourite horse or hound is not impossible. But Marko's conversations with his falcon seem to show a more intimate relation. The wounded bird settled on Marko's shoulder and cried ceaselessly. Marko riding home with it asks: *"How art thou, my falcon, without a wing?"* and the falcon said : *"I am like one that has no brother. Had I a born brother I would not lament my wing, for he would avenge me...".*

And Marko said: *"Fear not, my grey falcon. An thou hast no brother, thou hast Marko, who will be no worse than a brother to thee."* Marko arrives home and sends for a doctor, who dresses the falcon's wound. News comes that seventy Turks have been harassing a neighbouring village. Marko, single-handed, kills every one of them and returning home remarks: *"Now fear not, my falcon. Thou knowest thou hast a brother. So long as Marko lives the Turks will never forget thy wing."* Marko was an historical personage (end of fourteenth century), son of Vukashin, chieftain of Scutari, in Albania, when that district fell under Serbian rule. That is, he hails from the very district where the falcon legend still prevails.

In one ballad, *'Childe Jovan and the Daughter of Tsar Stefan'*, we seem to have a reminiscence of actual descent from a falcon. The local colour is medieval Serbian. Tsar Stefan of Primen must be Stefan Dushan, who reigned from 1336-1355. But the tale is obviously an ancient one tacked on to a later celebrity. Briefly, the Tsar's daughter is found to be pregnant. Charged by her father, she confesses. According to custom she lives shut up in a sort of harem. *"One morning , I arose early . . . I went out on to the white tower and put the crown upon my head, to see how it suited me, until the sun rose in the east. When the crown saw the sun, beams of light flashed from the crown . . . as far as the Shar mountains where the falcons nest. And the beautiful Vilas (fairies, spirits) are with them. . . . When night came . . . a grey falcon came flying, and with him seven swans from the Shar Mountains and Jastreb. The swans alighted on the tower, the falcon upon my window sill. The tower shook. Light streamed forth from the falcon so that my golden cage (harem) was light at midnight as at midday. The falcon shook its wings and stood there a youth in a thin shirt. He stayed the whole night, and left early at morn. Never again has he returned to me, and by him am I with child."* The Tsar drives out his daughter, and she seeks her lover. She is guided partly by the sun. By the help of his old mother she finds the tower of her falcon lover, and upon it is a golden ball with falcons' wings (Is this a trace of Egyptian cults?). His mother, to prevent her son from again flying away, steals his falcons' feathers while he sleeps, and he is killed by the jealous Vila, who will not permit him to have a human wife.

Has this tale of a falcon and the sun any remote connection with the bird chariot of the sun found in Bosnia? Has it been handed down from prehistoric times to the now completely Slavised population? The tale is evidently fragmentary, for we are never told whether the falcon's child is born.

In the two versions of another tale: *'Sekula Changes Himself to a Dragon'* (Vuk Karadjitch Collection, Vol. 2, p. 498) we find an actual statement of relationship to the falcon. The tale purports to be an account of the second battle of Kosovo, that fought by Janos Huniades against the Turks on 17th-19th October, 1448. Knolles, writing in 1620, says: *"Zekell Huniades, his sister's son, was the first of the leaders there slain in the thickest of the Turkes."* The ballad clothes this historical fact in a myth. Huniades figures in Serb ballads as Sibinja Yanko (John of Sibinj, or Hermannstadt, in Transylvania, of which he was Voyvoda) Yanko makes ready to ride to Kosovo, and takes with him his sister's only son young Sekula in spite of the urgent remonstrances of his sisters and his mother. The maidens of various places they ride through foretell Sekula's death, and beg him to stay with them, in vain. When they reached Kosovo plain they spread their tents and Voyvoda Yanko said *"Up with ye, my falcons! Keep guard against the Turks while I sleep a while."* Sekula said to Yanko: *"Oh, uncle, (ujko = mother's brother), go thou now and sleep a while. I will steal to the Turkish camp and change myself to a six-winged dragon, and will bring thee the mighty Sultan in my teeth in the form of a falcon. When thou risest up from sleep, oh uncle, do not let reason give way to madness ! Shoot not the six-winged dragon, but shoot the grey falcon."* Yanko slept, and Sekula stole to the Turkish camp, changed himself to a dragon, and duly alighted on Yanko's tent with the Sultan in his teeth in the form of a grey falcon. All the warriors roared at once: *"In an evil hour hast thou lain down, oh Voyvoda Yanko, and in a worse hast arisen"*. Yanko leapt to his feet and seized a golden arrow. He thought at once : *"Why should I shoot the grey falcon, for I am myself a falcon, and of the race of falcons. Better that I shoot the six-winged dragon."* He shot an arrow from his golden bow, and shot the six-winged dragon . . . it hissed and loosed the falcon. The falcon arose to the clouds and flew to the Turkish camp. The dragon fell to the ground Voyvoda Yanko hissed for rage, and his sister's son Selcula said to him *"Oh, Uncle Yanko, did I not tell thee not to change reason for madness - that thou shouldst not shoot the six-winged dragon but shoot the grey falcon?"* Sekula dies of his wound, and the tale ends. The fact that Sibinja Yanko, who was not a Serb but a Vlach, should claim kinship with the falcon is at first puzzling. But the fragments of a much more elaborate versiom explain it.

In this version, when Yanko awoke and saw the dragon on his tent he called to George Ban Despot (the Brankovitch), who was then Prince of the Serbs under Turkish suzerainty: *"Oh, my brother in God, George Ban Despot, dost see the great marvel upon my white tent? A six winged dragon hath seized a grey falcon.The falcon is hissing like a serpent. "Shall I kill the dragon or the falcon?"* And George Ban Despot said to Yanko of Sibinja : *"Are we not of the brood of falcons, and the Turks are a brood of dragons?" Strike the dragon, do not strike the falcon."* Yanko shoots three arrows. The dragon only looses the falcon when mortally wounded by the third arrow. Sekula, dying, upbraids his uncle as in the former version. This version is in all probability the original one. For here it is the Serb, George Brankovitch, who claims kinship with the falcon, and obtains the liberation of the Sultan. Historic truth lurks beneath the allegory, for George betrayed Huniades, and so led to his defeat at Kosovo.

That eagle plumes were actually recently worn as a mark of heroism is shown by the following account taken from *'Les Quatres Premiers Livres de Navigations Peregrinations de Nicholas de Nicholay'*, 1568. He was French Ambassador to the Sultan, and gives a detailed account of the many types of people he came across, with elaborate drawings. Among them one of a *'Deli' (brave fool,crazy warrior)* (Fig. 2). These formed part of the retinue of the Pashas and Begs, and were, in fact, the Bashibazouks of those days. "These" he says, "*are adventurers who follow the Turkish army voluntarily and without payment, except that they are fed and kept at the expense of the Bashas, etc. , who have each a number in his suite. These fellows are inhabitants of Bosnia and Serbia. The first I saw was at Adrianople. His coat and large breeches were of the skin of a bear with the fur outside. On his head, he wore a bonnet hanging over one shoulder, made of a leopard skin well spotted, and in front of it, to make him look the more furious, he had fastened the great tail of an eagle. And its two wings were fastened with gilt nails to his targe, which he wore slung at his side. I was curious as to his country and religion. He said he was of the Serbian nation, and as to his religion, he was now living with the Turks and so dissimulated, but by birth and heart he was a Christian. I asked why he went so strangely clad, and he said it was to make himself look the more furious to his enemies. As for the plumes, none might wear them but such as gave proof of valour. For among them these plumes were esteemed as the true ornament of a valiant man of war.*"

Nicholay's description is confirmed by one of the ballads of the celebrated Heyduk, Old Man Novak, who carried on the profession of brigandage with great *éclat*, at about the end of the fifteenth century, in Bosnia. In *'The Marriage of Gruitz Novakovitch'* (Vuk Karadjitch Collection, Vol. 3), Old Man Novak, when going out to fight the Greek whose bride he has snatched for his son Gruitz, dresses himself *'in terrible clothing'* made of a bear's skin. A wolf's head with an eagle's wing in it forms his cap, and his eyebrows are made of owl's feathers.

Another celebrated chieftain, Relja, who ruled the Novipazar district, and is said to have died about 1343, is known in the ballads and in national tradition as *'Relja Krilatitza-Relja'* *(the winged bird)* or as *'Relja Krilati'*, *(winged Relja)*. Thus, in *'The Sister of Lek Kapetan'* (Karadjitch, Vol. 2) *'now shalt thou behold a beautiful bridegroom, Winged Relja! A winged warrior is no joke!'*

In a great number of songs, the various heroes are described as wearing fur caps, with silver plumes called chelenka in them. These are described as being given as rewards of valour, some wearing ten or a dozen. A few specimens of these old chelenka are in the Sarajevo Museum. I give sketches of two (Fig. 3). They have coloured stones set in them, which at first sight suggest peacocks' feathers. Nevertheless they may, I think, be taken as a stylised wing and tail.

The bodyguard of the late king of Montenegro was formed of picked men who were known as *'Perianitzi'*, (from *perianik, a plume wearer*). I was told that until recent years these men wore eagles feathers in their caps.

I possess a Montenegrin *'gusle' (musical instrument)* carved by a peasant of Nyegushi as lately as 1902. Its head is formed by a grotesque carving of Milosh Obilitch, who killed Sultan Murad in 1389. On Milosh's cap sits a dicky bird, which, I was told, represents the *'sivi soko'*, and indicates that he was *'dobar junak' (a great hero)*. It is a far cry from the prehistoric bird-chariot of Bosnia to my Montenegrin *'gusle'*. And it would be rash to say that they have any connection.

But that a form of bird cult has existed continuously for a very long period on the western side of the Balkan peninsula seems clear.

The very recently formed gymnastic clubs of the Czechs, which have been the most popular and eflicient form of nationalist propaganda, are called *'Sokols'*, and the members wear a falcon's feather in their caps. But whether the Czechs have a falcon tradition of their own, or if they adopted the term from their Slav neighbours further south, I have not been able to ascertain.

M. Edith Durham

Man, June 1923
Some Balkan Taboos
by M. E. Durham

The Name Taboo

In many parts of the Balkans which I visited, the taboo on mentioning the name of husband or wife was still strictly observed. In Montenegro, old peasants would not give the name of their husband or wife.

In the case of the men it was usual to apologise for mentioning a wife at all. She was referred to as *"Da oprostish, moja zhena"* *('If you will excuse me, my wife')*. Nor was this only in the peasant class. All females were regarded as an inferior order of beings, and a man who had no sons, but several daughters, would state emphatically that he was childless.

Nor did the *'chelyad'* (a collective for womenfolk) eat with the men in the older fashioned houses. Even in the house of a Voyvoda his wife, and daughter-in-law humbly waited on the men and on me, fetching, carrying and not daring to sit down. They ate up what was left in private afterwards. When it was decided that I ranked as a man, mainly I believe, because I wear my hair short(!), women often would not eat with me, and explained it would be *"shameful"* and would degrade me. My guide in Montenegro always ate with me. When he was absent from home for a week I vainly tried to induce his wife to take her dinner with me. She burst into tears when I pressed the point and said it could not be done.

An example of the name taboo is given in one of the Montenegrin peasant tales by Savo Vuletitch, himself a Montenegrin. *'Petar Radisitch, though he had lived on the best of terms with his wife for full twenty years, had never called her by her name nor even spoke to her as if to a human being on any subject if it were possible for a stranger to overhear. If he had to speak to her in public about anything, he uttered it through his teeth. And she did the same to him. To do otherwise would have been shameful.'* In this tale, even when the wife is dying, Petar cannot speak to her in the presence of the neighbours who come to aid her. He retains a stern front and breaks down afterwards when it is too late.

When I was doing relief work and having to catalogue and identify long lists of refugees, this taboo was a constant difficulty. A dozen or more women were, perhaps, all called Maria and all refused, with tears running down their cheeks to give any further clue to their identity, or gave the name of the father in a distant village. *"They are ashamed. You must not ask them!"* I was told, and found that I had asked an indecent question. *"Ask another woman. She will tell you."* And when the Maria in question discreetly retired, another woman revealed the horrible secret of the husband's name. This constantly occurred both among the Macedonian peasant women and the Albanian.

When I arrived among the Moslem Albanians at Vuthaj, where they had never before entertained a strange female, there was a very long pow-wow as to the correct course to pursue. It was decided I was far too important to feed with the harem. I was to rank as a man and feed with the chiefs. But to satisfy their sense of fitness I was helped last of all, even after my horse-boy, and so honour was satisfied.

Both the name and the food taboos being even to-day so common in the Balkans, it is strange to find Herodotus mentioning them as a peculiar custom of the Ionians, and accounting for it thus: *'Even those who esteem themselves the most noble of the Ionians, on first settling in the country brought no wives, but married a number of Carian women, whose parents they put to death. In consequence of this violence, the women made a compact which they delivered to their daughters, never to sit at meals with their husbands, nor call them by their appropriate names'* (Book 1. cxlvi). As he expressly states *'these Ionians appear to have been of very mixed origin'*, and says that *'Molossians, Pelasgians. of Areadia and Dorians of Epidaurus'* were mingled with them, it seems probable that the custom is one common to the early inhabitants of the Balkans. Judging by the present Balkan peoples, it is certain that the custom was far more likely to have been enforced on the captured women by the men.

Taboo on childbirth

In Montenegro, a woman may not make bread or cook food after childbirth until she has been churched. This is done forty, or less, days after confinement. I was told that any food prepared by an unchurched woman would be quite uneatable - unclean in fact. She was, nevertheless, forced to do very much harder work than cooking on the third day after confinement, having to resume the water and wood carrying that is considered particularly women's work. Wood and water I was told would not be affected by her condition. But I have known this severe work to cost the wretched woman her life, violent haemorrhage ensuing.

And I was so frequently asked to *"give a medicine"* to cause the birth of a second child, that I concluded that this too early hard work was the cause of severe displacements and other complications. One child and never another seemed a fairly common state of things. And if the one was a girl, this was a catastrophe indeed.

In Montenegro also, it is in the highest degree unlucky for a married woman to be delivered of her child in the house of her parents. Should this occur, every kind of misfortune would fall upon her brothers. This idea prevailed even among the *'intelligentzia'* of Cetinje. The wife of a Montenegrin Minister I knew was not permitted by her grandmother even to pay a call at her old home, for her confinement was very near and the grandmother was terrified lest it should occur there. As her husband had been summoned abroad and she had temporarily no home, she was forced to stay at a hotel until the event was over. *"It is no good my trying to go home,"* she told me, *"for in the future all misfortunes that happen to my brothers will be considered to be my fault."*

Among the Albanian women I found that a woman was very frequently known only as the mother of her son. Thus I was on very friendly terms with poor old Sokol Batzi of the Gruda tribe, and often went to his house. The son and daughter were exceptionally well educated for these lands and spoke both French and Italian. But the old mother was always known as *"the mother of the son of Sokol Batzi"* or as *"Kol's mother"*. This latter was what I called her. I never learnt her real name.

M. Edith Durham

Man, June 1923
Bride Price in Albania

Sir,

Some notes of my own observations in Albania may be of interest as an addition to Hasluck's comprehensive article (Man, 1933, 203). They date from 1908, when the mountain tribes had been very little influenced by the outer world. Throughout the northern tribe groups (Maltsia e madhe, Pulati, Dukagini and Mirdita) wives were obtainable by purchase only. The women of the tribe were the tribesmen's property, and as saleable as an ox, an ass or a rifle.

My first experience was at the house of a well-to-do Catholic of Hoti. He pointed to a swaddled babe in a cradle and said, with pride, that he had just sold her and received about £4 (= 59 Austrian florins) and would have the balance when he handed her over. His price for a girl was 20 napoleons at least. Some would sell a girl for 16 naps; he called that giving her away. He would not send the girl away till she was sixteen. Some did at twelve or thirteen, but it was not healthy. Nor would he let a youth have a wife before eighteen, unless the house needed another woman to do the work. Then a boy of fifteen or sixteen might be married. But it was better not.

I met two men once who looked like brothers. They were father and son. The father was thirty and the son fifteen. The father said that when just fifteen he had been married to a woman of twenty-eight. Now she was old, and he could not get rid of her.

My old guide observed that the Church had now forbidden priests to marry girls against their will and forbade the sale of infants. Our host was contemptuous. Unless arranged early, suitable alliances could not be found. Women could and should have no voice in the matter.

Infant sales were so common up-country that, unless a baby were bought in good time, it was impossible to find any wife but a widow. The Bariaktar of Nikaj lamented to me that his youngest son, though twenty five, was unmarried. He had bought wives for the four older ones when they were born, but had put off doing so for the youngest. Now all the daughters of good families are born betrothed. This was quite true, as *"I will buy the next girl you have'* was a not uncommon bargain. He said he must have *"good blood"* and did not mind paying a bit more for a woman of good stock. A woman of bad stock caused endless trouble. He was looking for a suitable widow. The mountain children knew all about sales.

A cheeky boy of Shala said to me: *"You have bought the girls a goat. Now you must buy me a wife. I am nearly old enough and they have not bought me one yet."* A little girl was crying bitterly. We asked, "Why?" She said the boys had told her that she was sold to an old man, who would beat her every day and make her work very hard. And as the boys continued to shout this at her, she could not be consoled. Even widows were not easily obtainable, for two reasons. If a widow had children, she and the children belonged to the tribe and she had to stay and rear them and she also became the levirate wife of her late husband's next male relative or, if he did not want her, of another in the house. An unmarried man could thus get a wife without paying for her, and the tribesman stuck to the custom in spite of the thunders of the Church. The man sometimes had a lawful wife already, but this did not prevent his taking his sister-in-law. I heard of one man who had taken on his uncle's widow and his sister-in-law, and then proposed to marry the girl who had been sold him as a child. But the Church intervened.

If the widow were young, and had been married but a short time before her husband was shot, and had not yet borne a child, she was regarded as eligible. One reason for this custom, I think, was to enable her to have one. I never got anyone to admit that such a child would rank as child of the deceased. But they shuffled and did not deny it.

In one case, the priest had excommunicated a household of some forty persons because a son was cohabiting with the widow of his elder brother who had been shot recently, shortly after marriage. It was a strange scene. The whole family begged the Franciscan to remove the ban. They offered candles for the Church, beeswax, corn, sheep. He was obdurate. The woman must be sent back to her family. By aid of my old guide, Marko, I got the young man aside and asked why he had done this. He said very earnestly that his honour *(nder)* made him. It was the "*Canon*" *(the Mountain Law)*. It would be dishonourable to refuse to live with her. They all dreaded the excommunication, but honour *(nder)* must come first. At last it was agreed he should live one year with her. Then he would part with her and marry the girl who had been bought for him. The year presumably was to give time for the birth of a child?

A childless widow was often sent back to her home as no good. I learned that in old days marriage did not take place till it was certain the girl was pregnant. Sometimes not until she had borne a son. The birth of a girl was always considered a misfortune. Very little price could be got for a widow believed to be sterile. She went back to her tribe, and the head of the house sold her for what he could get; an old-fashioned rifle in one case. But I heard of a young man who sold his aunt three times, and was thought to have done rather well out of her.

They had no mealy-mouthed ideas about bride wealth."*Kam blé*" ("*I have bought.*") applied to women and other animals. Neither youth nor maid had any voice in the transaction. The elders on either side drove the bargain for purely political purposes to make a strong alliance with another tribe; for they are strictly exogamous. That the price can be regarded as compensation for the loss of the girl's services is untenable, for until lately the girl was handed over at twelve or thirteen (as soon as puberty showed, but cohabitation was sometimes deferred), and till then she was chiefly occupied spinning and knitting for her own outfit. It might perhaps be regarded as compensation for the outfit, but was never so spoken of.

An odd psychological feature of these arranged marriages was that, whereas the girls not infrequently resisted strenuously and refused to go to their husbands, I never heard of a case where the young man had refused the bride bought for him. In answer to many inquiries, I always received the answer: *"But why should I? God made all women alike."*

A girl could escape by swearing perpetual virginity before twelve conjurors (in the church, if Christian, and in the mosque, if Moslem), but only after very severe measures had been taken to compel her - tieing up, beating and starving. For a family to refuse to surrender a girl, even if the bridgroom had grown up to be a thorough bad lot, entailed a blood feud.

A *'romantic marriage'* was a thing unknown. All were *'political'*, for the benefit of the tribe rather than for the parties most concerned.

Till the day before yesterday, almost all Royal marriages were arranged on exactly the same lines and the bride's feelings no more considered than in the Albanian mountains. Queen Charlotte was betrothed to George III when she was eleven. The Grand Duchess Marie of Russia, in her recently published reminiscences, tells how her marriage with a Prince of Sweden was arranged without their having met, and carried out in spite of her fears. She was helpless, and the unsuitable match was later annulled.

I put up for the night in a Mirdite house. A girl crouched like a wild cat in a far corner. They did not speak to her, but, threw her some food at supper. The father told us with fury that she had refused to go to the house to which he had sold her. The enlightened and civilized Abbot of the Mirdites had intervened and had persuaded the insulted bridegroom to swear not to take blood-vengeance and to return the money that had been paid. He stated, too, that either party was free to marry another and the girl need not swear virginity. The father was angry beyond words. But he dared not disobey the Abbot. *"A girl,"* said he, repeatedly, *"marries for the good of her house, not for herself. My honour is blackened. Where shall I find another such match?"*

Primitive savagery? But how many students of anthropology know that girls were sold thus as infants and forcibly married as late at least as the second half of the seventeenth century in England ? A very notable case is that of Mary Davies, the Pimlico heiress, after whom Davies Street, W. 1 is named. She was sold twice before she was twelve. First for £5,000 to Lord Berkeley of Stratton, for his son Charles, aged eleven. Mary was seven. Charles died of smallpox and Lord Berkeley, having no use for Mary, demanded his money back. But Mary's relatives had spent the lot and also fattened on the revenues of her estates. They were hard put to it and hawked Mary around. There were several offers. They accepted that of Sir Thomas Grosvenor. After much bargaining he repaid the £5,000 to Lord Berkeley and £1,500 as interest on it. He released Mary's relatives from giving an account of what they had done with her revenues. He settled a life annuity of £50 on the aunt who had had charge of her, and Mary, aged thirteen, was married at St. Margaret's, Westminster, to Sir Thomas Grosvenor, aged twenty-one, on 8th October, 1677. And thus the huge London estates of the Dukes of Westminster came into being.

Save that the sums are far greater, the marriage differs in no way from those of the Albanian tribesmen. In Mary's case it ended disastrously. So far as *'savage customs'* go, we have lived in very much of a glass-house till just the other day, and can't afford stone throwing. The tribesmen looked with contempt upon the townsmen who *'sold themselves'* for a dowry. The marriages in Scutari were just as much arranged by the elders as those of the mountains. But the bride's family found the money (as still in France, Italy and other lands). In Albania, I think the custom is a foreign one introduced from without. For centuries the towns along the Coast were under foreign influence - largely Venetian and had a considerable foreign population, whereas up in the mountains, the Canon of the Mountains and the ancient customs prevailed. But in Scutari, the bridegroom gave the bride a necklace made of silvergilt filigree from which hung three large gilt coins (*dupa*), and this probably was a reminiscence of the bride price.

Similarly, in Montenegro, where the marriages, too, were arranged by the elders - an apple or orange with a gold coin stuck into it was given by the bridegroom's people - a symbolic payment. It had degenerated into an orange without a coin when I was there!

M. Edith Durham

Man, July 1923
A Bird Tradition in the West of the Balkan Peninsula
by M. E. Durham

A further point of interest in *'The Ballad of Childe Jovan and the Daughter of Tsar Stefan'* (see Man, 1923, 33) is the fact that she is described as having *'grown up in the cage for fifteen years'* and it is in *'the cage'* that her father visits her. On the word *'kavez'* (a cage), Filipovitch, in his edition of the ballads of Kralyeviteh Marko (Zagreb, 1899) gives a note stating that this was the name given to the pavilion in which the Royal princesses of Constantinople were brought up, thus suggesting a similarity between the Byzantine and Serbian courts which doubtless existed. In *'The Ballad of the Sister of Lek Kapetan'*, however, we find a similar reference which throws a different light on the *'cage'*. Here. we are told *'the maiden, they say, has grown up in the cage; has grown up for fifteen years and never has seen the sun or the moon.'*Probably Tsar Stefan's daughter, too, was encaged to keep her from the sun and moon. For it is owing to her going upon the roof of the tower and attracting the light of the rising sun by putting on the glittering crown that misfortune befalls her. The falcon comes from the spot where the sun rises. And the tower in which he lives at Orluyevatz reflects the light of the sun from the golden winged ball upon its roof and the light of the moon from the metal of the roof itself.

These stories may be referred to the Danaid group of Märchen, which Hartland, in discussing the belief in impregnation by the sun and the custom of female seclusion at puberty, points out is common in the Mediterranean area. He quotes an Epirote story from von Hahn (*'Griechische und Albanesische Märehen'* 1, p.295) in which a maiden, who has been promised to the sun, is shut up by her mother in a tower in which all apertures through which light might enter have been closed; but the sun sends a beam of light through the keyhole, which had been overlooked, to fetch her.

The fact that the Bird tradition is strongest in Albania, whose inhabitants call themselves eagles, and in Montenegro where the Montenegrins call themselves falcons, together with the fact that the Serb ballads in which the falcon appears are principally those of Kosovo and Montenegrin districts, whereas the term *'soko'* scarcely appears in the later and strictly Serbian ballads, led me to suppose that the tradition is probably one of the South rather than the North, one already there when the Serb invasion took place. Had it been brought in by the Serbs, we should expect to find it strongest in the North. Whereas it is in the mountain districts in - the South West, to which the older inhabitant would naturally flee, that the tradition is still alive.

The doubtful point of this theory was the fact that the gymnastic societies of the Czechs, by means of which the national idea has been strenuously propagated for some time, are known as *'Sokols'*. It seemed, therefore, possible, that the falcon was a Slav tradition.

By the courtesy of Mr. F. Marchant, I have now learnt that the Sokols were founded as recently as 1862 by Miroslav Tyr and Jindrich Yagner. Tyr made a journey into Montenegro and was struck by the fact that the Montenegrins called themselves falcons and often wore falcons' feathers, and adopted the title for his gymnastic societies. Further, that there is no bird tradition in Czech literature

This seems to show the falcon or bird tradition belongs to the Mediterranean group of cults and is pre-Slavonic in the Balkans.

M. Edith Durham

Man, September 1923
The Making of a Saint
by M. E. Durham

Chance has thrown into my hands a pamphlet published at Cetinje, Montenegro, containing a number of State documents recently discovered in the palace of the late King Nikola. Among them is the original Proclamation of the sainthood of Vladika (Bishop) Petar I, the King's great-great uncle, who died on 19th October, 1830.

It is still customary among many members of the Eastern Orthodox Church to open the grave from three to four years after burial - at such time when the corpse may be reasonably expected to have decayed - cleanse the bones and store them in an ossuary. And in many places until quite recently, it was customary to put food upon the grave and hold funeral feasts at stated intervals so long as the body remained in the grave: a custom possibly not yet extinct. I found it flourishing thirty years ago.

In the rare cases in which the corpse has become mummified the fact is looked on as a miraculous sign that life everlasting among the saints has been attained and the corpse is accordingly venerated. This was the case with Bishop Petar Petrovitch I.

The pamphlet is entitled '*Spomenica*'; it is edited by Dushan Vuksan and printed at Cetinje, 1926. The passage in question runs as follows:

'The Proclamation of the Metropolitan Petar I as a Saint'

The Proclamation of Vladika Rade (his popular name) in which it is told that the body of Petar I was disinterred on 18th October, 1834, and on that occasion was found to be quite complete, was printed in Cetinje in 1834. But whether this Proclamation which was made to the whole nation of Montenegro and the Brda* went beyond the frontiers of Montenegro, is unknown to me. (the Editor).

I found in the archives of the Palace, in the fascicle of the year 1834, one single copy of this Proclamation and herewith publish it in entirety. It is printed on blue paper of large format and on it is the autographed signature of the Vladika (Petar II). The Proclamation announces:

From our Vladika, Petar Petrovich
To the whole nation of Montenegro and the Brda
A PROCLAMATION AND A GREETING

"We give ye to know, o Godfearing nation, how we, on the 18th of this month on St. Luke's Day did open the blessed grave of my holy Predecessor and your Archpriest (Arhipastir) Petar. And when we had

opened the grave, we found complete the holy body of our Archpriest.

Therefore, o Godfearing nation, joyfully do we proclaim to you this fortunate event; for we know that ye will give thanks to the Omnipotent Creator who has sent among you the good father and mighty pastor of the Church and the Christian flock, your protector and saviour, in his complete body. That, just as when in his mortal body he was ready to give his soul and body for you, so now we pray to him that, as a Saint and one favoured by God, he will pray to Almighty God for us as for his own sons.

I think o Godfearing Christians that ye remember the words of St. Petar who said to you: "May ye live in accord and peace and unity." I think every one of you has kept these holy and godly words in his heart since this man, so beloved of God, no longer lived among you.

And now I hope especially that you will keep them, for you see him that spoke them is amongst you, sainted and complete. And you are assured-I think that if any Montenegrin will not preserve 'accord, peace and unity' St. Petar will be his accuser both in this world and in the other; but let those that have enmity between them (i.e., blood feud) agree and make peace and thus they will be pleasing both to God and your Sainted Petar.

Recommending you to God and His favourite and newly proclaimed Saint I remain,
To each of you, the well wisher,
Vladika of Montenegro and the Brda,
Petar Petrovich.
St. Luke's Day, Cetinje, 1834

St. Petar Petrovitch was deeply revered by the Montenegrin peasants who almost always swore "*By God and St. Peter*". And, in fact did not distinguish him from the great St. Peter. I have seen men strike their heads against his tomb and even against the door jambs of the Monastery church where he lies.

The other popular saint of Montenegro, St. Basil of Ostrog, a bishop who fled from Turkish persecution and lived in a cave in the mountain side at Ostrog, likewise derived his sainthood from the fact that his body was found to be intact. When I made the pilarimage to this shrine, the body was packed in carbolized cotton wool. One foot was uncovered for me to kiss.

Such saints, I believe, are purely local and almost unknown to other branches of the Orthodox Church.

The Vladika of Montenegro had no temporal power. Such government as existed in his time was purely tribal and conducted by the tribal headmen. The Vladika's power, which was very considerable, consisted in his power of blessing and banning. His curse was greatly dreaded and, if we may believe local tradition it was most efficacious and the stern old man applied it freely.

Thus, being wrath with a recalcitrant tribesman he said *"I wish you may die."* The man contracted smallpox and died soon after.

Again, the Vladika owned fishing rights in the lake and the fishermen had to supply a tribute of fish to the monastery. None arrived. The Vladika asked, Why? The fishers replied that they had been unable to catch any. Time passed and still no fish. Again the Vladika asked and was told there are no fish in the lake. *"No,"* said he firmly, *"there are none and there never will be any more."* And there were no more, till the terrified fishermen implored the Vladika to remove the curse and promised a plentiful supply of fish in the future.

As the fish in the Lake of Scutari are extremely plentiful at certain seasons and slacken between whiles, we can only suppose the holy man timed his curse skilfully.

The skilful use made by his nephew and successor, Vladika Petar II, of the fact of the canonization, in order to stop the blood feuds which raged between the tribes at this period, should be noted. The Proclamation of 1834 is perhaps the last instance of sainthood by natural mummification. But how deeply rooted the idea is in the minds of peoples brought up in the Orthodox Church is shown by the immense reverence paid by the Russian people to the artificially embalmed body of Lenin. The tradition lives, though times have changed.

M. Edith Durham

* *Brda, a group of partly Albanian mountain tribes, annexed to Montenegro in the 18th century and now slavized.*

The Contemporary Review, November 1923
Croatia and Great Serbia
by M. Edith Durham

When we went to war in 1914, we were repeatedly told that we were fighting to destroy militarism and to liberate oppressed peoples. We are said to have come out of the struggle as '*victors*', but it becomes daily clearer that we did not achieve either of these ends. The arrival of M. Raditch in London, burning with the grievances of Croatia and begging for justice, gives us a good opportunity for examining the war's results in that part of the war's theatre in which the first scenes of the world's tragedy were played.

Among the masses of documents that have come to light on the causes of the war, very many deal with the mines of explosives which lay hidden all through Europe, but almost none have added to our knowledge of the deed that set them all ablaze - the murder of the Archduke Franz Ferdinand. By comparing the latest document on the subject of the murders with the statements of M. Raditch, we may arrive nearer to explaining the very unsatisfactory state of things in Jugoslavia and the Balkans in general. The war was actually precipitated by the failure of the Serbian Government to make any attempt to trace the crime and its refusal to permit Austrian officials to take part in any such search. Serbia did not take the opportunity of triumphantly proving her innocence to all the world. Those of us who were old Balkan hands asked ourselves anxiously what it was she dreaded would be discovered.

M. Stanoye Stanoyevitch, Professor of History at Belgrad, a man of some reputation as an authority on Serbian history, has just published what he asserts to be an exact account of the murder. His object, he says, is '*to present a few facts quite impartially and establish their historical truth and indeed the whole historic truth so far as is known to me. ... The material upon which the part of the book which deals with the murder of Franz Ferdinand is based, is derived from the persons who took part in the events described. They are chiefly officers who shared in the conspiracy of 1903 against King Alexander, and who were afterwards either members or opponents of the secret revolutionary society 'Union or Death' (known as the 'Black Hand'). I obtained, as well, statements from persons to whom Colonel Dragutin Dimitrievitch of the Serbian General Staff, the organiser of the murder of the Archduke, told some details of his part in the affair. I have not accepted these statements without criticism, nor left them unconfirmed. Where I cannot confirm their truth, I have stated my doubts and objections. I can say that this book is truthful in every word and can be verified.*"

M. Raditch states that the guilt of Colonel Dimitrievitch has long been well known in Croatia, and that, so far as it goes, Professor Stanoyevitch's account is entirely reliable. Briefly, it is as follows. He begins with an historical preface, intended to justify subsequent events, and starts, oddly enough, with the emigration of vast masses of Serbs, refugees flying from the Turks, into Austro-Hungarian territory in the sixteenth and seventeenth centuries. That they were given land and protection and saved from annihilation he admits, but his opinion seems to be that, having been allowed to settle, they should also have been given complete national freedom, and that Austrian attempts to incorporate them in the Empire justify all subsequent action. We are reminded of the fable of the husbandman and the viper. If the Professor's contention be righteous, it is a warning to all nations not to shelter refugees. Naively he tells us that the Serbs fought on the side of Austria because without aid they could not hope to beat the Turks, but that their sympathies were with Russia, and they accepted Austrian help only so long as they needed it. After some very one-sided historical chapters he passes to his main theme - the Sarajevo murders. Three groups, he says, were concerned in the crime: (1) the national party of the youth of Bosnia, (2) the group of Belgrade officers, (3) a group of Austro-Hungarian officials. Of the third group he can tell but little. Count Tisza is reported to have said of the crime: '*It was the will of God and we must thank Him for all things.*' The part of the youth of Bosnia, he considers, is explained by his historical chapter. He does not mention the fact that their hatred was stimulated and intensely cultivated from Belgrade, as I saw for myself so long ago as 1906, when I wintered in Sarajevo.

The Professor repeatedly refers to the Archduke as '*our worst enemy*', but gives no reason for so doing. The reason, in fact, was that Franz Ferdinand's publicly expressed policy was to make of the Dual Monarchy a Triple Monarchy by erecting a self-governing Slav State within the Empire and satisfying the aspirations of the Austrian Slavs. This the megalomaniac party in Serbia, which wished to reconstruct the medieval empire of Tsar Dushan, dreaded of all things, and they did all in their power to make it impossible. The Professor tells in detail how in 1903 the conspiracy against the pro-Austrian Obrenovitches was planned and carried out by a group of eighty officers and some civilians, who murdered the King, Queen Draga, and her two brothers. He regards these murders as the starting point of Serbia's success. The murderers were '*led to join the plot by honest patriotism*', but he admits that '*not all the conspirators had only idealistic aims*' and tells how '*having created the new régime they had to protect it*'. Until England refused to resume diplomatic relations unless they were discharged from office, they had in fact ruled the '*government*' they had set up. Their '*dismissal*' to please England meant merely that they retired behind the scenes for a while, but the gang was not broken up and met occasionally. It reappeared in force when the Young Turk revolution in 1908 precipitated the annexation of Bosnia by Austria and the proclamation of Bulgaria's independence.

On the day following these events the Serbian Minister for Foreign Affairs, Milovanovitch, called a great meeting at Belgrade which resulted in the formation of the Narodna Odbrana (Society for National Defence). Stanoyevitch, an active member of this, declares its objects were '*to collect material relative to the conditions in Austro-Hungary and to enlighten the Serbian population on the ideals, tasks, and duties of Serbia and the Serbian people.*' And, therefore, not revolutionary but entirely legitimate. This would, however, depend entirely upon the way in which '*ideals and duties*' were expounded to the '*Serbian population*' and here he does not enlighten us. By Serb refugee students in England I have been assured that one of the Narodna Odbrana's activities was paying for the education of Bosnian, Montenegrin, and other Slav students at Belgrade University; that those students met and had their meals at the inn of '*The Green Garland*' and were there often visited by officers and other patriots. Indirectly, therefore, the Narodna Odbrana may be more responsible for revolutionary methods than the Professor admits. He explains that the wilder spirits among the officers, particularly the old murder gang, were angry with the Government and the Narodna Odbrana for not taking more active steps, and in 1911 formed the secret revolutionary society '*Ujedinjenje ili Srmt*' *(Union or Death)*, popularly known as the '*Black Hand*'. The head of it was Colonel Dragutin Dimitrievitch, one of the organisers of the murder of King Alexander, and it consisted of some 300 members, most of them officers. They organised and trained and led komitadji bands in Macedonia. The hideous cruelty of these bands can be best studied in the Carnegie Report of the Balkan wars. The Professor refers always to the '*Black Hand*' as "*secret*" but its existence was known both in Serbia and abroad.

The dynasty and Government having been put in power by this gang of officers was powerless to suppress them. The old story of the Praetorian Guards was in fact re-enacted. Moreover, as the Carnegie Report points out, '*it was a distinct advantage to the regular Government to have under its hand an irresponsible power like this which could be repudiated if necessary.*'

Stanoyevitch describes Dimitrievitch as '*gifted, well-educated, honourable, an eloquent speaker, capable and industrious. He had immense influence on his entourage, was an admirable organiser ... but also vain and affected. ... He loved danger and secret meetings, and was so entirely convinced that he was right that he thought all who disagreed with him neither honourable nor patriotic. Restless and thirsting for adventure, he planned several murders. In 1911, he and Tankositch sent a man to Vienna to kill either the Emperor or the Archduke.'* This failed, and all trace of the agent was lost. In February, 1914, he planned with a revolutionary Bulgarian committee to assassinate Ferdinand of Bulgaria - a plan which was also abortive. The Professor describes Tankositch as weakly in appearance and dull witted, but very wily, raw, and undisciplined. He took an active part in the murder of the Obrenovitch and was a notorious komitadji leader in Macedonia.

The sweeping success of the first Balkan war so filled the officers with ambition and self-confidence, he tells us, that they were completely uncontrollable. The *'Black Hand'* at once came in conflict with the Government, which, to avoid war with Bulgaria, wished to come to terms over Macedonia. This the *'Black Hand'* would not hear of. In this I can corroborate the Professor. I was in Ochrida in 1913 a day or two before the second Balkan war broke out. The Serbian officers angrily and emphatically declared that they would not cede any of the land they occupied; that they would not accept arbitration; that they meant to fight Bulgaria, and were only waiting the signal to begin.

Having, with the help of Greece and Bulgaria, beaten their former allies and obtained the coveted territories by the Treaty of Bukarest, they became more uncontrollable than ever. They ruled the whole of the annexed lands with savage brutality and came into constant collision with the *'Government'* which wished to substitute civilian for military rule and promulgated an order to that effect. The officers broke into open revolt and there were fierce quarrels both at Uskub and Monastir.' *The Russian Minister Hartwig appears to have been mixed up in the affair,'* states Stanoyevitch, *'and the order was withdrawn.'* That Hartwig, reputed all-powerful in Belgrade, should have intervened on behalf of the *'Black Hand'* is significant. One of his predecessors had watched, unmoved, from the Legation windows the attack upon King Alexander's palace in 1903.

I can corroborate Stanoyevitch's account of the officers in Macedonia by a letter I received in February, 1914, from my former dragoman, who, shortly before, had rejoiced at the departure of the Turk. He now wrote: *'I write from Monastir, or, I should say, Bitoli, for there is no city of the name of Monastir in the vast Servian Empire whose Emperor Petar Karageorgevitch is wheting (sic) his sword sharp to deal a blow on the old Austrian Emperor. The conquest of Bosnia and Herzegovina and the creation of a vast and powerful Servian Empire is occupying the minds of all army men. Taxes are tremendous; this city must pay 1,000,000 francs war-tax. This will go to the War Office, for in Servia the army has twofold duty, to fight and to rule. There is hardly a country where the military have concentrated so great power in their hands. The King, the civil authorities, must needs comply with the wishes of the officers. The Servian officer has no respect for anyone. ... You cannot but pity us who are ruled by such men. ... Corruption in all branches is the essence of Servian rule'*

I never heard of him again. He doubtless fell a victim. It is clear he had heard plots against Austria discussed. I too heard similar talk at the dinner-table in the inn at Podgoritza during the first Balkan war. All who stood in the path of Great Serbia were, as it was delicately put, 'to be sent to visit the Obrenovitches'". Ferdinand of Bulgaria was named as one of these though at the time Bulgaria and Serbia were still '"Allies'. All this seems to show that Stanoyevitch's tale is true.

About this time, King Petar retired in favour of the Regency of his son the Crown Prince Alexander. Whether this was brought about by the officer gang it would be of interest to know. They may have hoped for a forward policy from a younger man. The Regency at any rate must have been with their consent. We now approach the climax. While the *'Black Hand'* was in something like open revolt, its head, Dimitrievitch, was Head of the Intelligence Department of the Serbian General Staff, and thus received from the Russian General Staff the information that at their meeting at Konopischt the Kaiser Wilhelm and the Archduke had planned an attack upon Serbia. This determined Dimitrievitch to kill the Archduke, *'our worst enemy'* and thus, declares his apologist, save Serbia from war. We should like to know the terms of the telegram and of subsequent ones from Russia. The narrative is here compressed and much is obviously glossed over and omitted. Just as Dimitrievitch, we are told, had decided to keep peace in this singular manner, Tankositch informed him that two youths representing the youth of Bosnia had asked him to help them to carry out a plan to murder Franz Ferdinand. Dimitrievitch at once empowered him to arm, train and otherwise aid them.

This was done, and they were smuggled into Bosnia. How, the Professor does not state. The Austrian Government severely blamed the Serbian frontier officials. They may be still living, and Stanoyevitch says nothing either of this or of the youths. By refugee Serb students I was told that they were students at Belgrad and that Princip was selected because he was so tuberculous that he could not in any case live long. Having sent the wretched boys on their fatal errand, Dimitrievitch called a meeting of the executive of the *'Black Hand'* and revealed the plot. A hot discussion took place and the majority of the members opposed it. Dimitrievitch in the end promised to stop it and, says Stanoyevitch, *"it is said he tried to do so."* In any case he failed, and, with the help of Daniel Ilitch, a schoolmaster, the murders were committed. Ilitch was found guilty and hanged by the Austrian Government.

Stanoyevitch's tale, which, as we have seen, can on many points be corroborated, completely explains all that followed. The guilt of Dimitrievitch and Tankositsch must have been known to many persons. The plot could easily have been traced. I could not when in Serbia go from one village to another or sketch a baker's shop without being pounced on by the police for my passport and reasons for my conduct. But in the case of the Archduke's murder no one was pounced on; no arrests were made. In reply to Austria's inquiry on June 30th as to what steps were being taken, M. Gruitch gave the reply: 'The police up till now have not occupied themselves with the affair.' The Crown Prince, in one of his dispatches to Russia, says he would punish the criminals if he only knew who they were. But he mentions no attempt to find them. The *'Black Hand'* which had raised his dynasty to the throne could by the same means depose him. The Serbian Government dared not act. To expose to Europe that the crime had been planned by the Head of her Intelligence Department and that the land was ruled by an irresponsible secret society of officers would have ruined Serbia and stultified all her schemes for aggrandisement. What advice Hartwig gave on this occasion we do not know. That he again supported the officers is not improbable.

For a whole month Serbia did nothing towards assuaging Austria's wrath. No arrest was made till Austria insisted upon that of Tankositsch. But when in the ultimatum she insisted also that Austrian officials should take part in tracking the crime in Serbia, the Government, only too well aware of the skeleton that must be found in the cupboard, preferred with Russian support to risk war. *"And you must admit,"* said a patriotic young Serb to me, *"that the plan has completely succeeded and Great Serbia is made."* Many are in fact proud of it. A Serb boasted to Lady Boyle that he had helped teach the murderers to shoot, saying *"Did I not teach them well?"* Space prevents giving other instances which corroborate Stanoyevitch. Dimitrievitch made yet more murder plans, he continues, and sent a man from Corfu in 1916 to kill King Constantine, but this failed. In 1917, he was himself arrested with several others of the *'Black Hand'* on the charge of plotting to overthrow the Crown Prince Alexander and substitute a military government, condemned to death with five other officers at Salonika on June 11th and executed. Others of the arrested, notably the notorious regicide Damian Popovitch, the instigator of many atrocities, were condemned to long terms of imprisonment and very shortly afterwards released. Tankositsch was killed early in the war.

When the war was over the object for which these men had plotted and murdered was obtained. The Powers gave all and even more than all the coveted lands to Serbia. And many members of the *'Black Hand'* survive to carry out their former policy. M. Raditch puts the matter briefly when he says: *'Croatia has been plunged from the twentieth century and civilisation into the barbarism of the Middle Ages. A Western and civilised people has been put under an Eastern and barbarous one.'* All who were once subjects of Austria - Croats, Slovenes, Dalmatians, and the Catholics and Moslems of Bosnia and the Herzegovina - are now subject to just such a military tyranny as we have described.

The Croats, says Raditch, had a local Parliament (Sabor) which administered their internal affairs and they expected very shortly the establishment of Trialism within the Empire which would have given them all they wanted. For them the murder of the Archduke was the greatest catastrophe. Nevertheless they hoped and expected that when united with Serbia they would have at least the freedom they had enjoyed hitherto. They had a civilised code of law; courts in which justice could be obtained and a very flourishing University. Their Croatian officials are replaced by Serbs; their civilised code by one that inflicts brutal punishments abolished in Croatia a century ago. Flogging of the severest description is inflicted for even the smallest offences, mercilessly, and men have died under the lash. They are treated not as a *'liberated'* but as a conquered and annexed people. Justice is non-existent and blackmail frequent. The teaching of the Serbian dialect is enforced in the schools, despite the fact that Croatia, in literature, is far in advance of Serbia. Under Austria, the Croats were recognised as a people *(narod)*, so were the Slovenes, whose dialect is very different from that of Serbia. The Serbs do not permit the recognition of any such narod. *'We are not Serbs,'* said Raditch, *'our culture is Western. We are Catholics. The outlook of the Serb and his religion are Byzantine. The Serb tried to 'divide and rule'.'*

The Croat is conscripted into the Serb army and taken from Croatia. He is bidden to hold down the Macedonians or the unfortunate Montenegrins and may be flogged to death if he disobeys. Each of the annexed peoples is used to hold down the others. People are robbed of their lands and Serbs are settled upon them. Of the Karageorge dynasty M. Raditch spoke with the greatest bitterness. They were put on the throne by murder, he says, and by murder they hold it. Nothing has more horrified the Croatian peasant than being bidden to swear fealty to the present King Alexander Karageorgevitch who deposed his grandfather King Nikola of Montenegro, seized and sold his goods, even it is said the carpets of his palace, and usurped his throne. Among the peasants Djed (grandfather) is the great man of the family. He sits in the one comfortable chair and is respected and consulted. No peasant can have aught but contempt and horror for the King who has acted so impiously. Not one Croat member will go to Belgrade to acknowledge the rule of such a man and sit in the Belgrade Parliament.

To all the Serbian attempts at forcible *Serbianising,* the Croat presents an unbroken front of passive resistance. 'We will not copy the brutal methods of the Serbs. We are opposed to bloodshed and bloody revolution. We were a million times better off under Austria but we are ready to form one of a federated Slav State in which each narod has its rights. The Moslems of Bosnia are now throwing in their lot with the Catholic Croats and Dalmatians. Together we outnumber the Orthodox Serbs. The Serbs intended to put an end at once to the Moslem problem by extirpating the Moslems. These Moslems are not Turks. They are Croats whose ancestors became Moslem. They are some of the ancient inhabitants of the land. The Serbs began when they had 'liberated' Bosnia by burning seventy Moslem villages and slaughtering a number of people. It is certain that they mutilated 140 Moslem women. But they found the task of extirpation too great.*

If they are so much hated how did the Serbs obtain a majority for their Government in the last election? That is simple. They timed the election for the season when the corn supplies in the highlands were all exhausted and the new harvest was not yet due. Then they promised the starving people so much corn for so many votes. The Government waggons of kukuruz (maize) went only to the village that voted for the Government. No other corn could be obtained. The wretched people voted to save their lives. In Croatia we had corn enough and our peasants voted against the Government. Twenty thousand of our peasants have been imprisoned, often in heavy chains, and most of those imprisoned have been frightfully flogged. But they will not yield. We ask that violence shall give way to justice; that we may be treated as human beings and not as swine. We drew up a Protocol of our demands and Pashitch sent some Serb delegates to discuss them with us. We came at last to an agreement, and the Serbs, and we too, signed the Protocol. We believed that the delegates had power to accept the terms. Three months passed and no amelioration took place. We asked Pashitch 'Where is our Protocol?' He replied, 'There is no Protocol.' He and his Government in truth fear the military and dare not go against them.'

If Croatia suffers, the people in Macedonia and Montenegro suffer much more. The Montenegrins, who had been independent for years and who are proud-spirited, resisted and Montenegro has been devastated. Fifteen per cent of all the houses of Montenegro have been burnt to the ground by order of the Serbian judges. About one third of the population is in very bad prisons, and another third lives wild upon the mountains fighting and robbing the Serbs. Of the remaining third many are dead - others are young lads whom the Serbs are training. They appoint a lad of sixteen as governor of a district. The Serb army rules and declares that the local governors are all Montenegrin. The Serbs line the main road with troops whenever they bring a convoy of provisions or ammunition along it. The land which was peaceful and happy and safe for travellers a few years ago is now filled with misery. As for the Macedonians, none of them are Serbs. They are Bulgars and Wallachs and Albanians. *"Under the Turk,"* the peasants say, *"Macedonia was a cup of blood. Under the Serb it is an ocean of blood."* Under the Turk, the Bulgar had his own schools, and very fine ones; his own churches, priests, and Bishops. The schools are closed. The Serb language is enforced. The churches are closed, the priests and Bishops are dead or expelled. Even people's names are turned into Serbian. Death or flogging and prison punish all who resist.

According to figures provided by M. Raditch, out of a population of 11,992,912 in Jugoslavia only 5,554,245 are Orthodox Serbs. The others are Croats, Slovenes, Bulgars, Roumanians, and Albanians, with a few Turks, gypsies, and others. The attempt, therefore, to make a Great Serbia of it with a centralised Government at Belgrade is manifestly unjust. The war which was waged 'to *liberate small nations*' has resulted only in transferring them to a worse régime. M. Raditch begs that the Powers who brought about this situation will intervene and make of Jugoslavia a true Jugoslavia, that is, a confederation of the South Slav peoples each working in its own way for the development of Slavdom, free from the grip of a military autocracy. The military power of Serbia has been greatly strengthened by the advent of a considerable part of Wrangel's Russian army, and Cossacks are said to have been playing a part similar to that they played in the days of the Tsars. That Russians take part in military operations is proved by the fact that some were captured by the Albanians in one of the raids made by Serbs into North Albania - an invasion which brought about the intervention of the League of Nations. Though thwarted on that occasion, the ambitions of the Serb military are not diminished.

One of the most important steps taken by Albania towards gaining complete independence has been that of forming an autocephalous Orthodox Church of Albania. According to the rules of the Orthodox Church, a group of Orthodox Christians of sufficient size can become self-governing and has the right to conduct all religious services in its own tongue. The Serb, Roumanian, Bulgarian, and other national Churches are all thus autocephalous. The Serb Government has, however, refused to recognise the Albanian Church, and is insisting upon forcing a Serb Bishop into Scutari to protect the interests of the handful of Serb tradesmen in that town and the people of a small village hard by. These, curiously enough, descend for the most part, as they have often told me, from refugees who fled into Turkish territory in former days because 'they owed blood' or more recently from persons who crossed the border to escape the Montenegrin police. They have always been permitted to have their own priest and a small Church and school sufficient for their needs. Nor has there been any question of curtailing these rights. As is well known to all students of the Balkans, the advance of a Bishop always means 'check to your King'; it is a political step. The Bishop needs an establishment, then a bodyguard. Later he is 'insulted' or has 'rights' and a casus belli can at any time be brought about. The Albanians, protected by the League of Nations from a military advance on the part of Serbia, now see themselves confronted with an ecclesiastical advance which may have sinister consequences, and they refuse to recognise this Bishop.

The best possible solution of the difficulty would be to exchange the small Serb population for some of the many Albanians who are under Serb rule, and so get rid of what can only be 'a thorn in the side' of both parties. If this could be effected by the League of Nations a real step towards peace would have been taken. Situated as she is between Greece and the Serbs, both of which wish for Albanian territory, Albania's lot is far from easy. Though there are many points of friction between Greece and Jugoslavia they would undoubtedly agree upon any policy which would facilitate the fulfilment of their respective aspirations in Albania. Thus the news of Albania which is telegraphed from Belgrad and Athens is always of a nature to prevent foreign capitalists from investing money in Albania. Not long ago it described a great revolution which never took place at all. Serbia in old days suffered thus from the Press of Vienna. Recollections of this, however, have not roused a fellow feeling and kindness. They have caused her only to adopt Viennese methods.

Reviewing the situation, we are forced to admit that our war 'for the rights of small nations' has not been a success. We have created a Jugoslavia and a Greece much greater than either Serb or Greek could have made for himself unaided, and have thereby encouraged the megalomania from which both suffered. Moreover, from the Balkan point of view the success of the Serb is founded upon the success of the murder of the Archduke. It is a bad precedent. If one State can thus fulfil its national aspirations, why not another? Nor can any stability be expected until it is clearly laid down that each Government will be held responsible for the acts of the komitadji bands and revolutionary societies whose existence it tolerates and 'can *repudiate when necessary'*. The owner of a dangerous dog is responsible for the injury it inflicts. No allowance need in this case be made for the *'first bite'* for it was bitten long ago. Political murder must be recognised as a crime to be tried by an international Court. The injurer must not be permitted to be his own policeman.

We who remember in 1913 hearing Serb and Montenegrin boast: *"If we do not get all we want we shall set all Europe on fire,"* realise even more strongly than others how unflinchingly the threat was carried out.

M. E. Durham

The Contemporary Review, January 1925

Fresh Light on the Sarajevo Crime

by M. Edith Durham

On June 28th, ten years had passed since the crime which precipitated the most terrible war that the world has known. The immediate cause of the war was the fact that the Serbian Government refused to permit the origins of the crime to be inquired into by Austrian agents, upon Serbian territory. To the few of us who had lived long in Balkan lands and had heard *"our next war with Austria"* loudly discussed both by Montenegrins and Serbs, there was no possible doubt as to why Serbia refused to permit this inquiry. We had even been told '*We have the whole of the Russian army behind us and you (England) can do nothing!*' Little did we then dream that instead of '*doing nothing*', England would ultimately be dragged in to support the plan.

At the time of the crime Serbia was, to the general public, a practically unknown land. Though it should have been common knowledge that the history of Serbia was punctuated with political murders; though the Carnegie Report of the Balkan wars of 1912-13 had amply exposed the atrocities of the organised gang of Serbian military, known as the '*Black Hand*'; though, in short, there was sufficient reason for doubting Serbia, yet, at this critical moment, she was taken at her own valuation. Great Britain was represented in Belgrade by a newly-appointed Minister, who had had no possible time in which to fathom the depths of Serbian intrigue, and at the critical moment he was absent from Belgrade. The Chargé d'Affaires who replaced him was also new to the land. Serbia shouted her innocence. *"Therefore,"* cried a band of enthusiasts, *"she must be innocent."* Viscount Grey, then Minister for Foreign Affairs, had had no Balkan experience whatever. The Serb mentality was a sealed book to him.

Those of us who had lived long in the Balkans asked in vain *"How is it possible that in a land riddled with police spies; where the simple tourist in pre-war days was asked for a passport in every village; dogged by the police; could not photograph a cow or speak to an old woman without the police noting the fact and wanting to know the reason - how is it possible that in such a land this ubiquitous police force has been totally unable in three weeks to throw any light on the crime?"* Between June 28th and July 23rd, not an arrest was made; not an explanation given. Slavko Gruitch, when asked by Freiherr von Storck, on behalf of the Austrian Government, what steps the Serbian police had taken or were taking to trace the crime, merely replied: *"The police have not concerned themselves with the affair."*

When Austria, her patience worn out by Serb indifference, insisted that Austrian officials should take part in a search for the criminals, Serbia preferred to risk war, rather than to risk the exposure that must necessarily follow. We could only conclude that the exposure would have been a very bad one. The innocent would cry: *"Open all my cupboards and see how clean they are."* From this belief we have never swerved. And the evidence which bit by bit has been piling up has only confirmed it.

It is now possible to show that Austria's suspicions were correct and her demands justified. Had Europe enforced such an inquiry on the spot - as was made recently in Greece, also in a murder case - the history of the past few years would have been very different.

Last year, Professor Stanoje Stanojevitch, of Belgrade, published for the first time the fact that the Archduke's murder was organised by Colonel Dragutin Dimitrijevitch, Head of the Intelligence Section of the Serbian General Staff at Belgrade, after a communication received by him from the Russian Intelligence Department. Dimitrijevitch was the leading spirit of the *'Black Hand'*, a society the main object of which was the break-up of Austria-Hungary. He took an active part in the murder of King Alexander and Queen Draga in 1903. As England resumed diplomatic relations with Serbia on condition that the murderers should be dismissed from office, we may fairly ask how he came to be appointed to such an important post as Head of Intelligence.

The main facts of Stanojevitch's book appeared in the Contemporary Review of November, 1923. His argument is that, the crime being the work of a *'secret society'*, the Government could in no way be held responsible. He fails to recognise that a Government which permits the existence of such a notorious society and fails to punish its crimes becomes at best an accessory. Dimitrijevitch employed as his right-hand man Major Voja Tankositch, says Stanojevitch, thus confirming the truth of Austria's accusation. He tells much, but he leaves untouched the question: Had the Serbian Government, or any members of it, any previous knowledge of the plot?

'Murder will out.' The veil that covered the days between June 28th and July 23rd, 1914, is now lifted by the Serbs themselves. To celebrate the tenth anniversary of the outbreak of the World War, a book of short articles by leading Serbians has been published at Belgrade under the title *'Krv Slovenstva' (Slav Blood)*. It tells almost all we want to know. The first article is *'After Vidovdan, 1914'* by Ljuba Jovanovitch, President of the Serbian Parliament. We will quote it freely, italicising the more important passages.

'The outbreak of the war found me Minister of Education in the Cabinet in M. Pashitch. I have written some of my thoughts and impressions of those days. From these for this occasion, I now make extracts, for the time has not yet come for publishing all.' [The extracts, we may remark, are sufficiently strong for a first dose.] 'I do not remember if it were the end of May or the beginning of June when, one day, M. Pashitch told us that certain persons were preparing to go to Serajevo, in order to kill Franz Ferdinand, who was expected there on Vidovdan. He told this much to us others, but he acted further in the affair only with Stojan Protitch,* then Minister of the Interior. As they told me afterwards, this was prepared by a society of secretly organised men, and by the societies of patriotic students of Bosnia-Herzegovina, in Belgrade. M. Pashitch and we others said (and Stojan Protitch agreed) that he, Stojan, should order the authorities on the Drin frontier to prevent the crossing of the youths who had left Belgrade for the purpose. But these frontier authorities were themselves members of the organisation and did not execute Stojan's order, and told him, and he afterwards told us, that the order had come too late, for the youths had already crossed over. Thus failed the Government attempt to prevent the outrage (attentat) that had been prepared.'

It is thus clear that the whole Cabinet knew of the plot some time before the murder took place; that the Prime Minister and the Minister of the Interior knew in which societies it had been prepared; that the frontier guard was deeply implicated, and working under the orders of those who were arranging the crime.

One order, which was disobeyed, was the sole effort made by the Government to stop the course of events. Had Pashitch and his Cabinet wished to prevent the murder it is obvious that their first steps would have been at once to inform the Vienna Government and the police of Sarajevo, giving the names of the criminals which it is clear they knew; to arrest and try the frontier guards; to make searching inquiry into the incriminated secret societies and arrest all suspected accomplices of the plotters. A few hours' energetic work would have stopped the affair. But Ljuba Jovanovitch's reminiscences tell of no such steps. We can only suppose that Pashitch and Protitch had no wish to stop it. Ljuba then remarks:

'There failed also the attempt of our Minister at Vienna, made on his own initiative, to the Minister Bilinski, to turn the Archduke from the fatal path which had been planned. Thus the death of the Archduke was accomplished in circumstances more awful than had been foreseen and with consequences no one could have even dreamed of.'

It has been claimed by certain defenders of the Serbs, notably by the

French author, M. Denis, that the Serb Government warned the Austrian Government and thereby freed itself from responsibility. Ljuba Jovanovitch makes it clear that no official warning was given. The Minister acted '*on his own initiative*'. We are left to imagine whence he derived his information. He makes yet one more of the official Serbs who knew of the plot.

As Minister of Education, Ljuba came in contact with the numerous '*emigrant*' students from the Slav provinces of Austria-Hungary. From one of the students, who was a refugee in London during the war, and from other sources, we have learned that these '*emigrants*' were mainly boys who had been expelled from Austrian schools for grave breaches of discipline. They were welcomed in Belgrade, where their schooling was often paid for by the various patriotic societies, or by individuals, and used to meet at the eating-house in Belgrade known as the '*Green Garland*' where a violent anti-Austrian propaganda was carried on by the '*Black Hand*'. ex-komitadji leaders and officers. Ljuba tells us that he was personally acquainted with Princip, the chief murderer, and that he encouraged him and his fellows to complete the classes in the school in order to be the better prepared '*to be of value to the nation and in general the better serve their ideals.*' That he was unaware of what went on in the '*patriotic Bosnian and Herzegovinian circles*' in Belgrade is in the highest degree improbable. The ugliest feature of an ugly tale is the fact that these men in official positions, deliberately and in cold blood, incited a pack of raw youths to commit crimes that must at least entail the death of the criminal, and sat calmly by and watched results. The refugee student above quoted stated that Princip was chosen because he was in such an advanced state of tuberculosis that he could not in any case have lived long. *"I saw him in the park just before he left and he looked very ill."*

Ljuba, after describing Princip, continues:

'*On Vidovdan (Sunday, June 28th, 1914,) in the afternoon I was at my country house at Senjak. About 5 p.m., an official telephoned to me from the Press Bureau telling what had happened at Serajevo. And although I knew what was being prepared there, yet, as I held the received, it was as though someone had unexpectedly dealt me a heavy blow. When later the news was confirmed from other quarters a heavy anxiety oppressed me. ... I saw that the position of our Government with regard to other Governments would be very difficult, far worse than after May 29th, 1903 (the murder of King Alexander). I feared the European Courts would all feel themselves aimed at by Princip's bullet, and would withdraw from us with the approval of the monarchist and conservative elements. ... I knew that France, and much less Russia, was not ready* to match itself with Germany and her Danubian ally, for their preparations were not to be complete till 1917.'

He describes his agony of terror. That military circles did not take so gloomy a view appears next:

'Terrible thoughts overwhelmed me from Vidovdan (Sunday) till Tuesday at noon, when a young friend, Major N, to whom I told my fears, said in beautiful, soft but truly inspired tones: *Gospodiné Minister! I think we need not doubt. Let the Austrian-Hungarian Government attack us. It must come sooner or later. Now is an inconvenient moment for settling the account. But now it is not for us to choose.'"* [Why not? Had the Serb military already decided to risk war and not to allow their *"Black Hand"* to be interfered with?] *"If Austria-Hungary chooses it - well, so let it be! It may possibly end badly for us. But it may be otherwise.'*

One can only suppose that by this time the Serb army was already sure of the support of some Power or Powers. Thus cheered by Major N-, Ljuba sat up again, and took notice, with high hopes, that the Russian Press was friendly; 'one knew in advance that it represented the Government ... Russia does not withdraw her hand from us and after Russia will come her friends. Thus it came about and was.' In this astonishing autobiographical fragment there is no attempt to conceal Serbia's bloodguiltiness. The '*inspired*' tones of Major N. suggest that he knew very well what he was talking about.

Meanwhile, Nikola Pashitch and Stojan Protitch had not been idle. Their main idea was to conceal all trace of the crime and pose as innocent. Serbia was, indeed, so much accustomed to political murders that it is possible they imagined one more or less did not greatly matter. Ljuba details their efforts with singular simplicity. He seems to take it for granted that no one ever imagined Serbia was innocent, but that the public would like to know how the thing was done.

'M. Pashitch hoped that somehow we should surmount the crisis and he - and all of us - strove that Serbia should get through the giving of these unlucky satisfactions to Austria cheaply. ... As is well known, the Government did all it could to show our friends and the rest of the world how far apart we were from the Serajevo criminals (atentatori).'

'Thus Stojan, on the very same evening when the news came of what Princip had done, gave orders, and the Belgrade police forbade all singing, and rejoicing in public places, and all was stopped and something like official mourning began.

When Mass was celebrated in the Catholic Church of the Legation on

June 20th (O.S.) at the time of the funeral of the deceased Archduke and his wife, some of the Ministers represented the Serbian Government. I, too, was among them. I wanted to show that even I, about whom it might be thought that I approved Princip's deed, was on the contrary in entire agreement with what our Cabinet was doing." ... [Here one asks, "What was it doing?" And can only reply, "Shamming mourning and trying to deceive Europe."] ... *"Nevertheless this short stay in the church was unpleasant to me. I felt myself to be among enemies who would not make peace with us.'*

What a picture is this of the man who, knowing of the murder plot a month beforehand, during which time he does nothing to prevent it, goes to church in pretended mourning for his slaughtered victim and is hard pricked in his conscience; aware that as Minister of Education and as a leading light in the Narodna Odbrana, which inspired the teaching of Young Serbia, he was himself already bloodguilty; would have the blood of the young criminals also on his head, and terrified lest, at the long last, he would be answerable for yet more blood. Autobiography has seldom produced a more vivid snapshot. Ljuba Jovanovitch's colleagues, however, were less sensitive.

'They still thought war could be avoided ... they would give satisfaction to Austria, and postpone the conflict till the time when we were again ready for war, from which we had emerged with glory and great gain last autumn.'

To those who do not know the Near East it must be explained that the death of the Archduke was but the last of a series of political murders upon Austrian territory, committed by youths whom Austria had every reason to believe had been armed and incited in Serbia. In all these cases, Austria had refrained from pressing the point and had limited her action to protests. It had come to such a point that Austria's cowardice, as both Serb and Montenegrin believed it to be, was a bye-word. *"You can do what you like to Austria. She dare not fight!"* was remarked contemptuously as each fresh outrage was duly applauded in the Serbian Press.

Pashitch and Protitch continued their efforts to make things safe: *'When,'* says Ljuba, *'The news came from Vienna that an employé of the Serbian Ministry of Works, Milan Ciganovitch, had helped the criminals to go to Serajevo, M. Pashitch asked Jotza Jovanovitch, who held that office then, what this employé of his was. M. Jotza did not know him, nor did anyone in the Ministry.'* [This is strange, for Ciganovitch was a member of the 'Black Hand' said to be known as No. 412, and in fulfilling its orders must, with or without leave, have been frequently absent from his post.] 'As M. Pashitch insisted, they found Ciganovitch after some trouble, in some administrative post on the railway. I remember that someone - Stojan or Pashitch - said, when Jotza told us this: 'There you are! You see it is just what folks say. If a mother loses her son, let her look for him in the railway service!' After this we heard from M. Jotza that Ciganovitch had disappeared somewhere out of Belgrade.'

This is a very important admission. It shows that the Government could, had they chosen, have arrested Ciganovitch. He had been accused by the murderers, in their confessions, of being the man who introduced them to Major Voja Tankositch and, by his orders, gave them lessons in pistol-shooting and bomb-throwing, Tankositch supplying the pistol. Ciganovitch, they said, also furnished them with four Browning pistols, six bombs, enough ammunition, and a tube of prussic acid, with which to commit suicide after the deed and so preserve the secret. He then gave them a letter to Major Radé Popovitch at Shabatz, who arranged with the frontier-guard for the safe passage of the youths and their weapons into Bosnia.For these very sufficient reasons Austria demanded the arrest of Ciganovitch. The Serbian Government replied that Ciganovitch had left Belgrade on June 15th (O.S.) and could not be traced. The Austrian inquiry was made some three days after the crime. Ljuba shows that Ciganovitch was then still in Government employ and that it took a little time to find him. He was not arrested, but mysteriously 'disappeared'." It was clear to Austria that, unless her own agents acted, no arrests were likely to be made. By conniving at the escape of Ciganovitch, the Cabinet became accomplices after the crime as well as guilty of foreknowledge of it. Austria's insistence on taking part in the inquiries raised an outcry among those who did not know the Balkans. To those who did, it seemed the one necessary clause.

Ljuba continues:

'Stojan for his part carried out a certain investigation. Among the things remaining in the post office at Belgrade, a postcard was found, 'poste restante,' written from Serajevo by one of the criminals, before Vidovdan, to one of his comrades in Belgrade.'

Here follows a long row of dots suggesting that one of the passages which are not yet ripe for publication is here omitted. Here was yet another opportunity for the arrest of one of the accomplices. Needless to say nothing was done. On the contrary, Ljuba says cheerfully: 'On the whole it could be expected that Vienna would not succeed in proving any connection between official Serbia and the event on the Miljacka.' The Cabinet then seems to have felt all was safe and to have awaited events happily.

Space does not admit of quoting more of the article. The carelessness with which Pashitch and most of the Ministers went up country electioneering, after having, as they thought, safely buried all tracks: the anxious cry by telephone of M. Patchu, the Minister of Finance, who was left in charge, telling that the Austrian Note is about to arrive and begging Pashitch to return; his reply *'Take it yourself,'* and his obstinate persistence in starting for Salonika; his final detention at Leskovatz by an urgent message from Gruitch telling the contents of the Note, are all detailed. He returned. The shuffling reply was drafted in which all points of little importance were conceded, but in which the guilty gang refused to allow any dangerous inquiries to be made in Serbia. The Russian Chargé d'Affaires was summoned, and begged to ask for the support of the Russian Government for Serbia. It is all an ugly tale.

One thing is clear after Ljuba's revelations, and that is that an inquiry at the Hague would have been a mere pantomime, staged by Pashitch and Co. with, perhaps, some distinguished members of the *'Black Hand'* to act as chorus.

It is melancholy now to read the criticisms then made in England on these events. Austria relied on the righteousness of her cause and supplied each of the Powers with a very detailed dossier of her charges against Serbia and the evidence obtained from the captured murderers. But in the Blue Book, published at the beginning of the war, this is condensed into a few lines. And there is nothing in the Blue Book to show that the dossier was ever seriously considered. We find Sir Edward Grey (as he then was) writing on July 24th to Sir Maurice de Bunsen at Vienna that *'the merits of the dispute between Austria and Serbia were not the concern of H.M. Government.'* And on July 29th: *'The Austrian Ambassador told me to-day he had a long memorandum which he said gave an account of the conduct of Servia to Austria and an explanation of how necessary the Austrian action was. I said I did not wish to discuss the merits of the question between Austria and Servia.'*

This was what Germany wished - that the question should be left to be settled between the two. But Sir Edward felt himself so tightly bound to Russia and France, whose protégé Serbia was, that we find him writing to Mr. Crackanthorpe, at Belgrade, on July 24th that he thinks:

'Servia should promise to give Austria full satisfaction if it is proved that Serbian officials were accomplices in the murder of the Archduke, and 'she certainly should express regret and concern.' For the rest, the Servian Government must reply to Austrian demands as they consider best for Servian interest." [Was it probable they would not?] *"It is impossible to say if military action by Austria can be avoided by anything*

but unconditional acceptance of her terms. ... Only chance appears to be avoiding absolute refusal and replying favourably on as many points as the time limit allows. Servian Minister here has begged H.M. Government will express their views, but I cannot undertake the responsibility of saying more than I have said above, and I do not like to say even that without knowing what is being said by the French and Russian Governments. You should therefore consult your French and Russian colleagues as to repeating what my views are as expressed above.'

To this Mr. Crackanthorpe replies that, his French and Russian colleagues having received no instructions, he has not offered the advice to the Serbian Government. Thus, for fear of upsetting France and Russia, it appears that Great Britain dared not even tell the Serbs to say they were sorry.

It is melancholy, too, to turn to the reflections of others who also did not know the Balkans and judged the Serbs by the standards, it would appear, of Oxford and Eton. Thus the anonymous author of 'Who provoked the War?' in Vol. I of New Europe, says: 'The Serbian Government denied the indictments of Austria, but no time was left for Serbia to conduct a regular trial of the persons denounced by Austria-Hungary.' But, as we have seen, the said Government had time to suppress the incriminating postcard, to cause the disappearance of Ciganovitch, and plenty of time to punish the frontier guards had they chosen. Ciganovitch, by the way, is not reported to be dead and may yet favour us with his reminiscences.)

The only report we have been able to find on the Austrian dossier is written by Sir Charles Oman, who, it is clear, has had no Balkan experience and ascribes Western standards to Near Eastern minds. He thinks that the evidence given by the captured murderers is probably 'concocted' because he is haunted by the idea that schoolboys do not 'tell' of each other. He is indignant that Austria should pass over 'the full and satisfactory promise of the Serbian Government to bring to trial anyone accused of complicity in the Serajevo crime' without a word. But a lecture in a haughty tone is delivered on the objection that Austrian delegates in the inquiry would be contrary to the Serbian Constitution. He is deeply shocked that Austria should add 'If the researches were properly carried out the results would have been of a kind unpleasant to themselves (the Serb Government).' So, indeed, they would have been, for the Cabinet, the Head of the Intelligence Section of the General Staff; the Executive Committee of the *'Black Hand'*; the officers of the frontier guard, and who knows how many more, might have appeared as prisoners at the bar accused of complicity either before or after the crime. Sir Charles' indignation culminates when *"it is alleged that the Prefect of Police caused his (Ciganovitch's) disappearance and could have found him if he pleased. In short, there is a blank accusation of bad faith made against the Serbian Government.*' Compared with Ljuba's picture of Jotza finding Ciganovitch; Pashitch and Stojan joking about lost youths found in the railway service, and Stojan's remark later *"that he had disappeared somewhere"*, the difference between the real and the imaginary would be ludicrous, were it not that failure to realise that Austria knew what she was talking about caused Europe to be drenched with blood and cost millions of innocent lives.

"Yes," said a Serb refugee student calmly, *"it is a pity so many were killed. But you see the plan was quite successful. We have made Great Serbia."* As it is always of interest to 'see ourselves as others see us', two more Serbian remarks may be added. *"We made you break up Austria and Germany for us. Now nothing stands in the way. The Slavonic plans will be realised. You cannot stop us."* Lastly, *"Oh, you English! You think you are honest, but you are so very, very silly. Anyone can deceive you."*

Deceived we were. It is evident that our course should have been to support Germany in insisting that no other Power should intervene; and give France and Russia plainly to understand that we would on no account fight on behalf of their protégé. France, as we know, had been steadily arming and financing Serbia ever since 1906. Serbia had formed an important element in Russian plans ever since the Serb military gang had murdered King Alexander and put Russia's choice, the Karageorgevitch, upon the throne in 1903. There are, indeed, hints that there was pre-knowledge of the murder plot in Russia, a report that Artamanov, the Russian military attaché at Belgrade, was informed of it by Dimitrijevitch; that he asked for delay while he communicated with Petersburg, and a few days afterwards informed the Intelligence Section of the Serb General Staff that, whatever happened, Russia would support Serbia. *"We trembled,"* said my informant, *"to the innermost depths of our being at the words of the Russian military attaché, for we knew that now the axe would be laid to the stem of the Austrian Imperial family."* Leopold Mandl makes this statement in the Neues 8 Uhr Blatt of July 1st, 1924. As he does not name his authority, we note it only as a point which requires further elucidation. The Russian correspondence between Belgrade and Petersburg has not yet been revealed.

Had France known for certain that she would receive no help from England if she went to war on behalf of Serbia, it is unlikely that she would have dared to support Russia; and had France accepted the often repeated entreaty of Germany to join with her in an intervention at

Petersburg the matter might yet have been localised. Isvolsky reports Germany's efforts with a chuckle: '*The Minister of Justice has not for one moment admitted the possibility of taking a moderating action at Petersburg. ...The Minister has refused to agree to the German proposal.*' Viscount Grey would not '*discuss the merits of the question between Austria and Serbia.*' Isvolsky wanted his war and he got it.

'*Never in history has there been a better outlook for the Serbian nation than has arisen since the outbreak of the war!*' cried M. Pashitch triumphantly on August 13th, 1915 (Tribuna, Belgrade, No 1771). Half Europe rushed to his support. The success of the murder plot surpassed his wildest expectations. We English, as the Serb remarked, were very, very silly. Let us learn from the past and on no account allow ourselves a second time to be dragged into a plot for Slavonic aggrandisement. But he was kind enough to add that we think ourselves honest. Let us then be honest and admit that Germany was not alone responsible for provoking the war.

M. Edith Durham

The Contemporary Review, September 1928
Fresh Light on Serbia and the War
by M. E. Durham

In July, 1914, when the Austro-Hungarian Government presented a copy of the Note to Serbia to the British Government, it presented also a detailed explanation to show that Serbia's aggressive policy made strong steps necessary. Briefly: that in spite of solemn promises, Serbia continuously carried revolutionary and terroristic work within the Monarchy for the purpose of disrupting it; that Serbia was the focus of criminal agitation; that societies both public and private, whose members included generals, diplomats and government officials, existed in Serbia for the above purposes; that Serbian journalism aroused and spread hatred of the neighbour State; that Serbian agents corrupted the youths of the border States of Austria-Hungary; that the Serbian Government had taken no steps to suppress this criminal action which had culminated in the murder of the Archduke. Details were given about his murderers and about other political attentats. This important document seems never to have been duly considered. It did not appear in the Press. Sir Edward Grey (as he then was), apparently without reading Austria's well-documented reasons, at once replied to Count Mensdorf that he thought the Note '*the most formidable document I had ever seen addressed by one State to another that was independent.*'

That he had never before had to consider a case in which such formidable provocation had been given he appears not to have realised, for he refused to consider the document on the ground that '*"to discuss the merits of the dispute"* (a very mild term to use in such a case) *"was not our concern. It was solely from the point of view of the peace of Europe I should concern myself with the matter.*' How he hoped to preserve peace without knowing the basis of the trouble is inexplicable. None of the British Documents indicate that Sir Edward ever realised that '*Sarajevo*' was not a mere assassination but a challenge hurled by the Slav at the Teuton. The Near East knew this very well. The Austrian dossier was, it seems, submitted for an opinion later, only to Sir Charles Oman, whose personal knowledge of the Balkans was - as his report shows - nil.

That Austria was amply justified in all her charges is now shown by the Serbs themselves. That the Serbian Government of 1914 knew of the plot to murder the Archduke we learnt in 1924 from Ljuba Jovanovitch, the truth of whose well-known article has never been shaken. When challenged, he offered at once to produce documentary evidence, whereupon his opponents dropped the matter hastily. Now full details on the whole criminal work have been published in the review Nova Europa (Zagreb) during the past year by men who led or took part in it. Serbia had long hoped to achieve her ambitions by means of a European war. In Serbia's Task (Belgrade, 1894) Zhivanovitch points out that Europe is rapidly arming: he calls on all Serbs to unite to create Great Serbia: only by war can this be done. *'Europe will be regenerated by blood. ... we have always been the declarers of war. The fruit of these wars is the Kingdom of Serbia ... force must be met with force, be it on the Carpathians, the Lim, the Drin, the Save, or on all at once. ... Fearful will be the storm. Blessed he that successfully survives. Serbia will perhaps be the centre of the fight.'* She must prepare. He quotes *'one of our leading statesmen'* as saying *'we want all Bosnia'*.

The Nova Europa articles show how this *'task'* was carried out. *'Serbia's resurrection'* is dated from May 29th (Old Style), 1903, the murder of King Alexander Obrenovitch. While the Austrophile Obrenovitches were on the throne, anti-Austrian work was impossible. The writers glory in that murder. The murderers are fondly called *'the May Men'*. Nova Europa (Oct. 11th-27th) gives a long account of those bloody shambles and the treachery and savagery of those same *'May Men'* who used to celebrate the anniversary of their deed by an annual dinner at Restaurant Koloratz, when Dimitrijevitch-Apis, who later organised the Serajevo murders, sat at the head of the table. Dushan Semiz, a member of the revolutionary party (N. E.: Oct. 11th-27th) lauds Apis and calls on the nation to honour him as the creator of Jugoslavia. The May Men, he says, *'opened a new page of Jugoslav history'*. They began to work at once in Austrian territory. He himself met the Serbian revolutionary agent Lj. Jovanovitch-Chupa (journalist, a founder of the *'Black Hand'*) in Mostar in 1904. *'I then joined the revolutionary movement. ... The May Men opened Belgrade's gates to youths from all parts. Inspired Jugoslavs swarmed in. The officers fraternised with them and vowed to live and die together for the liberation and union of the nation. All who still believe that the youths' revolutionary Jugoslav movement at the beginning of the twentieth century arose and developed independently in Austrian territory, deceive themselves. It derived its moral and partly its material support from After-May Belgrade. Thus, after May 29th the Shumadija (central Serbia) revolutionaries set fire to our whole race."* Austria's efforts to suppress this he calls *'persecution'*.

A Herzegovinian from Trebinje told me how schoolboys were worked upon. Danilo Ilitch (afterwards Black Hand agent at Serajevo and hanged as accomplice to the Archduke's murder) there taught the violin and preached revolt. *"We were so young - so ignorant. They told us we were oppressed and we believed it; that it was heroic to defy our masters. I shall never forget how, when I was only fourteen, Ilitch told me that it* was not enough to kill Austrians. We must torture them. He drew his finger across his face and said we must cut the skin of their faces with a knife and drag it upwards and downwards. I was terrified. I did not join the revolutionaries. He loved cruelty. Many of them did."

Marco, the pen-name of ex-Colonel Bozhin Simitch, 'May Man' and member of the 'Black Hand', also lauds Dimitrijevitch-Apis (Nova Europa XVI, Nos. 1, 10, 11), and dates all success from the glorious May 29th. *"Already in July, 1903, komitadji bands were organised in Macedonia, and the swearing-in of Austro-Hungarian youths for revolutionary work was in full swing."* He details the reconstruction of the Serbian army, *"exclusively the work of the young officers among whom first place belongs to Dimitrijevitch-Apis'* He tells how at patriotic meetings held in Belgrade: *'the officers were present in numbers in the front rows. This especially strengthened the belief of the youth across the Drin and the Save, that war with Austria-Hungary was - so to speak - on the doorstep. Thus the first seeds of the revolutionary movement were sown ... Vladimir Gatchinovitch, spiritual leader of the youth of Bosnia-Herzegovina and member of the Black Hand (No. 217), only became a true and hardened revolutionary after close contact with certain officers. He often said the youths of Austria-Hungary could not become serious revolutionaries till they had walked Belgrade's pavements. ...All who say that the revolutionary work of the Bosnian youth was spontaneous and worked independently of revolutionary Belgrade are either much mistaken or wish to hide something.'*

'Spomenitza V. Gatchinovitcha' (Serajevo 1921) tells how this man used to travel between Vienna, Sarajevo and Belgrade inciting the students to revolution, and swearing them in. *'We were once and forever bound to a great and mysterious existence. We felt it existed but knew not of what it consisted. I well remember the Browning on which one's hand was laid.'* Gavrilo Princip, one of the Archduke's murderers, was one of Gatchinovitch's recruits for the Black Hand. Milosh Vidakovitch similarly was 'Black Hand' agent in Paris. Possibly his presence there was connected with M. Poincaré's firm insistence that no examination of Serbia's skeleton cupboards would be permitted by France.

Mere lads were urged to commit murder. Oskar Tartaglia (first Catholic member of the Black Hand) in Veleizdajnik (Zagreb-Split 1928) and in Nova Europa, tells how the attentat on Commissary Chuvaj was planned. In February, 1912, Tartaglia and two others went to Serajevo, where *'by our temperamental speeches we inflamed the Sarajevo youth's.* On February 21st, they arranged a bloody demonstration led by Jukitch. As participant in this demonstration Princip had to leave the Serajevo school. Jukitch was introduced to Tartaglia and said that he wanted to murder Chuvaj at Zagreb. '*I advised him to ask for a private interview and to stab Chuvaj in the breast or fire some shots into him.*' Jukitch, craving for notoriety, insisted on a public spectacle. '*When an excursion was made to Belgrade we arranged to take Jukitch. ... In Belgrade I introduced him to Dimitrijevitch-Apis who at once agreed to an attentat on Chuvaj, and, without much more consideration, handed him to Tankositch, who taught him revolver shooting and bomb throwing.*'' (Tankositch also trained the Archduke's murderers later.) "*I visited Tankositch at his quarters next day and arranged the whole affair with him. Jukitch kept the revolver. The bombs were carried secretly to Zagreb. I told certain leaders of the Serbo-Croatian party of Jukitch's intention to commit the attentat.*'

On June 8th, Jukitch fired at Chuvaj when driving in the street, missed him and killed his secretary, Hervojitch, and also a gendarme. Jukitch was condemned to death, but owing to his youth the sentence was changed to life imprisonment. He was released after the war and lives in Bosnia. The Austrian police traced Jukitch's visit to Belgrade and found many of the Serbian arsenal bombs in the Save river. Complaints to Belgrade met with protests of ignorance and innocence. The Black Hand next arranged an attentat by Dojchitch who had come from America, hoping to put the Austrian authorities off the scent. '*Others by Shefer, Planinschak and others followed, but without success,*' says Tartaglia. Austria protested vainly. Belgrade lauded the attentators. Tartaglia, while denouncing Austrian '*tyranny*', boasts that his hatred was such that he would not learn German. This '*tyranny*' permitted him to receive his education in his own tongue - a privilege not enjoyed by the Bulgars, Albanians, and Kutzovlahs in the lands '*liberated*' by Serbia.

Ex-Colonel Chedo Popovitch (May Man and member of the Central Administration of the Black Hand) describes in Nova Europa (XVI, Nos. 5, 10, 11) the fear of the Serbs lest the Young Turk régime should succeed and thwart their plans to obtain Turkish territory. Intensive work was started to make it impossible for the Turks to maintain order. At the end of 1910 a system of "*frontier officers*" was arranged on the Bosnian-Herzegovinian and Turkish frontiers. By the influence of Apis, Black Hand men filled the posts. Each had a zone across the border in which to work revolution. Popovitch was at Uzhitza, for work in Bosnia. During the annexation crisis he "*had carried on a certain mission in Bosnia ... I therefore knew our work would find support on that side of the Drin because we were officers. The belief of the Bosnians that they would see their salvation in the Serbian officers was well known to me.*" He then makes an important revelation about the Narodna Odbrana, which defenders of Serbian innocence have represented as a "*purely cultural society.*" When it was started during the annexation crisis, the revolutionary officers belonged to it. It organised a komitadji school and taught rifle shooting and bomb work. Austria's protests, when Europe recognised the annexation, caused its fires to be apparently banked down. In fact, the '*Black Hand*' was formed and worked under cover of this so-called harmless society. Says Popovitch: '*The changed rôle of the Narodna Odbrana after the annexation, its turn from revolutionary to purely cultural work, was not accepted as true by our people over the border. They firmly believed it was merely the usual trick to strike any reason for complaint out of the hands of the Austrian officials. Thus, after the annexation, the Narodna Odbrana, in the eyes of the Bosnian-Herzegovinians, was the same as during the annexation crisis, i.e., a revolutionary organisation preparing war against Austria. Therefore I told my comrades it would be inopportune to introduce men to our organisation (the Black Hand), and very inopportune to say that the latter and not the Narodna Odbrana was leading the revolutionary work.*' It was decided unanimously that the Black Hand should work under cover of the Narodna Odbrana.

Serbia in her reply to the Austrian Note agreed to dissolve the Narodna Odbrana, knowing that the work could go on all the same under the Black Hand. The reply was '*merely one of the usual tricks*' - an impudent tissue of prevarication. To Popovitch's plan to work under cover of the Narodna Odbrana Dimitrijevitch-Apis replied: '*You have done well. It is better not to notice small differences. For us the work is the main thing.*' Apis quickly combined the work of the two societies by appointing Milan Vasitch, a member of the '*Black Hand*', as secretary to the Narodna Odbrana. As Head of the Intelligence Department of the General Staff, Apis had immense influence. The '*frontier officers*' adopted a password and a cypher for correspondence with Bosnia '*In order to preserve secret connection with our people over the border, 'canals' were made, by means of trustworthy people through whom we could arrange to meet, send information etc. The 'canals' were very safe, and worked undisturbed alongside of the active spying of Austria and her gendarmes.*'

By these '*canals*' the Archduke's murderers reached Sarajevo. The youths enticed into Serbia by the officers were sent to be trained at a komitadji school with Tankositch at its head. It was in an out-of-the-way spot at Prokuplje. '*Many recruits came bare-foot and ragged. Money was needed for the school. Our pre-war Government was stingy to miserliness in this matter. The Black Hand had to give of its own means.*'

The Government thus was clearly aware of the school's existence and made no effort to suppress it. The official report of the Salonika trial shows that the then Foreign Minister, Milovan Milovanovitch, was kept informed of the '*Black Hand's*' activities and favoured them.

Komitadji training was explained to me by Pavle Bastaitch, a Croat member of the Black Hand. It ended by his instructor, Voin Popovitch, taking him to the cellar of the Narodna Odbrana house at Vranje. Here, tightly bound, were two schoolmasters captured on Turkish territory and accused of betraying the movements of the Black Hand men, who were spying there, to the Turks. Voin swung up a hatchet and bashed in the heads of the helpless victims, saying: *"This is how we treat traitors"* - a hint to Bastaitch to hold his tongue. By the rules of the Black Hand money for this work was often obtained by force.

About the students in the universities who were subsidised as revolutionary agents by the Serbian Government and the Narodna Odbrana, we have a mass of information in the dossier of the trial of the Czech Klofatz and his accomplice Giunio, arrested in September, 1914, for high treason. Both worked in connection with the Serbian revolutionaries. The dossier quotes hundreds of documents seized in Belgrade by the Austrians in the houses of Pashitch and of Pavlovitch, head organiser of spy work, and at the State Archives. Pashitch's and Pavlovitch's lists of the subsidised students include Bogdan Zherajitch (who went to murder the Emperor Franz Josef when he visited Bosnia in 1910 and, failing to find a chance, fired at Vareshanin, Governor of Bosnia, missed him and blew his own evil brains out); Gatchinovitch, whom we have already mentioned, and V. Chubrilovitch, one of those who smuggled the Archduke's murderers through the *'canals'*.

The subsidised students in Austria sent reports to Belgrade of military movements, etc. Many subsidised journalists are also on the lists. The contents of this dossier deserve a whole volume, but we have no space. Ex-Colonel Chedo Popovitch, having described the triumphant success of the Balkan wars (1912-13) and the excitement thus caused in Bosnia-Herzegovina, says: *'From this we drew the necessary conclusions and at the beginning of 1914 drew up a plan definitely to prepare our people for the armed conflict with Austria which was expected in the future. ... But our Government, fearing our work, thought fit to stop the 'frontier officers" work by transferring us to the interior. Nevertheless our comrades in Belgrade so far as possible kept up the existing connections exclusively that Bosnia should neither know nor suspect that the work was checked at the moment when they expected the most intensive action from Serbia.'*

It is clear that the Government knew what was going on and thought it going too fast. Pashitch indeed is reported to have warned General Putnik about Apis' activities. The withdrawal of three Black Hand men from the frontier made no difference. Those who replaced them, when they received orders from the Black Hand, passed the murderers through the '*canals*' from the Serbian frontier posts. It is obvious that in June, 1914, the Serbian Government could at any moment have laid hands on the whole criminal gang. But as the whole of the Government and high military circles were involved in responsibility for the crime which was, as we have seen, the result of ten years' intensive work, it is equally obvious that only by means of foreign police agents could the criminals be traced. Members of the Belgrade police force were themselves Black Hand men and therefore useless. A Hague inquiry at which Serbian officialdom and the Serbian General Staff - '*merely the usual trick*' - would have sworn innocence and ignorance and France and Russia would have supported them, would have been quite futile. Ciganovitch, whose trial would probably have resulted in disclosing some of the truth, was concealed by the Serbian Government and a lying reply returned that he could not be found.

M. Grouitch similarly lied to our Chargé d'Affaires when he said (Brig. Docs. 80) '*that of Princip the Serbian Government knew nothing*', though he was well known to the Minister of Education as one of the subsidised students. Grouitch's statement that '*it was impossible to adopt definite measures before learning the findings of the Sarajevo Court*' shows that Serbia did not intend to disclose anything not already discovered by Austria.

The Serbian Government relied on two things. One was the certainty of Russian support. Pashitch in his speech to the Radical Party (v. Politika, April 26th, 1926) stated: '*after the Peace of Bucharest I received from Russia the formal promise that Serbia would always be defended if Austria attacked her*'. M. Grouitch revealed this to our Chargé d'Affaires on July 19th, 1914 (No. 61 Brit. Docs.) But Sir Edward Grey ignored it. The second was that, as Semiz, '*Marco*' and others state emphatically, it was confidently expected that the result of the swearing-in of revolutionaries would be that Austria would find herself faced with a great revolution and be unable to use her Croat and Bosnian regiments. Bitterly do these writers blame the failure of their agents to rise. With Russia behind them and Austria crippled they had feared not at all. Says Marco sadly: '*the revolutionary action had not yet ripened and had not penetrated the wide circles of the intelligentzia*'. It was in fact confined to a set of ignorant and irresponsible boys worked upon by unscrupulous journalists and the Belgrade gang. "'*Since the annexation,*" said the Bosnian doctor under whom I worked in 1912-13, "*now that we have our Parliament and Constitution, we have little to complain of. I greatly regret that a party of hotheads keeps up agitation.*" So too may all Europe regret. It has cost Europe dearly. And, the Serbs having learnt that murder leads to success, it may cost yet more.

M. E. Durham

The Observer, May 22nd 1938
The Albanian Language

Sir,

'Dalmatic' asks how the Albanian language has been standardised. Few languages have survived so many difficulties as has Albanian. Under Turkish rule the language was forbidden, and both the teaching and the printing of it were severely punished.

In Albania itself, the language could only be printed under the protection of a Foreign Power. With a view to future partition of the land, the Italians, Austrians, and Greeks all ran propaganda schools protected by their various consulates, and in these taught Albanian. But, having no desire to help the formation of a united Albania, all these schools were given, by their promoters, different alphabets.

The Jesuits in North Albania had their own printing press and a special alphabet as early as the eighteenth century. The British and Foreign Bible Society translated the book of Genesis into Albanian and one of the Gospels, using a peculiar alphabet of freak letters adapted to the southern dialect of the language.

The book of Genesis was popular. I once assisted at the sale of seventy copies, mostly to Moslems eager to read the tale of Potiphar's wife! Sometimes the Turkish authorities interfered and seized the copies, but as the society had the right to sell its publications in Turkey, many got into circulation. Then came, in 1908, the Young Turk revolution, and freedom of the Press was proclaimed. The effect in Albania was amazing; schools and newspapers sprang up like mushrooms all over the country. Enthusiasm was unbounded; so much so that the Turkish Government took fright and tried to restrain it.

But it was too late. The Albanians recognised that an alphabet for the whole country must be fixed on. A congress was summoned in, I think, 1910, at Monastir (now Bitolja), in Macedonia. There was then a very large Albanian population there, and it was hoped to include the town in Albania.

A large number of schoolmasters, writers, and others of the 'intelligentsia' met. It was decided to throw aside such forms of orthography as were suited mainly to either the North or South dialects, to steer a middle course, and to use the Latin alphabet with no freak letters.

Literary work was, of course, hampered by the outbreak of the Balkan War (1912-13). But one of its results was the recognition by the Powers of Albania as an independent and neutral State. The Great War, following close on this, almost ruined Albania, which, though it had been declared independent and neutral, was invaded by Italian, Austrian, Greek, French, English, and Serb armies, and threatened with partition.

It says much for the pluck and determination of the people that so soon as rid of the invading forces, educational work was again taken in hand and many good schools opened. By the time that Achmet Zogu came to the throne as King Zog both language and education were on a secure footing. He found, however, that schools '*benevolently*' run by certain foreign Powers were striving to undermine national unity, so a few years ago all foreign schools were closed. Unfortunately, it was not possible to discriminate, so several very good American schools, which, naturally, had no annexationist plans, had to be closed, too, which was a pity, but under the circumstances unavoidable.

Yours, etc.

M. E. Durham
London, N.W.3

The Manchester Guardian, June 13th 1940
Albania and Italy
'Opportunity to Right a Wrong'

Sir,

In to-day's *'Manchester Guardian'*, you publish an appeal, signed by a number of influential persons, under the heading *'The Allies' opportunity to right a wrong'*. The signatories ask that Italy's sovereignty over Ethiopia should no longer be recognised and that the Ethiopians should be helped to evict the invaders. But they omit to make a similar appeal for Albania, a small country invaded and seized without the smallest right or excuse.

For years before the actual seizure took place, our Government looked on while British influence was forced out of that country, much against the wishes of the population. Thus the British gendarmery officers were forced to leave. The flourishing Boy Scouts instituted by the late Lady Carnarvon were stopped and the boys ordered to join the Italian Balilla, and in other ways English influence got rid of. Albania is now filled with Italian troops, and can be used as a jumping off ground for war in the Balkans. The Italians have long been hated and feared by Albanians, who did not believe England would let them be victimised.

Yours, &c.,

M. E. Durham
London, June 11

The Manchester Guardian, September 11th 1940
Position of Albania

To the Editor of the Manchester Guardian

Sir,

I should like to confirm the statements in the letter of Mr. Duma in your issue of September 6. It is strongly desirable that the Albanians should be relieved from their present anxiety, and assured that when the Allies achieve victory Albania too shall be restored to independence. The position of the Albanians is most painful. They detest Italian rule. Now they are told by Italy that in case of Italian defeat, Albania will be partitioned between Greece and the Yugoslavs. This they are well aware would mean the annihilation of Albania and all its hopes. In the Albanian districts, annexed in 1913 by the Greeks and the Yugoslavs, not a single Albanian school has been permitted. The bulk of the Moslem Albanians have been reckoned as Turks, their lands and possessions confiscated, and themselves sent destitute into Turkey. Whole districts which were almost solidly Albanian when I visited them are now colonised by Serbs. As things stand the Albanians are threatened with destruction whichever side wins. They are fine fighters, and if assured that they would gain freedom by so doing would give the Italians even more trouble than they are now doing. Sporadic risings have done much sabotaging. But a general rising can hardly be expected if its success means 'out of the frying-pan, into the fire'.

The Albanians, both North and South (Tosks and Ghegs), have succeeded in preserving their strong individuality and their language from prehistoric times. They are some of the oldest peoples of Europe. They have survived the Byzantine Empire, the short medieval Serbian Empire, and the Turkish Empire, and on the overthrow of the last in Europe achieved independence. They were loyal members of the League of Nations, but we took no steps whatever to protect them when they were suddenly invaded by huge mechanised Italian forces against which, though they put up a good fight, they had no chance.

Abyssinia has been promised independence. It is time that Albania, Mussolini's other victim, should be assured that we are truly fighting for the freedom of all nations suffering under Axis tyranny. Let the B.B.C. inform them of this as soon as possible. The Italians will then find their situation difficult. Above all, let us not, when peace is achieved, give away any territory that does not belong to us, either to 'appease' an enemy or to reward an ally. The giving away of territories after the last war was one of the causes of the present one. - Yours, &c.,

M. E. Durham, London, September 8

The Manchester Guardian, November 14th 1940
Albania's Cruel Fate
The Tragedy of Koritza

Sir,

Just indignation is aroused by Italy's unprovoked attack upon Greece. But let us not forget that a yet more cruel and unjustifiable attack was made on that fatal Good Friday by Italy upon Albania. More cruel, for it causes Albania to be the battleground upon which the Italo-Greek war is to be fought out. As a member of the League of Nations, Albania was entitled to the help of her fellow-members. But not a finger was stretched to save her from the greed of Mussolini, whose object was to secure a strong strategical position from which to advance to further acts of brigandage. It was clear from the first that he was aiming at Salonika and control of the Aegean.

Hopelessly outnumbered and held down by huge armed forces, Albania has seen her fertile plains ripped up, regardless of private ownership, by military roads. Worst of all, aerodromes and munition stores have been made near her towns, thus making them military objectives. It is the homes of the Albanians that are imperilled, not those of the Italians. Those of us who remember Albania's brave struggle for freedom, as brave as that of any other nation that revolted against the Turks, hear with pain and grief of the bombardment of her towns.

At the beginning of the present century Koritza was the home of Albanian nationalism in the south as was Scutari in the north. Albania was then part of the Turkish Empire, and the Turks, by forbidding the printing or teaching of the Albanian language under heavy penalties, were striving to check the rising national spirit. A remarkable family led the language campaign. George Kyrias, an employee of the British and Foreign Bible Society, translated large portions of the Bible into Albanian, and the society published much of it. The Society had leave to sell its publications in the Turkish Empire, but the Turks had not reckoned on an Albanian version.

A journey I made through the length of Albania with one of the colporteurs, had its adventures. At one place our stock was confiscated by the police, but we obtained a fresh supply. Christians and Moslems alike flocked to buy the forbidden books. All wanted to read their own language. I remember on one morning selling seventy copies of the Book of Genesis and the joy of a young gendarme who said that now he could teach his younger brother to read. It was largely by the help of these publications that South Albania learned to read its own language. Koritza was then the only place in South Albania which had an Albanian school.

George Kyrias had a sister, a woman of great courage and intelligence. Helped by the American mission she went to the United States, returned a fully trained teacher, and was made mistress of a girls' school protected by the American mission. Koritza when I first visited it in 1904 was a clean, stone-built little town with a considerable trade. The school was well equipped and attended both by Moslem and Christian girls. Miss Kyrias used books printed in English. All written exercises in Albanian were destroyed after the lesson, and the Turkish police searched the school in vain for books in the forbidden language. The girls taught their brothers The enthusiasm for education and the struggles made to obtain it were something truly remarkable. To the tireless energy of the Kyrias family and of the patriotic priest Fan Noli Albania is deeply indebted. They gained, too, financial aid from America and contributed largely to Albania's obtaining independence.

And now we hear that Koritza, which was then called 'the Beacon', for it lighted the way, is bombarded - for no fault of its own but because it has unwillingly been made an Italian base. When I remember the bright hopes of 1904 and the pluck of Koritza it seems to me that never were an innocent and patriotic people more cruelly betrayed. The outcome is undecided. Let us hope that when peace is made this martyred nation will be liberated again and her shattered towns rebuilt Albania survived the Roman Empire, the Byzantine Empire, the Turkish Empire. She must survive Mussolini and his Empire, and along with Belgium, Denmark, Holland, and Norway be restored.

Yours, &c.,

M. E. Durham
London, November 11

The Sunday Times, November 17th 1940

Albania

Sir,

In our indignation at the unprovoked attack of Italy upon Greece, let us not forget that an even more dastardly attack upon Albania was made by Italy on that fatal Good Friday in 1939 when huge forces of mechanised troops poured into Albania, which, being unprovided with anti-aircraft guns or other machinery of war, was completely overwhelmed.

Though she was a member of the League of Nations, not a hand to help her was held out by her fellow members. Italy was thus able to take possession of a very strong strategical position commanding the entrance of the Adriatic, and a jumping-off point for further brigandage in the Balkans.

That her aim was Salonika and command of the Aegean, there could be no doubt from the first. Now, though Italy is being bombed, the brunt of the suffering falls upon the innocent and unfortunate Albanians. The Italians have made their aerodromes and munition dumps near the principal towns. Those of us who know Koritza must grieve to hear of its bombardment.

It is earnestly to be hoped that, when peace is made and the Italians driven from the land they so brutally seized, Albania may be restored to her former frontiers and her ravaged towns and lands repaired. She has suffered enough already under the Italian yoke and must not be made to pay for Italy's crimes.

M. E. Durham
London, N.W.3

The Manchester Guardian, November 28th 1940
Albania's Independence Day

Miss M. E. Durham writes:

All who know the Albanians and their long struggle for independence must rejoice that in Koritza November 28 can be celebrated freely. The Italian yoke is shattered and a small people can again lift its head. In the fifteenth century Skenderbeg, known as the Champion of Christendom, kept the Turks at bay for long years. At the beginning of the nineteenth century the Albanians, under their chieftain, Ali Pasha of Tepeleni, freed all South Albania from Turkish rule and reigned over it from his palace at Yanina. There he was visited by Lord Byron, Sir Henry Holland, and other travellers, and he entered into diplomatic relations with Great Britain. But again Albania was overwhelmed by Turkish forces, and it was not until November 28, 1912, that the Powers recognised Albania as an independent State.

A ride through the length and breadth of Albania in the summer of 1913 was an inspiring experience. Provisional governments had been set up in every town and perfect order reigned everywhere. One met enthusiastic people determined to drop all feuds and to work for the unity of the State. There was but one cloud on the horizon. Would the Powers give Albania a sporting chance? Or would they dig in their claws and throttle the young nation?

The Albanian Spirit
England was very popular, America very helpful, and Albania very hopeful (continues our correspondent). No one dreamed that one day Europe would stand by and watch the invasion of the land by Italy and offer no help. On the edge of the sea near Valona stood the small house where Albania's independence was proclaimed and where the Provisional Government was established. There were then no quays, munition stores, or other military equipment. A road led from the sandy shore to the town through the olive gardens. In the town little wooden shops carried on a lively trade. No more peaceful spot could be found. Now, through no fault of their own, the Albanians see their homes bombarded. I photographed Independence House. Have the Italians allowed it to exist? I doubt it. But the memory of that day will not fade. Let us hope that a new Albanian Provisional Government has been set up in Koritza and that, as of old, Albanian culture will radiate from that little town. Certainly in hundreds of houses still under Italy's yoke the day will be celebrated - secretly if need be.

M. E. Durham

The Times, November 29th 1940

Albania

A Committee of its Friends

To the Editor of The Times

Sir,

For nearly two years the Albanian people have endured an Italian military despotism. Their leaders have been exiled, killed, imprisoned, degraded, and dismissed from the public services, and their country has been turned into a bridgehead for the unprovoked attack on Greece. In this ordeal they have lost none of their ancient pride and love of freedom. Many of their young men died resisting the treacherous invasion of Good Friday, 1939, and since then every chance of hitting back at the Italians, whether by passive resistance or sporadic revolt, has been taken by them.

This small, liberty-loving race is thus an ally in our struggle; but an unacknowledged ally. The Under-Secretary of State for Foreign Affairs said in the House of Commons on August 7 last that the Government would co-operate sympathetically with any association of persons representative of the Albanian people; but there, for the moment, the matter rests. A declaration from the Government, backed up by suitable action, would, we feel, encourage the Albanians in passionate resistance to their temporary masters, and raise up a formidable threat to the communications on which Italy depends for success in her war against Greece. An unbroken link between the Albanian and the British peoples is the love and trust that the people of the mountains have had for English men and women (from the days of Byron), and one of the memories to which Albanians cling fondly is the good work done by the Anglo-Albanian Committee of 1920.

On November 28th, every Albanian, whatever his religion or politics, secretly celebrates the anniversary of the first declaration of his country's independence in 1912. The day is sacred to him, and to mark the occasion it is proposed to create a committee of '*Friends of the Albanian People*'. In the meantime, we would strongly urge that this country should espouse the cause and inspire the spirit of a brave and far from helpless people.

Yours, &c., (Signed)

Cecil, Vernon Bartlett, Victor Cazalet, M. E. Durham, R. M. Hodgson, Geoffrey Le M. Mander, E. C. De Renzy-Martin, Philip Noel-Baker, F. W. Pethick-Lawrence and Ben Riley

Proceedings of the Royal Institution of Great Britain, Volume XXXI, 1939-41*

Albania

by Miss M. Edith Durham

I would plead for justice for one of the oldest and now one of the most unfortunate peoples of Europe. Sympathy is warm for the Poles but the Albanians, who have suffered yet more brutal dismemberment at the hands of their more powerful neighbours, are now the battlefield of two rival Powers and threatened with annihilation in a quarrel which is not their own.

The Albanians are descended from the tribes who dwelt in prehistoric times along the Western side of the Balkan peninsula- the Illyrians and the Epirots- before the arrival of either Romans or Slavs. They were not and are not Greeks.

Strabo, writing about the beginning of the Christian era, gives details which show that their tribal system resembled that which has existed until recent times. He states that the frontier of the Greeks was South of the Ambracian Gulf, now the Gulf of Arta. That is further south than today. Albanian territory was taken by the Greeks in 1913. The Illyrians and the Epirots are now known as the Ghegs and Tosks. They speak the same language, have the same customs and form a united nation.

When Rome conquered the Balkan peninsula Christianity reached the Adriatic coast and Illyria formed part of the Patriarchate of Rome. When the decline and fall of the Roman Empire began Roman rule was replaced by Slav rule, the peninsula was invaded by the ancestors of the modern Serbs and for a short time in the Middle Ages they ruled a large part of it.

A contemporary account by the Dominican, Father Brocardus, 1331, shows the Abbanois, as he calls them, speaking their own language, clinging to their Church and 'very harshly oppressed' by their conquerors. The laws enacted by the Serb Tsar, Stefan Dushan, in 1349 show that they were classed as herdsmen serfs. The Serb Empire was short-lived. At its greatest, it lasted but 25 years, the reign of Stefan Dushan. On his death, the conquered peoples and rival chieftains speedily broke it up and the inrush of the Turks destroyed it completely. Meanwhile the Venetians had crept down the coast. Albanian chieftains rose to power in the mountains; together with the Venetians, they long

* Reprinted by courtesy of the Royal Institution of Great Britain

defended Scutari which finally fell in 1478. But the Albanians were the last of the Balkan peoples to be subdued. Led by their great hero Skenderbeg, famed as the champion of Christendom, they offered a magnificent resistance from his stronghold at Kruja. On his death of the fever in 1467, they were leaderless and forced to accept Turkish suzerainty. Their position differed from that of the other conquered peoples as they retained a semi-independence under their own chiefs. Race instinct, that blind unreasoning instinct of self-preservation, drove them against their old oppressor and they sided with the Turks in the endeavour to expel the Serbs. The position of the Serbs in the Kosovo district was made untenable. Led by the Bishop of Ipek, they migrated en masse into lands in Hungary allotted them by the Emperor. The Albanians re-occupied the lands from which their ancestors had been evicted and retained them till 1913.

Turning Moslem in considerable numbers, the courage and intelligence of the Albanians enabled them to rise high in the Turkish army and Government. As did the Roman and the Serbian Empires, so did the Turkish Empire reach its zenith and wane. Towards the beginning of the nineteenth century the subject peoples began to think of independence. Ali Pasha, a mighty chief in South Albania, born at Tepeleni in 1744, revolted, defied the Turks and for some fifty years ruled all South Albania from his capital at Janina; entered into diplomatic relations with Great Britain and France and received many distinguished visitors, notably Lord Byron and Sir Henry Holland. In his old age, he was overpowered by large Turkish forces and his head was carried to Constantinople as a trophy in 1822. I found his name still honoured when I was at Tepeleni in 1904.

Meanwhile Russia fixed greedy eyes on Constantinople and incited and aided Greeks, Serbs and Bulgars to revolt. The Greeks, aided also by Great Britain, were the first to recover independence and be given a foreign king. In 1876-77, came the Russo-Turkish War to liberate the Slavs. Again the Albanians sided with the Turks and put up a very strong resistance to Serb invasion, defending their towns of Djakova, Prizren and Prishtina successfully. Turkish resistance broke at Plevna. There followed the Treaty of Berlin and the Eastern Roumelian Commission. Much wholly Albanian land was allotted to the Serbs, Montenegrins and Greeks. The Albanians formed the League of Prizren, summoned their forces and saved much of it. The northern tribesmen kept the Montenegrins out of Gusinje. I knew fine old Marash Hutzi of Hoti who organized the defence. Dulcigno, a purely Albanian town and Antivari, inhabited solely by Moslem and Catholic Albanians, were handed over to Montenegro. The Janina district, however, was saved from the Greeks and Kosovo from the Serbs.

At this time Lord Goschen and Lord Fitzmaurice on the Eastern Roumelian Commission, strongly favoured forming a large and independent Albania to include all Janina vilayet, all Kosovo vilayet and a considerable part of Macedonia. Lord Fitzmaurice took very great interest in Albania and corresponded with me about it for some fifteen years. He maintained that had an Albanian State been then formed both the Balkans and Europe would have been spared much bloodshed ; each of the respective peoples would have had a fair share and balanced each other. But the prejudice against Moslems was then too strong. I became interested in the Albanian question in 1903. A revolt of the Bulgars of Macedonia who wished to join free Bulgaria was sharply suppressed by the Turks, leaving a mass of burnt villages and starving people. As. I had done much Balkan travel I was asked by the British Macedonian Relief Committee to act as their agent in the Ohrida Presba district. The Turkish Government gave permission and facilities. Our headquarters were at Monastir (now called Bitolj and included in Yugoslavia, but at that time there were no Serbs there). Our assistants, kavasses and interpreters were mostly Albanians obtained from the British and Foreign Bible Society which had a depot at Monastir. From them I learned of the strong nationalist spirit then at work. Without our capable and honest Albanian staff, the work would have been far more difficult. The Governor of Ohrida, too, Mehdi Bey Frasheri, was an Albanian, a just and kindly man who was a great help to me. I regret to say he is now interned in Italy for having opposed the Italian invasion: may he live to see his land restored to independence. When the relief work was ended in the spring of 1904 my Albanian friends begged me not to return to England but to travel through Albania and see conditions for myself.

At this time the Turkish Government, afraid of the rising national spirit of the Albanians, tried to suppress it by forbidding the printing and teaching of the Albanian language under heavy penalties. Faik Bey of Konitza published an Albanian paper in London which was smuggled into the country. George Kyrias, an employee of the Bible Society, prepared some books of the Bible in Albanian and the Society published them. The Society had leave to sell its publications in the Turkish Empire but the Turks had not reckoned on Albanian books. An Albanian colporteur was to try to sell these through the length of Albania. Would I go with him? I joined him at his home at Leskovik. It was an inspiring journey. I first visited Koritza, Korça as the Albanians call it. It was the active centre of the independence movement in South Albania, whose first object was to rid the land of all foreign influence.

A sister of George Kyrias, a brave and very capable woman, went to America aided by the American missionaries, was trained there and on her return was made mistress of a Girls' School under the protection of the American Mission. She used American textbooks, gave her lessons in Albanian and destroyed all writing after the lesson.

The Turks searched vainly for the forbidden language. Christian and Moslem girls flocked to the school, learned to read and write and taught their brothers. All worked hard to counteract the influence of the Greek school and priests which the Turks permitted by way of suppressing Albanian. We went on, wherever we found an Albanian Governor, we were welcome to sell as many books as we could. At Berati, where there was a Turkish one all our Albanian books were confiscated but as we had a secret store awaiting us ahead, this did not matter.

At Berati, I first heard of the efforts being made by the priest, Fan Noli, to form an autocephalous Albanian Orthodox Church and free the land of Greek priests. At Berati, the Christians complained that the Greek priest informed against persons possessing Albanian books. Fan Noli's long years of work were crowned with success after Albania became independent. The autocephalous Albanian Orthodox Church was legally established and there are now no Greek priests in Albania unless some have accompanied the invading Greek army. The clergy are all Albanian and the services are held in Albanian. The Head of the Church is Archbishop Kissi whose seat is at Tirana. The Church is thus on a par with those of the Serbs, Greeks and Bulgars, which are all autocephalous. Bishop Fan Noli is head of the Albanian colony in America.

I would emphasise the formation of the Albanian Orthodox Church as some newspapers describe the South Albanians as 'Greek Church' and its adherents as 'Greeks'. This is as incorrect as it would be to reckon all Roman Catholics as 'Italians'. Not only Christians but Moslems hastened to buy our books. At Elbasan, in about an hour we sold 70 to Moslems. *"Now,"* said a young gendarme joyfully, *"I can teach my young brother to read."* At Elbasan, I found a movement to form an Uniate Church in order to stop Greek influence.

Thus we peddled books through all the towns of Albania and reached Scutarl, travel-worn but satisfied. There were then no made roads, the journey was on horseback, fording rivers where horses nearly swam, plunging through marshy land where they were bogged to the shoulder and had to be dug out, and having to walk when the track was too bad to be safely ridden. Scutari was the centre of the independence movement in the North. Here there were more opportunities for education. Austria and Italy both coveted Albania and each tried to outdo the other in trying, to win over the Albanians. So there were schools both for girls and boys, a boarding school for the mountain boys, a technical school and a printing press all under Austrian or Italian protection. The Albanians profited and studied eagerly.

Then came the Young Turk revolution in the summer of 1908. It promised freedom and equality for all. The Albanians played a major part in its first successes. The Kosovo men marched on Uskub (now called Skopje but then a largely Albanian town). They evicted the old governors from the district and occupied the town. Our Vice-Consul, a friend of the Albanians, testified to the good behaviour of the Albanian troops.

The Constitution was proclaimed, Scutari was wild with joy. Thousands of mountain men, in finest array, marched into the town, were feted and feasted. We fired revolvers (I had one in each hand) into the air till not a cartridge was left. Not an accident nor any disorder occurred. Said the French Vice-Consul: *"What a people this would be with a good government!"* They went back to their mountains happy and hopeful.

There was to be freedom of the press. Albanian newspapers sprang up like mushrooms in the night. Schools were opened with great rapidity. A Congress for the standardization of the alphabet and orthography was held at Monastir and a universal one adopted. The foreign schools had used separate systems. Long live Albania! She was to have her chance at last. Never again shall I see such a joyous resurrection of a people.

I went over the mountains to Djakova which had long been closed to foreigners and over the Kosovo plain to Prizren, Prishtina and Mitrovitza, back through Mirdita to Scutari. Everywhere the Albanians meant to have freedom.

Alas! The Young Turks made every possible blunder. Rightly handled, the Albanians would have supported them as before against foes. But before the year was out the Albanians realised that no freedom was to be expected. I talked in vain to the two Young Turk Governors. Greece, Serbia, Bulgaria and Montenegro were all determined not to let the Young Turks succeed, for this would mean no more chance of land-grabbing. They formed the Balkan League to overthrow the Young Turk Government before it should have time to consolidate.

In 1910, the Albanians of Kosovo revolted, being encouraged to do so by the Serbs who promised them help. They were led by the gallant Isa Boletin. Glad news came to Scutari. Isa had made terms with the Serbs. A Serb officer and his men were aiding him, even sharing quarters with him. Serbia had recognised Albania's right to independence. The age-long feud between Serb and Albanian was to cease. Isa believed and trusted the Serb and was cruelly deceived. The Serb in question was

Colonel Dimitrijevitch, a leader of the gang which so brutally murdered King Alexander and Queen Draga in 1903, and head of the notorious Black Hand Society which planned a few years later the murder of the Archduke Franz Ferdinand and launched the World War in 194. One of the greatest criminals of his time. Disguised as Albanians, Dimitrijevitch and his men committed many murders, among them that of Popovitch, the Governor of Berani, who though a Montenegrin by birth was a supporter of the Young Turks and wished to make Berani a little model province. He was hacked to pieces and the crime was ascribed to the Albanians. But his widow, a Frenchwoman, declared to me that the Serbs had killed him. This revolt of the Albanians succeeded in completely alienating them from the Turks, as the Serbs intended it should do.

In 1911, the King of Montenegro offered to help the tribesmen of the Northern mountains to obtain freedom. They too believed him and rose. I was at Constantinople and returned in haste. The revolt was in full swing. King Nikola asked me to aid the crowd of women and children who had fled into Montenegro in wretched plight. Montenegro was supplying the rebels with arms, ammunition and advice. They put up a gallant fight but were crushed by the arrival of a large Turkish army. The Turkish Government ordered King Nikola to make peace at once. The dismay of the tribesmen whom he had promised to stand by till they were free was piteous. They were commanded to return at once to their burnt villages but refused. The situation was very critical and the Montenegrin Government asked me to act as intermediary. They made it a condition that I should go with them. Mr. Charles Crane gave me £200, I raised more money and spent an arduous winter in relief work.

Then came the Balkan wars of 1912-13. By their cunning policy the Serbs had cruelly tricked the Albanians. They had separated them from the Turks and used them to drive the Turks from Kosovo. Far from fulfilling their promises to help the Albanians to liberty, the Serbs and Montenegrin armies fell upon them with ferocity. The Albanians were trapped and unable to obtain ammunition from either side. The Serbs ruthlessly massacred wholesale. In Montenegro, at the inn dinner table I heard a Serb officer boast how his men had slaughtered men, women and children of the Luma tribe. *"You must kill the women,"* he said, *"they breed men"* and laughed till he choked over his beer. The Montenegrins cut off the lips and noses of prisoners and the dead and showed them as trophies, and burnt and looted. They boasted that when they took Scutari they would cut the throats of its inhabitants. The sad news came that Janina had fallen. Ismail Kemal, the Albanian leader in the south, appealed to the Powers and proclaimed the Independence of Albania, on November 28, 1912, at Valona. The claim of Albania was recognised and the Montenegrins were ordered to withdraw from the siege of Scutari. They obtained its surrender by means of a Quisling. Essad Pasha Toptani, a man detested save by the men of his own clan, was an officer in the Turkish army within Scutari. Terms were offered him through the medium of the Italian Consulate in Scutari. He and his men would be allowed to march out fully armed and he should be made Prince of a small Principality if he could contrive the surrender of the town. Essad then murdered the Turkish commander, Hussein Riza Bey, and admitted the Montenegrins just as the mountain men, who perceived too late how they had been tricked, were about to march to the town's relief. The Montenegrins set fire to the bazaar and looted it. The Powers ordered the Montenegrins to clear out. They made a last and strange attempt to hold it. Petar Plamenatz, who had been made Governor, offered me the Governorship of Scutari- he to be nominal and I actual Governor- if I would persuade the tribesmen to ask for Montenegrin rule. *"They will follow you,"* he said, *"speak the word, I implore."* He offered bribes. *"Impossible,"* said I. *"But why?"* *"Because,"* I said sternly, *"I have been lied to too often."* He showed no anger. He said, *"Alas, alas, Mlle. This time I swear I am telling the truth!"*

An international naval force steamed up the river and as Admiral Burney landed the Montenegrin army marched out over the bridge. Albania was saved. I spent the winter feeding and clothing the half-starved Scutarenes and mountain folk.

The mountains were full of Moslem survivors, escaped from the lands taken by the Montenegrins and Serbs, telling tales of horror. Men were roasted by fires to make them accept baptism. Women herded into church and their veils torn from them. If the poor, dazed victims did not answer next day to their Christian names they were beaten and in some cases raped. Two wretched widows told how the Serbs had cut the arteries of elbows and wrists of their husbands and danced round while their victims bled to death. The grisly pantomime by which they described it made its truth clear. Briefly, the Serbs called this cleaning the land.

I did my best, too, to keep the peace among the foreign armies of occupation which arrived and had jurisdiction for some twelve miles round Scutari. Intrigue was rampant. Luckily in some crucial moments the tribesmen consulted me and I was able to get them to listen to the Admiral, which enraged some foreign officers.

Mr. Nevinson, the well-known war correspondent and Mr. Erikson, an American missionary, arrived and asked me to ride with them through Albania. We found perfect order kept by a small provisional government in every town and were welcomed everywhere. There was dread of Essad the traitor and hopes that soon the Powers would send the promised King.

We went to Ohrida, where large Serb forces were making ready to fight the Bulgars, and thence to Koritza, where we went to the schoolhouse. Heavy Greek forces occupied the town. Orders were being given that shop fronts were to be painted Greek colours. We were hailed as saviours. The Greeks. held the telegraph lines and Koritza was cut off from the world. Save us from the Greeks we were implored. We visited the Greek commander, Colonel Kondoulis. He made no concealment of his intention not only to keep Koritza but to take the whole of South Albania up to Tepeleni, as he showed on a map. I protested that the lands were wholly Albanian and he had no right whatever to them. He replied, *"Appetite comes with eating. We have eaten and shall eat more!"* I said, *"He that eats too much gets the bellyache."* Nevinson said, *"Take care, those fellows are furious."*

On returning to the schoolhouse - the Greeks had closed the school - we learned that Greek soldiers were making a house to house visit, ordering every inhabitant to come to a public meeting to vote for what form of government they wished. This was obviously arranged to impress us. Lest we should be made fools of and put on the platform with the Greeks, we went out and the officer sent to fetch us was too late. We arrived late at the meeting. Surrounded by Greek troops the populace was said to have voted unanimously to be Greek and a telegram to that effect was sent to the Ambassadors' conference in London. From both without and within the town we were begged to save them. We hired a guide and started on a two and a half days ride over rough mountain tracks to Valona which was in Albanian hands. Nevinson drafted a telegram explaining how the Greek vote had been obtained. Koritza was allotted to Albania and saved. At Valona we were met with a deputation of fine fellows from the Chiameria, also occupied by the Greeks, who begged earnestly to be saved but their prayer was in vain.

I left Albania at Christmas, 1913 and returned to Durazzo in April, 1914, where the Powers of Europe had appointed the Prince zu Wied as King. Why they agreed to choose him is a mystery, since France, Russia, Italy, the Greeks and the Serbs had agreed together to expel him and permit no German influence in Albania.

Wied was a well-meaning man but was never given a chance. He fell into the hands of the traitor Essad Pasha, who went to meet him and so gained his confidence that he made Essad his Minister of War. I landed at Durazzo to find a whirlpool of intrigue. The French Commissioner, a Polish Jew born in Bosnia (Krajewsky), told me that France would never permit an independent Albania; a Russian journalist and Dr. Dillon were backing Essad. I had a long talk with Wied and begged him not to trust Essad but to make a tour of the country with me. He hesitated too long. Essad as War Minister had control of the arms; he armed the men of his own district and also a large force of refugees from Dibra, which had been given to the Serbs. They were told that if they would expel Wied, Dibra would be returned to them. They rose, the signal for attack being given by an Italian, Colonel Muricchio, waving a red lantern at night. The British Vice-Consul saw him and he was arrested. So was Essad, who ought to have been court-martialled and shot. The Italians made a great uproar, Muricchio had to be released and Wied feared to act. Each of the Powers had a warship lying off Durazzo and Essad was put on board the Austrian warship. The Italians claimed him and cleared decks for action. The world war might have begun then had not Austria released Essad, who was taken by the Italians to Rome, feted and decorated.

The attack on Durazzo was a failure in spite of Italian efforts. The town was well defended by the little body of Dutch gendarmerie appointed by the Powers as Wied's guard. The rebels sued for truce but hardly was truce made when there came news that the Greeks were invading South Albania and that Koritza was threatened. Sir Harry Lamb, the British Commissioner, sent me to Valona to investigate. It was too true. The Greeks and Serbs had planned a simultaneous attack. The refugees were streaming down to the coast. Valona was thronged. Under every tree or shelter for miles around men, women and children were falling exhausted from a flight for life from their burning villages. The detachment of Dutch gendarmes who were in charge of Koritza had resisted till overwhelmed by superior forces and then had fled with the rest. They gave terrible accounts of the sufferings and deaths that occurred in the rush over the mountains.

Athens, when remonstrated with, denied complicity and declared it to be a local rising of so-called 'Christian Epirots' against the Moslems. This was quite untrue; the local Christians did all they could to aid their Moslem brethren. As Sir Harry Lamb said, the so-called Epirots were in fact Cretans. The leader was a Greek, Zographos.

An International Committee, of which I was a member, toiled to save the starving, suffering people. I shall never forget the miserable children dying under the trees. I obtained but very little condensed milk and there were at very least 50,000 refugees. A small ration of bread per head per day was the most we could do.

The Greeks were said to be approaching Valona. Where the army was we did not know. Athens continued to deny its existence. So I went myself two days' ride up country to spy its position. Not far from Tepeleni on the opposite side of a deep valley when I crawled along the mountainside, I saw through field glasses, a large military camp with soldiers in khaki, tents and horses, as unlike a band of local revolutionaries as could well be imagined.

I returned in hot haste in one day, hoping to put pressure on Athens, and found that Russia and Germany had declared war. The Great War had begun. Austria's declaration of war on Serbia was greeted with wild joy by the Albanians. The Serbs would be justly punished for the murder of the Archduke and Kosovo would be restored to Albania. We were cut off from all news. I crossed to Brindisi to get news, meaning to return if all was well and learned to my dismay that we had declared war forty-eight hours earlier. There was nothing for it but to return to England.

The Serb attack on Albania ceased . . . the Italians landed at Valona and stopped the Greek advance . . . the French occupied Koritza, proclaiming a Republic. During the war, though Albania had been declared neutral and independent by the Powers, it was entered by Serb, Montenegrin, French, Italian, Austrian and British troops. The Prince of Wied left on September 3 and Essad returned. By now the rebels saw how they had been tricked and telegraphed to Wied to return; he never did.

In April 1915, the British Government made a secret treaty by which Albania was to be divided between Greece and the Serbs, Essad to have his Principality. He acted as French agent all through and was well paid. The secret treaty was published by the Bolsheviks in 1917. Colonel the Hon. Aubrey Herbert formed a strong committee to struggle for Albania's independence: Sir Samuel Hoare, Lord Moyne and Lord Harlech were members of it; I was Honorary Secretary. We had the support of Lord Cecil and later of Lord Balfour. After much hard work Albania was again made an independent state and a member of the League of Nations but unfortunately the Serbs were permitted to retain territory with some 800,000 Albanians and the Greeks also retained the wholly Albanian Ciameria.

Both Serb and Greek reckoned the Moslems as Turks, expropriated them and expelled them in numbers, penniless, to Turkey. Not a single Albanian school has been provided for those that remain. Their numbers have been so reduced as to make them powerless and they have been deprived of civil rights in Greece.

When I returned to Albania in 1921, a council of three Regents was ruling at the head of a Parliament. All seemed going smoothly; there was no national debt; Essad dared not claim his principality and to make sure that he should not do so, a young Albanian shot him in Paris, where he was living on French money. The outlook was hopeful and there was perfect order.

But oil was the undoing of Albania. It was believed to exist in large quantities. The wise priest Fan Noli thought it better for Albania to remain poor for a time than to grant large oil concessions to foreign Powers. Others favoured getting rich quickly. Ahmet Zogu of Mati, now known as King Zog and Fan Noli's rival for the Presidency, promised a big concession to the Anglo-Persian Oil Company and one to Italy. He obtained the support of Great Britain and the Anglo-Persian started boring.

In memory of her son, Aubrey Herbert, Elizabeth Lady Carnarvon started her noble work. She equipped a hospital at Valona, built and equipped a library, sent a scoutmaster to start boy scouts, which were very popular, and began anti-malarial work. British officers were appointed to train the gendarmerie. All looked well. Alas the Anglo-Persian found no oil worth working and withdrew. Italy, on the contrary, found good oil. Had we obtained the concession which the Italians did, Albania's fate would have been very different. As it was, it became Italy's sphere of influence..

The boy scouts were first suppressed and finally the British officers dismissed. Italy undertook to finance Albania and to make roads and bridges. Albania, which at first thought of Italy as a protection against Greeks and Serbs, became uneasy as Italy dug her claws in deeper and deeper. Some attempts to resist, made by the rising generation, many of whom had been educated abroad, were suppressed.

Then came the fatal Good Friday, when we all looked on and let a huge mechanised force overwhelm the little land and presented Italy with the control of the Straits of Otranto. At Durazzo, the gendarmerie and the cadets put up a brave fight. But the warships bombarded the tiny town and forced a landing. A pathetic incident was that when planes flew over Tirana, the populace thought they were English planes coming to their rescue. But they dropped leaflets saying that if further resistance were offered the town would be destroyed. Having no anti-aircraft guns- none could be offered.

Very briefly this is the sad tale of a small and fine people who want only to live their own lives on their own land. Should any further disrmemberment of their lands take place they are threatened with extinction, for neither neighbour has shown them any mercy.

In the years when I lived among them, I found the Albanians loyal, grateful and kindly. That they are highly intelligent is proved by the fact that those who have managed to come to England for education have taken good degrees at the London University. Their beautiful silver work and fine embroideries show them to be the artists of the Balkans. Do not let them be offered up as a human sacrifice either to appease our foes or propitiate our Allies.

[M.E.D.]

New Times and Ethiopia News, October 1941
Miss Durham and Albania

'Honour to whom honour is due.' May I correct a statement in your issue of September 20? I did not found the Anglo-Albanian Association. Its existence was due entirely to the initiative of the late Colonel the Hon. Aubrey Herbert.

He started work for Albania's independence during the Balkan war of 1912-13, when on the defeat of the Turks, this was an urgent question. The Serbs and Greeks had planned to divide Albania between them, leaving only a tiny principality for their tool, the traitor, Essad Pasha. Colonel Herbert's committee, with Mr. J. C. Paget as Hon. Secretary, worked hard to ventilate the Albanian question and push Albania's claims. I was not in England at the time and did not return till after Albania had been recognised by the Powers as a neutral and independent State.

The committee then lapsed, having no further work to do. Towards the end of the Great War it was again clear that Albania's independence was threatened by the Serbs and Greeks. On February 28th, 1918, Colonel Herbert called a meeting at the House of Commons and proposed to reconstruct a society *'for maintaining the rights and welfare of Albania'*. There were present Lord Lamington, Major the Hon. George Peel, M.P., Mr. H. W. Nevinson, Mr. Mark Judge and myself. Mr. Paget and I were asked to become joint Hon. Secretaries. An executive council was formed; Colonel Herbert as president, Lord Lamington vice-president, Dr. C. W. Cunnington, Mr. Morton F. Eden, Colonel the Hon. Walter Guinness, M.P. (now Lord Moyne), Colonel the Hon. Cuthbert James, M.P., Mr. Mark Judge, Mr. C. F. Ryder, Mr. E. McRury, Major George Paget and General George Phillips. The Hon. W. Ormesby Gore, M.P. (now Lord Harlech), Lord Treowen, Sir Samuel Hoare, M.P., Colonel Amery, M.P., and others were members of the Association. It met in committee rooms of the House of Commons and owed its driving force to Colonel Herbert and his influential friends in both Houses.

Finally, after many meetings and much hard work, Albania was admitted as member of the League of Nations. At a final meeting of the Association on February 17th, 1921, Colonel Herbert gave a short account of Albania's admission to the League, and it was agreed that the next step was to approach the League and obtain through it, if possible, the evacuation by the Serbs of the Northern Mountains and the Dibra district, which they had seized, and which were within the limits of the frontiers de-limited for Albania in 1913. This the League accomplished.

Italy had already withdrawn from Valona and renounced all claims on it. Albania being thus freed, the Association ceased to function, except that it raised the fund in December, 1923, to aid the starving populations of the Dibra district and the Northern mountains, which had suffered by Serb invasion.

My own part in all this work was purely secretarial - writing to the Press, to private individuals, and drafting questions as directed by the Council. It was not on behalf of Italy that France and Russia protested when Sir Edward Grey wished to send me to Albania in 1915 to collect recruits. It was because they both wished North Albania to be given to the Serbs, and the Serbian representatives here were against my raising the Albanians. As it happened, my health was too bad to permit of my going. Albania is again threatened with destruction. It is to be hoped that justice will again prevail, and this, one of the oldest of the peoples of Europe, be allowed to carry on an independent existence. In 1913, we guaranteed it as '*a neutral and independent State*'.

M. E. Durham

Dielli, Boston, Mass., July 29th 1942

Dear Faik Konitza,

I write in great anxiety as to the fate of your country. The matter is urgent. One thing only can save it and that is that the Albanians now in U.S.A. and England should present a united front.

All personal dislikes and differences of opinion must be dropped. There is one point upon which all can unite, and that is to demand and obtain the integrity and independence of their country. Party politics must not be permitted to dismember the country and bring it to ruin.

When the house is on fire it is madness to discuss who has a right to the best room in the house. It is a case of all hands to the pumps.

Your friends in England are surprised and grieved that you have not yet all joined in an All Albanian Congress, no matter who is its president. Get the American missionaries and school teachers to join in a great appeal to the U.S.A. Government.

President Wilson played a large part in obtaining Albania's independence. Try to get President Roosevelt to uphold that act of justice.

I hope and trust that my respected friend Mgr. Fan Noli will agree to this. Make an appeal to the love of the American people for freedom and independence and tell them that all Albanians - whether Orthodox, Moslem or Catholic - have but one desire, that their lands may be restored to them whole and free.

I implore you not to waste time over minor differences.

Please give my cordial regards to Mgr. Fan Noli.

All good wishes from your old friend,

(Signed) M. E. Durham

The Manchester Guardian, December 4th 1942
Albania

To the Editor of the Manchester Guardian

Sir,

On November 18, 1913, Albania's independence was proclaimed at Valona and subsequently recognised by the Great Powers. Albania was later admitted as a member of the League of Nations and her status as an independent nation confirmed. Nevertheless, when the small country was invaded by a large mechanised force, not one of Albania's fellow-members of the League intervened to save her. The Mediterranean Fleet lay idle and the Italian fleet poured in troops uninterrupted. In fact, we offered up Albania as a human victim to '*appease*' Mussolini, regardless of the fact that it is impossible to glut a greedy adventurer by giving him more food.

What has been the result of our action - or, rather, inaction? The Adriatic became an inland sea for the Axis, with Italy commanding its entrance. Until we break down that command the Axis can, and doubtless does, build U-boats and ships of all kinds in safety in the magnificent ports of Trieste (formerly the base of the Austrian Navy), Pola, and Fiume.

Meanwhile the Albanians have been left in most painful uncertainty as to the fate of their country. Now is the time to relieve them of anxiety and assure them that their independence will be restored and their integrity guaranteed. This alone is needed for a rising against the Italian invader to take place. Guerrilla fighting, sniping of Italians, and sabotage have gone on, but fear lest the departure of the Italians would be followed only by a partition of their lands between Balkan neighbours has caused and is causing great uncertainty among Albanians both in Albania and abroad as to the best course to pursue.

Remove this anxiety - let the Albanians assist at clearing the enemy from the mouth of the Adriatic. Guarantee Albania's integrity and independence and we shall have no more reliable and efficient allies than the Albanians. Assure them that the Atlantic Charter is not a meaningless document. Let them assist in opening the way to Pola and Trieste.

Yours, &c.,

M. E. Durham.
London, N.W. 3, December 1

The New Statesman & Nation, January 17th 1942
The Case of Albania

Sir,

I am glad that you have published a letter on the case for Albania, and endorse every word of it. It is a case that should be supported by all lovers of justice and freedom.

The Ethiopians and the Albanians were ruthlessly sacrificed by us in the hope that by so doing we should appease Mussolini. Both were members of the League of Nations and entitled to our support. Neither obtained it. Nor did we buy peace!

That we should see them both righted is urgently necessary if we wish to preserve - and deserve - our name as champion of the oppressed. Had the oil concession granted to us by Albania proved to be of value, it is unlikely that we should have allowed Italy to grab the land. Let it not appear that we champion only lands from which we expect immediate commercial benefit.

The Albanians are some of the oldest of the peoples of Europe. Through the Roman, the Byzantine, the Serb and the Turkish empires, they have preserved their language and their sturdy individuality. After each empire collapsed they have risen again undaunted. That they should not only be allowed, but also aided, to survive the tin-pot empire of Mussolini is but their due.

But, so far, our Government has not given them a definite promise. On the eve of November 28, Albania's Independence Day, I was called on the phone by the B.B.C. and asked to send a message of greeting to the Albanians. I replied that I wished them a speedy restoration to independence, and was told that the Foreign Office would not permit this message to be sent. I protested in vain.

Ill-armed and unaided, the Albanians have harassed and sabotaged the Italians. But they have had no encouragement to believe that by making a combined effort they would obtain liberty. Above all, they dread lest their land be partitioned and they themselves handed over as spoils of war. The Albanians are neither Slavs nor Greeks. They wish to live at peace with their neighbours, but not to be subjected to them.

If justice is to survive and the Atlantic Charter to be a valid and not a mere makeshift document, let Albania's claim to be independent be recognised at once. We shall thus gain a brave ally and save our reputation for honesty.

M. E. Durham

New Times and Ethiopia News, January 16th 1943
Albania's Fight for Freedom
by M. E. Durham

Miss Durham, authoress, social worker and traveller, is an authority on Balkan questions.

I.

Forty years ago, I first learnt of Albania's fight for freedom. But it had been going on much longer The Albanians survived the Roman Empire, the Byzantine Empire, the short-lived Serbian Empire, and even under the Turkish Empire never lost entirely a certain amount of autonomy, especially in the remoter mountain lands. At the beginning of the 19th century the great Ali Pasha of Tepeleni freed all South Albania for a time and ruled it from Janina. Finally overpowered and killed by a large Turkish army, Albania fell again under Turkish rule. But the struggle for independence went on.

After the Russo-Turkish war of 1877/78, new frontiers were drawn, and the subject races received extensions of territory. Bulgaria was freed, Serbia and Montenegro enlarged. At this time Lord Fitzmaurice, who was a member of the Eastern Roumelia frontier commission, was strongly in favour of creating a large independent Albania, full details of which can be found in the contemporary Blue Book. It was to include Janina and the provinces of Monastir (Bitolja) and of Kosovo, in which the Albanians then had a very large majority.

Lord Fitzmaurice, with whom I was in correspondence for many years, maintained that had this plan been adopted the various peoples of the Balkans would have been about equally divided, and that this would have made for peace. The Albanians of Kosovo formed the League of Prisren, to oppose the loss of lands with which they were threatened. Major George Paget, whose house still stands in Scutari, joined the League. Janina and Gusinje then were saved, but the wholly Albanian town of Dulcigno was torn from them by Mr. Gladstone, who sent a fleet of the European Powers to demonstrate off the coast in 1880 and order the surrender of the town to the Montenegrins, who had failed to take it. The Albanians had to yield to superior force and thus lost valuable coastland. Gusinje was saved by Marash Hutzi of the Hoti tribe, whom I knew well in his old age. He told how he rallied the northern tribesmen and drove off the Montenegrin troops that came to seize it.

Albania did not obtain independence then; but never gave up hoping for it. The Turks began to see Albania as a possible danger. The Greeks, the Serbs and the Bulgars had all been allowed to have their own schools and churches within the Turkish Empire. It became a race between the three to plant schools and appoint bishops in as many places as possible To move a bishop and say *"Check to your King."* Intrigue and jealousy raged. The Turkish Government, seeing how schools ended in producing revolts which the Powers supported, forbade the opening of any Albanian schools, and forbade under heavy penalties the printing and circulation of any papers or books in Albanian. But the Albanians were not without friends. Their intelligence and their honesty gained them the support of the American missionaries and of the British and Foreign Bible Society in the South, and in the North the Catholics were under the protection of Austria. Thus Skodra (Scutari) in the North and Korcha in the South became the two centres of Albanian Nationalism.

Such was the situation when I first was introduced to the Albanian question just over forty years ago, and promised the Albanians that I would do all I could to help them to achieve liberty. It has been a long journey. Many gallant men, much younger than myself, have fallen by the way. The champions of freedom with whom I worked in the North - Bairam Tsuri, the mountain chieftain, Hil Mossi, Gurikuchi, Ivanaj, Hussain Bey of Pristina, all are gone. In the South, Faik Konitza, whose whole life was given to the freeing of Albania, has just passed away. The gallant Kyrias and Dako families, heroes of Korcha; and perhaps the greatest of all Albania's champions, Mgr. Fan Noli, are still with us. Young Albania is awake and active. I have entered my eightieth year. I can no longer spend days on horseback and climbing mountains, but I hope to live to see Albania restored to freedom and her frontiers extended to include the many who now are under foreign rule.

Miss Durham on Albania

Miss M. E. Durham, the veteran protagonist of Albanian freedom, who has given forty years of devoted service in that cause, in an article published on this page rightly stresses the importance of schools in stimulating patriotism and love of liberty, and records that the two main centres of Albanian Nationalism were those in which education was not altogether denied to the people.

New Times and Ethiopia News, January 23rd 1943
Albania's Fight for Freedom
by M. E. Durham

Miss Durham, authoress, social worker and traveller,
is an authority on Balkan questions.

II.

Forty years ago I first took part in Albania's fight for freedom. I had already some Balkan experience, in Serbia, Bosnia and Montenegro, and had visited Scutari (Skodra), when I was asked in the winter of 1903-4 to go as relief agent to Macedonia by the British Relief Committee.

In 1903, the Bulgar peasants of Macedonia revolted against Turkish rule and desired union with free Bulgaria. The revolt was crushed by Turkish troops. Bulgar villages were burnt and looted; it was a bitter winter and suffering was intense. Our task as relief agents was hard. It was greatly facilitated by the able Albanian assistants recommended to us by the British and Foreign Bible Society, which had a centre at Monastir (now Bitolja). At that time the printing of the Albanian language and the circulation of any printed matter in Albanian was prohibited by the Turkish Government under very heavy penalties. The possession of an Albanian newspaper published abroad might lead to its owner's ruin.

The Bible Society had leave to sell its publications in the Turkish Empire. One of its employés, George Kyrias, a very cultivated man and a patriotic Albanian, prepared an Albanian version of a book of the Gospels and Genesis, and the Society published them.

In the Spring of 1904 our relief work ended. Another rising was expected, and the British government recommended all relief agents to return home or stay at their own peril.

I had been stationed at Ohrida, ably aided by a young Christian Albanian, Konstantin Tsillis, now dead, and by the local Governor, an Albanian, Mehdi Bey Frasheri, who was noteworthy for his justice and kindness. One, in fact, of Albania's best patriots and now alas interned in Italy. Through them, it was suggested that I should travel with an Albanian colporteur of the Bible Society from the South to the North of Albania, and assist in the sale of contraband Albanian Gospels.

Off I started, and picked up the colporteur and his pack mule at his native village. The first town on my route was Korcha, where I was put up at the American Girls' school. Here I was at once in the centre of everything. Korcha was, and is, the home of Albanian nationalism in the South. The Albanian school at Korcha existed under American protection. The American missionaries were allowed to work in the Turkish Empire - in fact the Turks were much more tolerant than they were usually given credit for. And that Mission had done a mighty work for numbers of Balkan people, not least for the Albanians. Sevasti Kyrias, the gallant headmistress of the school, was trained in America. She used American textbooks, but taught in Albanian. Both Moslem and Christian girls attended the school, which was known as the Beacon Light. The girls taught their brothers. All written lessons in the school were destroyed after the lesson. Turkish inspectors searched in vain for documents in the Albanian language. Dreading the rise and spread of a national Albanian movement, the Turks encouraged Greek propaganda. Having recently beaten the Greeks they did not regard them as a danger. In the Eastern Orthodox Church, unlike the usage of Rome, the use of the local language and local autonomy is the rule. Thus we find the Orthodox Church of Roumania, of Serbia, of Russia, of Bulgaria, etc.

The Christians of South Albania were now demanding the right to their own Church, their own priests, and their own language. The leader of the movement was the brave young priest Fan Noli. To this man Albania owes more than it can ever repay. He had to contend with the Turkish Government and the Greek priesthood, and risked his life in so doing. But he led his flock to freedom, and is now Mgr. Fan Noli, head of the Church of Albania. But in 1904, Sevasti Kyrias taught the girls of Korcha, and Fan Noli was working for an autonomous Church. Korcha was a centre of life and aspiration. Moslem and Christian were united in their efforts to free Albania. The Moslems of South Albania belong, for the most part, to the tolerant and charitable Bektashi sect.

The colporteur and I went our way, visiting all the chief towns between Korcha and Scutari, and some villages - Premeti, Tepeleni, Valona, Fieri, Berat, Elbasan, Pekinj, Durazzo, Tirana, Kruja, Alessio, Scutari. It was an inspiring journey, worth all the hardships and fatigues. All along our route our Albanian Gospels and Genesis had ready sale. Both Moslems and Christians bought, though they knew that both Greek priests and consuls would betray them to the Turkish police if they were detected.

At Berat, the governor was a Turk and we were brought before him at once by the police. He confiscated all our Albanian books and explained that he had no objection to Christianity as such. We might sell as many Gospels as we pleased in English, French, Latin - in anything but Albanian. The colporteur took it calmly, being aware that we should find a fresh supply which had been smuggled into Elbasan. But Berat folk complained bitterly of the work of Greek agents there.

At Tepeleni, the birthplace of the great Ali Pasha, we were very well received. His was still a name to conjure with. There were the ruins of his castle, and I was told how he had entertained Lord Byron. The local Governor was very friendly, and gave me a photograph he had taken of the rocky seat where the great Pasha used to sit. What Tepeleni wanted was independence as in Ali's day.

At Elbasan, where the Governor was an Albanian recently returned from governing Tripoli (the town now in the front of news), we were received with enthusiasm. The old man could not do enough for us. Sell our books? Yes, as many as possible. He was all for freeing Albania. He entertained me at his house, and arranged for me a visit to the district of Spata, which, as he said, was almost free already. Each man had two names - a Christian one and a Moslem one, e.g., Konstantin Suliman. When called on for military service, they used their Christian names and claimed exemption. When told to pay the poll tax, they gave Moslem names and refused to pay. I spent a most interesting day with them. The Elbasan Christians were strongly anti-Greek. They went so far as to try to form an Uniate Church, and had sent a delegate to Rome for this purpose. Rome granted their prayer and the delegate, with whom I had a long talk, was planning to build a church. He procured a site, but permission to build had to be obtained from the Turkish government and this he had not yet secured. Here we sold a great many books, many to Moslems. I remember the joy of a young gendarme who said, *"Now I can teach my young brother to read."*

Finally we reached Scutari, travel-worn and fatigued, for there were very few roads; we scrabbled over stony tracks, were bogged in mudholes, forded deep streams perilously, save where a dug-out tree trunk served as ferryboat. Inns supplied no food - nothing but an empty room. We picked up food at the local cookshop, save when given hospitality But it was worth the toil to see the uprising and rebirth of a people, the oldest inhabitants of the Balkans, second to none in courage and intelligence - a people worthy to take their place in Europe and be given a fair deal.

It was thus that I was initiated forty years ago into Albania's fight for freedom in the South. Of the struggle in the North with Scutari as centre, I must tell in another chapter.

New Times and Ethiopia News,
February 13th 1943

Albania's Fight for Freedom

by M. Edith Durham

Miss Durham, authoress, social worker and traveller, is an authority on Balkan questions.

III.

Just as Korcha was the centre of Albanian nationalism in the South, so was Shkodra (Scutari) in the North. And, as the Albanian language was protected in Korcha by the American mission, so was it protected in the Scutari by Austria and Italy. In the South, the enemy was Greece; in the North, the Serbs and Montenegrins.

The Christians of North Albania are Catholics, and have been for a very long time. These lands in ancient days formed part of the Patriarchate of Rome before the advent of the, then, pagan Slavs. Austria had a protectorate over the Catholics of Albania, and had established not only schools but a printing press worked by the Jesuits, which issued some of the earliest printed Albanian books.

The Franciscans not only had a school for boys (and one for girls managed by the Poor Clare sisters), but also trained Albanians as priests, and almost every Northern tribe had a Franciscan officiating in a tiny little church in the mountains. These men, having had part of their training in Austria, were missionaries not only of religion but of civilisation, and devoted themselves whole-heartedly to the task of training their flocks to better ways of life. I had many friends among them and cannot speak too highly of their patient and unselfish lives.

Naturally, to be freed from Turkish rule and make Albania independent was the deep-rooted desire of the Catholics.

Schools in the mountain regions are (or were then) almost impossible, the houses being so scattered and the tracks rough, but a boarding school for mountain boys was started in Scutari, and in the Mirdite tribe, under the Mitred Abbot of the Mirdites, Mgr. Premi Dochi, there was a small school. Also the priest of the Klementi tribe had a school. Thus under Austrian protection both girls and boys learned not only to read and write their own tongue, but also to speak and write some foreign language - German, or Italian, or French. The Italians started their work much later and tried hard to compete with Austria. When Austria opened a hospital - a very good one, too (I was there as a patient for two months, and the able Dalmatian doctor saved my life) - Italy retorted with a dispensary, and founded a good technical school and a boys' school. And in order to prevent unity among the Albanians used in her schools a different alphabet and orthography for Albanian. As the American school in Korcha used a third alphabet this was extremely confusing. The Albanians accepted gladly all and any advantages offered them and remained Albanian. Such was the situation in 1908, when the Young Turk revolution took place.

I was up in the mountains at the house of Dom Ernesto, the priest of Rechi, when the news came, brought hurriedly and excitedly. I returned at once to Scutari and lived through days of such rejoicing and enthusiasm as I shall never again see. Under the Constitution, we were told, all would be free and equal. Freedom of the Press, freedom for schools. Thousands of mountain men swarmed into the town in their finest clothes. Scutari feasted them nobly. And, in Albanian fashion, all showed their joy by firing revolvers in the air. Along with them I ran round the Cathedral with a revolver in each hand. And we fired for two days, until not a cartridge was left in the town. And save for a man who shot his own foot, not an accident occurred. All shouted *"Liria"* (freedom) till they were hoarse and finally retired to their homes, believing that an earthly Paradise would begin. Alas for their cruel disappointment!

At the beginning all went well. Schools were opened and newspapers sprang up like mushrooms in the night. There was a rush for education. A Conference of educated Albanian leaders was summoned to meet at Monastir (now Bitolja), which was then regarded as an Albanian town, to decide upon an alphabet for all Albania and unify the language. The Abbot Premi Dochi took an important part in it and had a long talk with me before setting out. It ended in the Latin alphabet being adopted for universal use, and the *'freak'* letters used by the American mission and the Bible Society were wisely dropped.

Peace was sworn all over the country. Tribal feuds were dropped. Travel in the Kosovo district had been difficult and almost impossible, as the Albanians there were very suspicious of all foreigners, whom they distrusted as possible spies, and, in fact, with much reason. The way was now open, so I started with my trusty guide Marko for Prizren and Djakova, both renowned Albanian strongholds. These districts, in fact, were almost autonomous and very jealously guarded.

I was the first stranger in Djakova for many a long year. I stayed at the house of the Catholic schoolmaster. Djakova was by a very large majority

Moslem. There were a few Serb Orthodox houses segregated on one side of the town.

The whole surrounding country was solidly Albanian and partly Catholic. The Catholic villages were visited by two priests and a Franciscan, Father Palitch, a cultivated and brave man. He died later as a martyr to his faith, bayoneted to death by the Montenegrins for refusing to make the sign of the Cross in Orthodox fashion.

In Djakova, I found already doubts as to the Young Turk Constitution. It was feared it might strengthen Turkish power, as the Powers of Europe were supporting it. And the Albanians of Djakova wanted independence. Space does not permit me to detail my journey. Suffice it to say that, all over the plain of Kosovo, I found that the few Serbs were a negligible quantity. When addressed in Serb they often replied in Albanian and talked it to each other. Only in the neighbourhood of Ipek (Pec) were they plentiful, but were in minority in the town. This was mainly Moslem Albanian, but the Franciscans had a small Catholic school.

Prizren was typically Albanian, its bazaar a wonderful sight, full of the magnificent gold embroidery and silver inlay for which the Albanians were famed. Arts which I fear will have been destroyed by the tempest of war. Prizren, like Djakova, was ready to fight for freedom and in great unrest. The Serbs had a theological college which I visited. Its head was from Belgrade. It was run as propaganda and students imported even from Montenegro. It was in Prizren that the League of Prizren was formed after the Russo-Turkish War of 1877-78 to save Albanian lands which had been allotted by the Powers of Europe to Greece and Montenegro, and saved much.

Lord Fitzmaurice, who was on the East Roumelian Commission for re-drawing Balkan frontiers, was strongly in favour of forming then a large independent Albania to include all Kosovo (which, as may be seen in the Bluebook on the subject, was then, too, all Albania), Monastir and Janina. As he told me, in the course of a long correspondence in his old age, he believed that had this been done and the peninsula been fairly divided between its various nationalities much subsequent trouble might have been spared. And to the end of his life he took the greatest interest in Albania's independence and especially in Mgr. Fan Noli.

Having explored Kosovo, employed a Serb to drive me about it, and having made a pilgrimage to a Serb monastery - Devich - and enquired as to whence came the pilgrims, and visited Grachanitza where there was a small Serb island, I can state emphatically that with the possible exception of the Pec district all south of it should be Albanian. Peace can only be kept in the Balkans by a just partition of its lands. In the districts which were torn from the Albanians in the wars of 1912-13 and 1914-18 both Serb and Greek have been *'weighed in the balance and found wanting'*. Their unwise policy of forbidding any Albanian schools and publications and the expropriation of Moslems under pretence that they were Turks and their expulsion threw Albania into the hands of Italy. When freed from Italy, it is to be hoped that some of Albania's lost lands may be restored to her. There is room in the peninsula for all, and only the unity of the various nations can save it from further invasions.

Neither Serb nor Greek will require *'lebensraum'* after the devastation of war.

Any people unjustly treated will call in foreign help. Injustice threw Bulgaria into German hands.

New Times and Ethiopia News, July 24th 1943
The Battle of Italy
by M. E. Durham

'The Spectator'

Sir,

Sir Odo Russell tells us *"the House of Savoy, who originally benefited by British support, are still there to reassume the lead and to save the Italian people at the eleventh hour."* That the House of Savoy owes its position in Italy largely to the aid lavished enthusiastically on Italy at the time of the Risorgimento is true. What gratitude has the House of Savoy now shown for that aid? What have its present representatives done to show that they are capable of leading Italy? Since 1922, King Victor Emmanuel has been a mere puppet dancing to the piping of Mussolini. No member of the House has objected. The King has acquiesced in all Mussolini's brutalities; accepted at his hands the title of Emperor, after making an unprovoked attack upon Ethiopia and obtaining victory by drenching the helpless population with poison gas; followed this up with the entirely unjustified seizure of Albania, though it was - as was Ethiopia - a fellow member of the League of Nations and as such bound to be respected by him.

Victor Emmanuel has sanctioned every one of Mussolini's crimes and is thus responsible for them and himself a criminal. His daughter is married to a Nazi. He and his House have accepted, as a symbol of government, a bundle of rods with which to flog and an axe with which to behead their opponents. Italy in truth started the present world catastrophe. Hitler modelled his Third Reich in every particular upon Italian Fascism. And copied its deeds. Having larger forces at his command he has surpassed his masters. But both Italy and Germany are equally guilty, and a proposal to entrust the leadership of Italy to the House of Savoy, and by so doing ignore its complicity in twenty years of crime, is inadmissible. It has been *'weighed in the balance and found wanting'*. Among the many honest men, whom the King has exiled or imprisoned, surely some can be found more fitted to lead what was once a great nation.

M. E. Durham

New Tlimes and Ethiopia News, July 31st 1943
Albania's Struggle for Freedom
by M. E. Durham

Since the invasion of Albania on Good Friday, April, 1939, Albanian guerrillas have never ceased to struggle against their Fascist oppressors. During 1942 the underground movement became intense. Mr. Eden, Mr. Cordell Hull and M. Molotov declared that the Independence of Albania would be recognised after the war.

This statement filled the country with wild enthusiasm. And now all are united in a common fight for freedom.

Copies of two *'underground'* newspapers have now reached London. One, called *'The Struggle for National Liberation'* dated Jan., 1943, is the right wing organ. The other, *'The Voice of the People'* is left wing. They contain, respectively, 11 and 20 pages and give full details of the great anti-Italian effort.

Complete unity has been effected between the different groups. At the end of last December, a General Council of National Liberation was formed with full power to organise and direct the resistance activities throughout Albania, by means of local councils and liaison officers. There are three types of units. The Partisans, the Volunteers of Freedom and the Guerrillas. The first two are well-trained groups of professional soldiers, intellectuals, students and peasants. The Guerrillas are mainly peasant forces and form a reserve ever on the alert and with arms and munitions hidden in their homes, ready to be called upon to fight and able to provide the fighting forces with information about enemy movements and also to supply food and shelter. Many women have joined the forces, both as nurses and as fighters.

The newspapers give details about the more important fighting groups. In South Albania, the Italians are harassed in the Valona area by two forces led by Hysni Lepenica, a former gendarmerie officer, and Skender Mucho, a prominent lawyer. The Gendarmerie officers, it should be recalled, were trained by British officers who were dismissed by order of the Italians. We may take it that Lepenica knows his job.

In the province of Korcha, the home and heart of Albanian nationalism in South Albania, the outstanding leader is Dr. Butka, who commands a volunteer unit and a force of guerrillas. In central Albania, the Italians have reason to dread Myslim Peza, who commands a very active and mobile force of Partisans in the Tirana Durazzo and Kavaja district. Near

Kruja, Major Abas Kupi launches constant attacks on Italian convoys and communications. And in the North Eastern mountains, the gallant Colonel Bajraktari, formerly Commander-in-Chief of the gendarmerie, commands a large guerrilla force. Besides these there are fighting units at Dibra, Scutari, Berat, Skrapar and Ghinokaster.

Colonel Bajraktari's guerrillas attacked a big motor convoy on the Puka-Prisren road in North East Albania, destroyed it, captured two guns and 12 machine guns and killed 97 Italians. Myslim Peza's forces have had several fights near Tirana. Recently, on the Tirana-Durazzo road, they attacked a military convoy, killing 42 Italians and taking 80 prisoners. Many declared with tears in their eyes that all they want is to leave Albania so soon as possible.

Details are given of fourteen other fights and of much sabotage. The telephone and telegraph lines are frequently destroyed. A house full of Italian officers was bombed at Valona and three officers killed. The Italians executed four Albanian prisoners as reprisals and a riot and fierce fighting ensued.

The offices of the Fascist paper Tomori have been bombed. Four other 'underground' papers are being published. When the publishers are short of paper they raid Italian offices. Lately the Guerrillas raided the Ministry of National Economy in Tirana and carried off four duplicating machines, 6 typewriters and carloads of stationery.

There are several more pages describing Albania's struggle for freedom. Enough has been quoted to show that it is a real and general struggle.

May it soon lead to victory and to well-deserved independence.

The Manchester Guardian, 9th August 1943
Albania's Struggle

To the Editor of The Manchester Guardian

Sir,

In no land has Mussolini's crash excited greater hopes than in Albania. When the Allied troops land there they will find enthusiastic Albanians ready to aid them to clear the land of Italians. Papers published '*underground*' and recently smuggled to London give many details about the well-organised Albanian resistance that is actively at work.

A General Council of National Liberation has been formed by complete union of all parties. It directs the resistance activities throughout the country. Some of its leaders are former officers of the gendarmerie, which, it will be remembered, was trained by British officers until Italian pressure forced their dismissal.

The forces consist of partisans, volunteers, and guerrillas. The two former are mobile and well-trained groups. The guerrillas are largely peasants, who give information as to the movements of the Fascist enemy, afford food and shelter to the partisans and volunteers, and are always on the alert and ready with hidden arms and ammunition. Many women have joined the forces as nurses and fighters.

There are some fifty fighting groups at work. They attack convoys, cut communications, and recently in a fight on the Durazzo-Tirana road broke up a military convoy, killing forty two Italians and taking eighty prisoners, many of whom declared with tears in their eyes that all they want is to leave Albania so soon as possible.

The day of liberation approaches, and the relieving army will find a reception even more enthusiastic than that in Sicily, and the General Council of National Liberation ready to co-operate in forming a new Government. Next to the Ethiopians, the Albanians have suffered most from Mussolini's greed.

Yours, &c.,

M. E. Durham
London, N.W. 3, August 6.

New Times and Ethiopia News, September 22nd 1943

Now that Italy has crashed - as crash she must - it is imperative that we save those patriotic Albanians whom she captured and interned soon after she grabbed their land. Many, both male and female, are reported to be prisoners in North Italy. Gallant old Mehdi Frasheri, who up till the last moment appealed to England and the League of Nations for help - which never came - was taken as prisoner to Rome.

When the first planes were seen to fly over Tirana it was hoped that the help was arriving. But the planes were Italian and dropped leaflets threatening the immediate destruction of the town if it did not surrender. It was devoid of anti-aircraft guns and helpless.

Let us make amends for the way we threw Albania, a member of the League of Nations, into the hands of Italy, by enforcing the release of all those who courageously opposed her.

The little nation is now attacked by Germany. It is reported that every Italian has been cleared from South Albania and that the German attack is being resisted.

Brindisi and Bari are now in our hands. Let us hope that the Allies will soon land in Albania to support the gallant Albanian bands.

M. E. Durham

New Times and Ethiopia News, September 25th 1943
Remember Albania
by one of her friends (M. E. Durham)

Italy's unconditional surrender has been greeted everywhere as the inevitable and just end of the foolish imperialistic policy adopted by Rome during the last twenty years. It has been hailed most of all by the Balkan peoples and the Muslims of the Near East. They knew, since the capture of Tripolitania and later of Albania, that the internal and international caesarism resuscitated by modern Italy was a deadly menace to their existence. Now this menace at least is no more. Neither the kidnapping of Mussolini nor the difficulties of the Italian campaign can bring to life again the menace of the Impero Romano.

Italy's unconditional surrender has been greeted with joy, hope and satisfaction by the Albanians. They and the Ethiopians know better than anyone else how real the danger has been. They have known it since 1915; they felt it in 1939, and since then they fought it without pause, though without any international help or recognition of their efforts. Now they see the boastful Italians prostrated.

The mountaineers of Albania once again see fulfilled the old saying transmitted to them by the past generations: *'Albania is a holy land, whoever assail it will perish'.* Once more a powerful conqueror trying to dominate this small people has perished.

Albania is now occupied by a new oppressor: the Germans. When the news of Italy's capitulation was made known, many thought the next move would be an Allied landing on the Albanian coast. The Albanian guerrillas prepared for it; but the German divisions arrived first.

Perhaps the requirements of the Italian campaign postponed the invasion of Albania. The guerrillas have now to fight the Nazis. It is less easy than to fight Italians; but they will do it.

It does not seem probable that Hitler will hand Albania again to his *'great friend'.* When Mussolini was preparing the glorious enterprise in order to *'wash out the shame of Valona in 1920',* Hitler encouraged him to take a bone that he could not then obtain for himself. But now Hitler has got it he will find no reason to abandon the prey. The legal argument is not lacking. Albania was tied to Italy only by a personal union of the two kingdoms.The *'republican'* fascist party cannot claim to personify such a union. Italian dynastic ambitions, said the D.N.B., can no longer impede German diplomacy; Mussolini is in such a position that he cannot demand anything of his saviour and master. Hence the proclamation of

Albanian *'independence'*. along with the forthcoming Greek one. Ribbentrop may perhaps give Albania to Bulgaria; it is already reported that a great part of Albanian territory has been handed over. But Germany will keep the rest in order to transform it into a battlefield, where she will try to defend the Reich. Albania knows what that means. During the last war she experienced the trial, and she paid for it with 100,000 lives. She knows, however, that freedom and independence must be paid for.

Albania is in exactly the same position as the rest of occupied Europe. She has the same oppressor, the same sufferings fall on her people as on the others. Why has she not the same rights and the same treatment?.

In 1914-18, Albania was occupied by the Central Powers; she endured the same evils as any other battlefield. She was, as now, in a state of war. Nevertheless, she was being ignored; when the Peace Conference came she was excluded and afterwards mutilated without being allowed to put her case before the world. This was because the secret treaty of 1915, which Italy secured as her payment for supporting the Allies, stood between Albania and justice. America did not permit this Treaty to be fully carried out; but the Ambassadors' Conference, where America was not represented, saw to it that the Treaty did not vanish altogether. Albania had to pay for the Treaty during twenty years, and is paying still. What now stands between Albania and justice? It is said there are no more secret Treaties. America will be in the proposed Mediterranean Commission; so will Britain and Russia. But Albania is still ignored.

In the terms of the Armistice, Badoglio undertook to put at the disposal of the Allies *'all Italian territory and Corsica'*. He cannot do it now, but the arrangement is there for the future. Albania cannot be considered as *'Italian'* territory in law. And the special mention of Corsica makes even more remarkable the silence regarding Albania. One could say that the liberation of Albania *"va sans le dire"*; Mr. de Talleyrand would have replied: *"Cela va beaucoup mieux en le disant."*

The Press maintains a strange silence about Albania and the deeds of the Albanian guerrillas. Albania has become a geographical expression. The Allied Commander-in-Chief Middle-East appealed to Greek and Jugoslav guerrillas; Mr. Churchill and President Roosevelt have appealed even to the Italians. No one mentions the *'brave men'* to whom, some months ago, Mr. Cordell Hull promised military assistance.

Actually we have the Anglo-Saxon and Russian declarations of December, 1942, promising independence to Albania. But the reservations contained in the English statement, the Greek interpretations of these reservations, the non-recognition of Albania's legal status and the present silence on Albania are disquieting signs. There is no doubt, there cannot be, that Albania will benefit, like every other nation, by the Atlantic Charter; but why not regularise the situation now and avoid complications later on? It is hard to believe that even the naming of Albania could be tabooed by any favoured government of the Democratic coalition. Such a concession to any Allied government would be unwise, and, in the end, harmful even to the gallant people represented by such politicians.

Albanians everywhere, inside and outside Albania, with one voice demand of the Allies the recognition of their right to be amongst the United Nations represented, as are the others, by a legal government. Before the danger to their country the Albanians are united; they think only of their country; they are determined. But now that the oppressor is more ferocious, they need encouragement, not only by words, but by needs The fact that even the Nazis try to create for Albania, as for Greece, a Quisling government, proves that such an organ can be of use. The Albanians urge that they may have their representatives, the real ones, in the Allied councils. It is not a favour they ask; it is the application of international common law, and of the principles for which this war is being fought by the Democracies. This common law, if applied, will make even greater than it has been the courageous Albanian contribution to the common cause.

New Times and Ethiopia News, November 4th 1943

May I corroborate Mr. Kerran's excellent letter on the status of Albania? Albania's right to independence and to representation as a member of the United Nations cannot be denied if truth and justice are to prevail. As Mr. Kerran rightly says, it was owing to the fact that she was not represented at the last Peace Conference that she was deprived, both in the north and the south, of wide lands and many thousands compatriots, many of whom have been expelled from their homes, and to none of those remaining have Albanian schools been permitted. Neither of Albania's neighbours has any right to more of her territory. Nor, as their loss of population in this terrible war has been very great, have they any need for more land. As for Italy - for a burglar to maintain he has a right to keep his loot is ludicrous - she has no more right to Albania than to Ethiopia. On the contrary, she should be made to pay reparations.

For an Italian, who himself fled from Mussolini, to jeer at King Zog is ignoble. The rulers of Norway, Holland, Jugoslavia and Greece all thought it best to quit their lands when unable to defend them and to work for their future liberation elsewhere. King Zog has done likewise.

He has also, as Mr. Kerran rightly points out, declared that he wishes the people of Albania to decide by a plebiscite the future government of Albania. King George of Greece and King Peter of Jugoslavia will also wisely be guided by the wishes of their subjects. How far the Balkan lands will be democratised we do not yet know.

But that Italy will continue to be ruled by the present Royal Family seems highly improbable.

Professor Salvemini would be better occupied putting his own house in order than by interfering with a poor neighbour.

M. E. Durham

New Times and Ethiopia News, October 30th 1943
Miss M. E. Durham: A Tribute

On December 8th next, Miss M. E. Durham will celebrate her 80th birthday. This has seemed to some of her friends and colleagues a suitable occasion on which to give expression to our grateful appreciation of her distinguished scientific and political work in the Balkans. It is proposed that subscriptions be invited to a fund which shall be presented to Miss Durham on behalf of the subscribers on December 8th, with the request that she will use the fund for some purpose which commends itself to her.

It is unlikely in these days that any large sum can be expected, and the proposal is to give to Miss Durham a list of the names of those who have subscribed, without reference to the amount of their individual contributions. This testimonial is designed to give some slight expression to the high regard in which we hold the personality and the activities of a brave and unselfish public worker, and a highly gifted woman.

Cheques or postal orders may be sent to Sir Edward Boyle, Bart., Cheselbourne Manor, Dorchester, Dorset, and crossed Miss Durham Testimonial Fund, Coutts Bank, Lombard Street.

Noel Buxton,
Mary Herbert,
Evan MacRury,
Edward Boyle, Hon. Sec.

Signs of the times - Lines on Italy's "co-belligerency."
*Shrewd are the words
The old salts say -
"When the ship is sinking
The rats swim away!"*

August 12th 1944
'Dielli'

36 Glenoch Road, London NW3, England
June 30, 1944

Dear Mr. Pani:

I should have written to you long ago to thank you and Vatra for your great kindness to me.

But ever since last October my health has been bad. Eighty years are a heavy burden to carry and I become weaker as time goes on. I am glad to say I can still manage to go to the shops to buy my rations, for they are near to this street. But I have to stop to rest halfway. The food parcels you have so kindly sent me have been very useful to me and as a token of the kind thoughts of my Albanian friends have given me much pleasure.

I cannot any longer attend any meetings of the Anglo-Albanian Association I am sorry to say but keep in correspondence with it through my old friend, Sir Edward Boyle.

I hope we may see the end of this hideous war before Christmas but do not feel certain of it.

When peace comes I hope that those in Albania who have fought so bravely against both Italians and Germans, will be free to elect the new Government for they will know best what the country needs.

The King of Greece has decided very wisely not to return to Greece unless he is invited to do so by the vote of the Greeks.

Here in England we are having raids of pilotless planes which are very tiresome. A great many are shot down before they reach London and I hope that this nuisance will soon be stopped.

It is not so bad as was the bombarding in 1940-41 but it does some damage and wakes one at night. But I was so often under gunfire in the Balkan war of 1912-13 that it does not affect me much. The victories of the combined English and American forces in France are very encouraging and when we get control of the North coast of France as we soon shall, I hope, no more raids of planes to England will be able to come over the Channel.

Russia is now advancing so quickly that I think the Germans cannot hold out through another winter.

We have been having a very dry summer. Almost no rain, so are short of water and are asked to economise and not to waste it. And also to economise in coal, gas and electricity as all this is needed for the army. We are better off, I think, than any other people in Europe for neither bread nor potatoes or fish are rationed and other things are shared very fairly so that everyone can get a ration. No one needs to go hungry. And the prices are regulated.

Please give my thanks and good wishes to all my Albanian friends.

With warm greetings, I am your old friend.

M. Edith Durham

The Englishwoman, Volume XVI, Oct-Dec 1912
Mary Edith Durham
by Charles D. MacKellar

'Our Queen has come back!' cried but a short time ago, the Malissori tribesmen, as a tired, wet, muddy, famishing woman rode into their midst; and greeting her in their wild way, the weirdly picturesque mountain warriors, armed to the teeth and keen for war, rode on with her, through the wet mist and. mirk of the night, till a rough mountain home received them, and their heroic but bedraggled *'Queen'* sat down with them to take her share in their rough meal of a sheep boiled almost whole !

And this is in Europe to-day-in prosaic, highly civilised, conventional old Europe - and this Queen of the wild Malissori, that fighting clan so renowned for valour, fierceness, and its blood-feuds, is nothing more or less than an English lady, and a Londoner to boot !

Who says romance is dead?

Then we see her next morning, after sleeping in wet clothes, no doubt, for she tells us that she had not had her clothes off for fifteen days- out amongst the Montenegrin soldiers, and being chaffed by them because she is devouring in hunger a crust of yesterday's bread carefully saved up, whilst they, the soldiers, have none and are yet cheerful and happy.

This no doubt sounds theatrical to the stay at home people, yet it is simple fact. Last year the writer saw the houses and villages of the Christian Albanians. being burnt by the Turks and their Mohammedan subjects; this year and month Miss Durham tells us that she rides through a blackened and desolate land, where the Christian tribesmen have taken their revenge on their onetime oppressors, and nothing but fire-scorched ruins a common sight there mark the way.

But on she rides through rain and discomfort into the camp of the Montenegrin Army, where the Princes who command give her a the cordial welcome. It is war - real war- war with the booming of cannon, the shells of the besiegers raining upon the Albanian capital, and, hissing through the air, the return shots of the besieged.

But Miss Durham who is combining her work with the the Montenegrin Red Cross with her duties as a War Correspondent at the Front, has no time for rest, and so, an as she tells us, it is on and on again in mud and rain till the thing becomes a nightmare; sleeping just anywhere, eating just anything, with the shells whizzing overhead,and the rattle of the guns unceasing, whilst the smoke rises from the belaboured and besieged town. She meets a woman who, recognising her, greets her and gives her day's meal of dried figs and a lump of bread; and be then when evening comes she finds herself under shelter with a band of those fierce people, who call her but one an name, *'Kralitza' (the Queen)* and they hold high revel, cooking seven sheep whole, hacking off the flesh with a sword bayonet, and, with a garnish of bread and salt, at devouring the meal which, as is the custom, they eat with their hands.

The strange fantastic costumes, heads bandaged, white garments elaborately braided with black knives, pistols and rifles, the whole lit up by the light of a burning house, and in the midst, the Englishwoman who has, through years, become the trusted friend of these warriors,it is a striking picture, which those who know the land can easily conjure up.

It is perhaps ten years ago, or even more, since Miss Durham first became a wanderer in these Balkan lands, and in that long space of time she has become very well acquainted with some of them, and especially with the mountains of Albania and the warlike tribes who dwell in them and at their feet. She has acquired the Serb language, and also a certain knowledge of the Albanian tongue, which is the ancient Illyrian. She has studied their customs and ways, their songs and legends, and made herself familiar with their hopes, their wrongs, and their ambitions. When first the young Englishwoman with the appeared amongst them riding alone, or with any guide she could find, through those wild lands where few foreigners could venture, and where no foreign woman had been seen before, she was received with wonder; but the Albanians are a chivalrous race, and because she so trusted herself amongst them she won their confidence and regard, and in time became their friend and adviser. She, therefore today can ride through those lands and anywhere dwell in security where none others can. Any one who knows her books, *'High Albania'*, *'The Land of the Serb'* and *'The Burden of the Balkans'* - books which should be read intelligently by every one at this moment- knows that she can wield the pen with fearless vigour on behalf of her people to plead their cause. to guard their interests, to point out their age-long unredressed wrongs and urge the statesmen of Europe to give them right and justice at last. But also she can wield the pen with fine humour, sometimes at her own expense, sometimes at the expense of others with a full appreciation of the quaintness of the situations in which she sometimes finds herself, and can also make her pictures living, moving scenes of colour for us, and portray the romance which lives in these mountain solitudes, where the customs and ideas of the people are as they were centuries ago.

She can argue with them in their own tongue, showing. of these them the fallacy of many of their beliefs, telling them of the customs and ideas of other lands and valiantly opposing the wickedness of their eternal blood feuds. She laughs with them as they fire their rifles over her head in salute of some joyful event, and she has all sympathy needful for the sufferings and wrongs they have endured from times immemorial. She binds and dresses their wounds for them; teaches mothers, imbued with the prejudices of ages. that light, air, and cleanliness are needful things for their babies and exemplifies precept by practice in doing for them what they ought to do for themselves.

Her present occupation of War Correspondent is but an episode in her life, in which there have been many episodes, some of which found her in unusual and dangerous situations. It is to the fact that she is so well known in Montenegro and Albania that she owes the special privilege granted to her.

Miss Durham does not reside continuously in the Balkans, but has become so familiar with some of those lands that she must feel at home in them. The Albanians are the children of her heart, and her endeavours on their behalf have been unceasing.

Montenegro is a civilised land, inhabited by a fine and chivalrous race, who are honest, gentle, and courteous of manner, kindly and, hospitable, and all born warriors. It is neighboured by Albania, which no one could describe as a civilised land. Albania and Albanians are but generalterms for a country of ill-defined boundaries. and a people composed of many different tribes of different origins.

There is no leader to weld all these tribes into one and this has probably been the cause why the Turks have never managed to subdue them, and they have never been able to raise themselves to a more free position. Unity makes force, and the Turks had no desire to see them become united.

The Albanians, speaking generally, are supposed to be ancient Illyrians, and they speak Illyrian today. The Romans, the Servians, the Venetians, and the Turks have all left some of their blood in the veins of these tribes, and have ruled, or attempted to rule, them through the centuries; but these fierce fighters have always managaed to retain possession of their mountain strongholds.

The land is a high, mountainous one, of the grey Karst formation so noticeable in Montenegro, with deep valleys lying between the ranges. At the end nearest Montenegro, and above the beautiful Lake of Scutari, lie the lands which have been most harried by the Turk, who has never ceased to oppress and tyrannise over this subject race. Warfare between them has been unceasing, as it has between the Montenegrins and the Turks, and the Albanians, therefore, have had continually to seek refuge over the Montenegrin frontier, and on this, frontier they have frequently been assisted by the Montenegrins in reprisals on the Turks. The *'frontier incidents'* have been unceasing and often much more serious than the outside world imagines.

The Turkish troops have frequently burnt houses and villages, destroyed the crops, and massacred the people. Therefore the Albanians have had to guard themselves in their mountain homes as best they could. There are no roads or railways in the country; it is in as uncivilised and barbaric a state as it was centuries ago. Taxes wrung from the people at the point of the bayonet have only gone to fill the pockets of the Sultan or the rich Pashas who dwell, far from them; not a farthing collected has been spent on the people or their land. Their wrongs for centuries have been great, and they still exist.

They have retained many old tribal customs and ideas. In a tribe there is no intermarriage, all descending from a common ancestor being deemed brothers and sisters. The institution,of Blood Brotherhood also exists, and this means that the relatives of those entering into a Blood Brotherhood are regarded as being of near kin and cannot marry. Partners for marriage must be sought in some other tribe. Frequently a destined bride is taken away from her own people and brought up in her betrothed husband's tribe until she is of age to live with him, when, however, marriage does not take place until it has been seen that she is capable of motherhood.

Blood-feuds are the breath of their lives. Blood shed must always be washed out by blood- a life for a life. This is a point of honour they will bear no tampering with; and the consequence is that nearly every boy and man is engaged in some such feud and has killed somebody. Life is of little value amongst them. Montenegrins, who have to a certain degree, the same custom, fly Into Albania, and Albanians fly into Montenegro to escape the pursuer, but the end is usually the same- the feud must be ended with blood.

There is here, however, no space to enter into details about the customs of these still untamed mountain warriors. It is amongst them that Miss Durham has often chosen to pitch her camp, living in wild and rough surroundings, enduring hardships, but gradually growing to be their trusted friend. She rides from place to place with her belongings, in her saddlebags, and has been a participator in various events of striking interest and of historical importance to them.

Whilst residing in Montenegro she has devoted much time to the hospitals and nursing and tending the poor and sick. and there, with her own hands, she rights what is wrong, bringing sweetness and freshness where before dirt and squalor reigned. It is little wonder her name has become a household word both in Montenegro and Albania.

Miss Durham is a very practical person, an English lady of decided character, who knows what should be done and sees that it is done, even, as so often happens, when she has to do it herself. She was present, by invitation, at the capitulation of the town of Tuzi, with the Montenegrin Princes; and it is characteristic of her that she at once went to the Turkish hospital, which she found full of wounded, and in a shocking state of neglect and dirt. She proceeded forthwith to wash and tend the wounded, and with her own hands to clean out the hospital; then, mounting her horse, she rode back to Montenegro to write and send off her dispatches as War Correspondent.

She is thoroughly conversant with the political history. ancient and modern, of many countries, particularly so with that of those wild Albanian lands to which she has been such a blessing. Nothing escapes her; she can see through the countless intrigues, and, wanting nothing for herself but merely justice for her people, can easily put her finger on the weak spot, or expose the shams and shames of interested diplomacy. Miss Durham is feared in some political circles; there is no deceiving her, and as her courage marches with her intelligence. She is not to be restrained from speaking or writing the truth.

The unfortunate Albanians have not only been great sufferers at the hands of the Turks, but have suffered severely through the ambitious intrigues of Great Powers, who have used them merely as pawns in a political game; and they have more than once been the victims of a so-called *'protecting'* Great Power. So they allege and believe, and with every appearance of truth. It will be indeed a dark and sad day for Albania if she is allowed to come, even in a remote degree, under the hands of Austria, the one Power which should have no say in anything pertaining to her. Miss Durham knows all this, many people know it, the Great Powers know it; and yet those Great Powers to-day, as before, would deliberate sacrifice Albania to their ideas of political expediency.

It would be enough to say of this Englishwoman that a whole land and a whole people speak of her, trust her, and believe in her; that she has been a true and noble friend to a land and its people in their days of adversity, so that they give her the only name they deem suitable, and that is *'Our Queen'*.

Amongst the customs of the Albanians is one common to all ancient and primitive peoples. Round the fires on long winter nights they love to sit and sing or recite the deeds of love or war of their forefathers, the doings of their heroes in a land of heroes, and the happenings of a daily life of unceasing war against the oppressor, or of the constant bloody feuds between clan and clan.

It is easy to believe, then, that in the legends to be told in time to come there will be strange tales of the Englishwoman who came from her far land to be with them and amongst them in all their trouble. She is to live in the hearts and legends of the Albanian clans and many a one may envy her that.

She has been so long familiar with the life of people of these lands that it is all natural to her; her fine spirit loves the freedom and the freshness of it all; the people have grown near to her, and their wild but chivalrous virtues to the strength, which is. yet womanly strength, in her nature. She is a very feminine person with a strong strain of real and good womanliness in her character, though she can ride as hard and shoot as straight as a man, and withal she is always an English gentlewoman. Her influence has always been for good amongst these Albanians, she being their best and almost their only friend.

Last year there was great trouble between the Albanians and their rulers the Turks, which resulted in thousands of Albanians seeking refuge in Montenegro; whilst the Turks, after burning, villages and houses, destroyed standing crops, slaying all they could get at, men, women, and children, and consigning many of their women to a worse fate, pursued the fugitives to the very frontier of Montenegro, and threatened the Montenegrins that unless they gave up these refugees they, the Turks, would follow them over the frontier. The Turks and Montenegrins are old hereditary enemies.

The sight of the Turkish army entrenched along their frontier but a few miles distant from, and visible from, the Montenegrin town of Podgoritza, naturally infuriated the Montenegrins, who were craving to take up the cause of the persecuted Albanians and attack the Turks. They had to feed the starving refugees, and tend their many wounded at Podgoritza hospital.

War seemed inevitable. The Great Powers, however, caring nothing for the wrongs of Montenegrins or Albanians, but afraid that a war between Turkey and Montenegro would inflame the other Balkan States and bring about a great European war, employed all their influence with the Porte and the King of Montenegro to prevent a formal declaration of war. Pressure was brought on the King to stop feeding the refugees. He could not let them starve, but eventually was forced by the Great Powers to announce that in two days all food - maize bread - would be stopped.

The danger of.the situation was that if the Turks and Montenegrins went to war - and King Nicholas could scarce restrain his people - that not only might other Balkan States join in, but that Austria, under the pretence of interfering to keep the peace might enter Turkey and march directly to Salonika.

The Albanians and the feelings of the Montenegrins had therefore to be sacrificed. The Albanians, after much negotiation by emissaries of the different Powers, were told they must go back to their own desolated land; would be allowed by the Turks to do so, and would receive aid in erecting shelters for the winter. They refused, trusting no Turkish or other promises; demanding that their safety and other claims should be guaranteed by the Great Powers, and that they should be allowed to return armed. The latter demand was refused, and things were at their worst. To the Albanian refugees, there seemed to be only death from starvation in Montenegro, or death at the hands of the waiting Turkish army entrenched on the frontier. They had been deceived too often and would not trust the Turks, nor would they trust any word of Austria. There was danger that they would either attack Podgoritza which sheltered them, or that the Montenegrins would join with them in attacking the Turks. War, therefore, with the Balkan States and Austria mixed up in it seemed inevitable, and the Great Powers and all concerned were driven to desperation, the Albanians refusing to listen to any one.

Miss Durham had been for some time at Podgoritza, attending to the wounded in the hospital, and assisting in. distributing the relief in food and money which the *'Macedonian Relief Fund'* and others in England had provided, money too being placed in her own hands to use as she saw fit.

When all else failed, she was appealed to to induce the Albanians to return to their own country, and after much persuasion, and seeing that there was nothing else to be done, she consented. It was touch and go whether they would listen, and that might have been a bad day for Podgoritza. However, they consented to go, the condition being now that they should go armed - a great triumph for them. They trusted in Miss Durham's word, where they would trust no one else, but they would only go if she went with them. So she had to lead those refugees back into their own land.

The war which is taking place now would have taken place last year and perhaps it would have involved the Great Powers or some of them. The

Albanians left Montenegro, the Turkish troops withdrew all pretence for interference on the part of Austria vanished, and a temporary peace reigned. This, beyond doubt, was owing to Miss Durham's influence with the Albanians and watchers of all these events saw clearly that she had saved a European war. That will be easily understood in the light of events now taking place.

Miss Durham then, accompanied by Mr. Nevinson, visited the mountain villages, or where villages had been, to afford help to the people, and to see that the Turks carried out their promises of giving food to the people and means to build some shelters for the approaching' winter. The destroyed crops and untilled fields promised dire famine for the coming year. She remained at Scutari during the winter, so as to be in touch with her people and to look after them; then went for a time to Italy, returning later to Montenegro to watch the proof events, and was, therefore, on the spot when war broke out against Turkey last October. Some day we may hope to have the account of these many doings from her own pen. So much of the recent history of Albania has passed under her eyes that it was fitting she should see and participate in the present phase. It will be seen that the Albanians have much reason to put faith in her.

The Turks spent the winter in fortifying Scutari, and that was warning enough to every one concerned what their promises really meant. The Balkan States are well on the way to bring the Balkan question to a satisfactory, right, just, and final solution, by which they attain their ambitions, drive the Turk from Europe, and set free these millions of Turkish subjects of varied races and religions who have suffered for so very long under Turkish misrule.

As we see, there is a disturbing element. It is Austria; and Albania is again the peg on which embittered ambitions and political intrigues are to be hung, if permitted. Set free from the Turk, it would be as well that much tried Albania should be set free also, and for ever, from Austrian interference. However desirable her coasts may be for ports-and for naval bases for ambitious Powers, it is more than time that an end should be made of all these intrigues, and the Albanians be allowed to rise and flourish, under freedom from Turkish rule, as the Greeks, the Bulgars, and the Serbs have done.

Now, in the high mountains of Albania, and in the rocky ridges and defiles of Montenegro, there is a keening and mourning for the braves who have died and are dying so willingly, gladly, and nobly for their countries; and though their women lament, as women must and will through all the ages, for the husband, the son, or the lover gone from them, their laments - have you ever heard them wailing through the wild lands? - are always tinged with pride, for these are Spartan women, the women of simple and primitive peoples, who think it their first, and a noble, duty to die for king and country. These women, who, despite all, must tell their rugged mountains and rocks the sorrow within thein, which even pride will not assuage, are heroines themselves; for they, too, have been under the fire of the enemy, have been wounded and bled for their country as they did what seemed to thein their natural duty, and toiled, heavily laden, many a mile through rocky defiles, or sunken paths deep in slush, to bring what food - and little enough it is - they could to the men who are fighting.

It is a proud thing, after all, to be the mother, the wife, the daughter, or the sweetheart of a soldier, to stand by him through thick and thin; to tell him, whatever comes, to go and do his duty, and to do it bravely and well and that is what the women of these lands are doing today.

But they are such poor lands these, so terribly poor; the breadwinners in many cases are coming back no more; a hard and cold winter is already with them - things are coming to women and children which are very hard to bear - have come to some already things - it is not comfortable to think of!

If you care- then be sure the means to alleviate something of this can never go into better hands than those of the understanding woman of whom this is written, and because she makes the name of Englishwoman a word of honour throughout the land, would not many of her countrymen and countrywoman express their debt to her in the way she would care most for, and that is in making it possible for her to aid and succour her people in the time of their distress?

Is it not possible that when at last the strenuous work is done, and peace comes, that Miss Durham may return to those lands, free at last from their oppressor, and with full hands and, be sure, a full heart, say to them, *"Look - the people of my land send you this'*?

There is Montenegro with her splendid and brave people, who for over 500 years have fought the foe at their very doors, unconquered, undismayed, as they are doing to-day. I who write know these people, their history and their life, and I know the dire want that has come and is still to come to them amidst the snows of Tchernagora. There are only 250,000 people in the whole land, and 50,000 of them are engaged in fighting for their country. It is easy to do a great deal with no such large gift in such a land, and the doors of the Montenegrin Consulate in the street of the Crutchedfriars in London Town are standing open to all who care to enter and give.

But Miss Durham's people, the Albanians, have no Consulate with open doors- they have her. and that is about all, the poor harried clans of the *'Accursed Mountains'* of Albania. At least one can plead for sympathy with them in their centuries-old troubles.

Miss Durham has been led by circumstances, perhaps, more than by her own purpose, into her present prominent position as the advocate and friend of the Albanians. The fact that it is an Englishwoman who does occupy this relation towards them ought to be pleasing to her countrymen and make them feel it is a duty to support the claims of these people, though there are sufficient grounds for it otherwise. The fact that in conversation in the Near East. they are often spoken of as *'Miss Durham's people'* speaks for itself; and it is often said that the two people - of this country anyway - who have the most extensive knowledge of the various Balkan nationalities are Mr. Bouchier, of The Times and Miss Durham. It is unnecessary to say what a great advantage knowledge of the speech of the people gives them over other travellers or residents there.

It may be said that there is little more to be told concerning this lady than is to be found in her own books, which so graphically and often so humorously, portray the curious adventures she has had in Albania. The country is not a normal one, so it could not be expected that her existence there would be normal.

When the Constitution was proclaimed in Turkey, the important Mirdite Clan gave no sign of being aware of it, which created some consternation in Scutari, the North capital. They had been expected to rejoice, as did other innocent Christian clans, who imagined something wonderful had happened to them. The Archbishop of Scutari was directed to inform the Abbot of the Mirdites that if they did not come down to Scutari at once, and accept the Constitution, they must take the consequences, the Abbot replied that he had only spiritual, not temporal power over them, and that they had a Prince who unluckily was not there.

Prenk Pasha, Prince of the Mirdites, had been taken to Constantinople when a youth, thirty years before this. and was therefore a stranger to his people. He was summoned back by the Young Turks, and the news of his return created intense excitement amongst his people. We will quote from Miss Durham to show what were the sort of incidents in which she was a participator, and how her brilliant pen describes them: *'The restoration of an exiled Prince to his people in a wild mediaeval land-in the twentieth century-was an event that for dramatic interest could have no rival. It cried to me, and I went.'*

With her guide, Marko, she halted at a *han* on the borders of the Mirdita, to await the arrival of the men who were coming to escort their Prince : *'In another half-hour they trooped at a double, all of a pack, firing as they came-small, dark men, for the most part, wiry and eager-the most notorious robbers and skilled cattle-lifters of the district. Rattle, clatter, over the loose stones, followed their priest's long black figure, on a strong white horse.'*

There they awaited the Prince.

'At first sight of the distant cavalcade there was a great cry, and a party rushed off to meet it. The remainder drew up in rude order by the wayside,tense, listening. Distant shots - the replying ones - he is coming, he is coming! In a cloud of white smoke, and the dan-dan-dan the rifle shots, Prenk Pasha, befezzed, and in uniform gold-corded, cantered up on a white horse with his escort, drew rein, and threw himself from the saddle. A roar of rifles rang out, as Mucla, in a solid mass, fired over our heads. And then it was obvious that Prenk Pasha was a stranger to the land. He recoiled, deafened from what, to the tribesmen and myself, for I had been under fire on and off for two months, was only a pleasing exhilaration.

Prenk Pasha had arrived. There was a certain irony about the fact that the man who had left as a prisoner - treacherously kidnapped on board a Turkish warship - was now returning to the land of his birth, in Turkish uniform, as aide-de-camp to the Sultan, and attended by two Turkish guardian angels - young Turks in officer's uniforms. The halt was short. It was already late. We remounted.

The Pasha, with his cousin Kapetan Marko, and his escort, pushed on, I following, up the valley of the Qjadri. We were stopped to receive hospitality at the house of a headsman- the most celebrated Cattle lifter of them all- where we sat on a scarlet carpet, drank rakia and ate tepid mutton with our fingers, the young Turks kindly pulling off lumps from the main animal for me.'

They proceed on their journey, and she dines that night at a priest's house with the Prince and his escort. On the evening of the next day she and her guide, Marko, arrive at the church of Kacinari, high on the hillside, and in the priest's house. *'The cavernous black raftered kitchen was full of company. We sat round a great fire that burnt in the middle of the floor; while one tinkled music on a tamboritza, another roasted coffee and turned the fragrant seeds, smoking and black and shiny, on to the carved shovelshaped tray to cool- and all talked.'*

The following day they arrived at Shpal, in the heart of Mirdita: *We arrived at the trysting-place just before the Pasha. The wood round* the little church, the heart of Mirdita, was full of tethered horses; the bare hillside beyond crowded with Mirdites, grouped according to their bariaks. The men and boys of Prenk Pasha's house stood foremost, anxious and eager for the first glimpse of their Head. And the man upon whom all hopes hung came at the head of his escort, upon his white horse, and rode around the great gathering. A mighty cry arose. Some thousand bullets ripped with a tearing swish between the hills as he passed. We thronged into the wood, where, under a great tree, was spread a carpet. He took his seat upon a chair, his crimson fez making a brilliant blot on the green-leaf background. Then all his male relatives-many born since he was exiled- were presented to him. I thought of the Forest of Arden, where they 'fleeted the time pleasantly as in the Golden Age,' as each in turn strode up, 'a hero beauteous among all the throng,' dropped on one knee and did homage, kissing his chieftain's hand with simple dignity. The tribesmen stood around in a great circle, the sunflecks dancing on their white clothes, and glinting on gun-barrel and cartridge-belt. . . . We awaited the coming of the Abbate. Mirdita without the Abbate is Hamlet without the central figure. Nor had we long to wait. His gold-banded cap shone over the heads of the crowd, that parted and let him through on his fat white horse, gay with a gold saddle-cloth, followed by the rest of the priests of Mirdita.

We went out on to the bare hillside. There was no room among the trees for the great concourse now assembled. . . . It struck me suddenly that among some two thousand five hundred armed men, I was the solitary petticoat. The Young Turks and I were the only anachronisms - blots on the old-world picture. . . . Soon none were left on the historic spot but the dead asleep in the lonely graveyard. A chill wind arose, and the autumn leaves fell in showers. For better or for worse, a page had been turned in Albania history, The summer had gone, the year was dying. I had seen the Land of the Living Past.'

These are but glimpses of the life Miss Durham lived amongst the mountain tribes. Her experiences have been manifold, and the end is not yet.

Charles D. MacKellar

The Times, November 21st 1944
Miss Edith Durham:
King Zog's Tribute

King Zog of Albania writes:-

I wish to pay a grateful tribute to Miss Edith Durham. In doing so, I know that I speak for every one of my countrymen who today cannot express freely even their sorrow.

She first came to Albania at a time when the country's name was nothing more than a geographical expression, to help human beings in need of aid and assistance. Open-minded and generous as she was, she speedily understood Albania's soul and grasped that, besides aid and assistance, she longed for - and merited - freedom and independence. Fearlessly and without compromise she told the world and its rulers, in books, articles, and conferences, what she had learned. Indeed, her whole life was devoted to Albania. She gave us her heart and she won the heart of our mountaineers, for whom she had especial sympathy. Even to-day her name is treasured by them. Albanians have never forgotten - and never will forget - this Englishwoman, for the memory of their true friends remains for ever with them. In the mountains she knew so well, the news of her death will echo from peak to peak - the news of the death of one who was loved there.

Sad it is that she should have died at a moment when Albania is again fighting for her independence and her liberty, her people again needing aid and assistance as was the case when she first came into contact with it. These recent days have, indeed, been sorrowful ones for the mountaineers she loved. But she died sure - as the Albanians are sure - that allied victory will bring liberty to Albania. This common confidence is yet another proof of her understanding of my countrymen.

New Times and Ethiopia News, November 25th 1944
Obituary: Miss M.E. Durham

We deeply regret to announce the death of Miss Durham, whose name often appeared in our pages. She was a friend of long standing of our Editor, to whom she frequently wrote, although not for publication, letters of advice, information, and encouragement.

The last letter we had from her, neatly typed as usual, ended with the words: *'I am getting weaker every day more.'* We all lose in her a trusted friend and a most valuable contributor.We reproduce below the notice which *'The Times'* gave of her death:

TRAVELLER AND WRITER

Miss M. E. Durham, traveller and writer, who died at Glenoch Road, N.W., recently, was an authority on the Balkans and particularly on Albania. A strong and fearless woman, she explored remote parts of Europe, moving freely among wild tribesmen whose respect she gained and kept. She made valuable contributions to the knowledge of the customs and usages of the most primitive Balkan peoples. Formerly she was a correspondent of *'The Times'*.

Mary Edith Durham, born in 1863, daughter of the late A. E. Durham, F.R.C.S., was educated at Bedford College, and at the Royal Academy of Arts. She painted well, exhibiting at the Royal Academy, the Royal Institute of Painters in Water Colours, and the Institute of Painters in Oils. Among the numerous books she illustrated was the reptile volume of the *'Cambridge Natural History'*. She became a wanderer in the Balkan lands in the early years of the century, her gift for acquiring languages helping her to make friends with the turbulent peoples among whom she lived. Her knowledge of Serb and Albanian was particularly good, her fluency in the latter language, combined with a genuine sympathy with the Albanians and their aspirations enabling her not only to make friends among the wildest clans, but also to exert a great influence for good. But while she championed the cause of Albania, urging in her writings the need of redressing their wrongs, she never hesitated to criticise some of their customs, and to condemn the endemic blood-feuds of the northern clans.

During the fighting between the Serbs and the Albanians in 1912-13, she did valuable relief work among the Albanians, and an account of her experiences was published in 1914 under the title of *'The Struggle for Scutari'*. Her book *'Twenty Years of Balkan Tangle'*, which appeared in 1920, did much to help the British public to understand the political and dynastic intrigues of two stormy decades, and her volume *'The Sarajevo Crime'*, published in 1925, was very critical of Serbia. *'Some Tribal Origins, Laws and Customs of the Balkans'* (1928) brought home to the reader the lack of civilisation among the Albanian clans, and dealt interestingly and informatively with Balkan cults and heresies.

Miss Durham had been a Fellow of the Royal Anthropological Institute since 1908 (later becoming a member of the Council), and in celebration of her eightieth birthday last December she attended a meeting of the Institute to receive a presentation in recognition of the many great services she had rendered it. She was, too, a member of the Royal Institute of International Affairs.

New Times and Ethiopia News, December 2nd 1944
Albanian Tribute to
Miss M. E. Durham

May we be allowed to express through your paper - which almost alone upholds Albanian rights without fear or compromise, and to whom our mutual friend has so often contributed - our deep dismay and sorrow at M. E. Durham's death.

Some of us are Albanian mountaineers, brothers of those whom M. E. Durham loved so much and so unselfishly; others come from southern Albania, whose real aspirations she understood so well and upheld so firmly.

We therefore feel entitled to express the sentiments of all our compatriots at the loss of a great friend of our country. We think that it is no exaggeration to state that among the mountains and valleys of Albania her death will be considered a day of national mourning.

The tribute that we pay here to-day is not what the Albanians owe to M. E. Durham. We know that one of the first acts of free and independent Albania will be to commemorate this *'Princess of the Albanian Mountains'*, but meanwhile the struggle for freedom goes on, and it is for the Albanian exiles, who are not given the opportunity to participate in it, to record, even with unsuitable words, what M. E. Durham did for, and what she meant, to Albania.

She came to Albania when the situation was much like that of to-day. She was young, courageous, anxious to help the distressed whom war for freedom and independence had reduced to destitution.

The situation was then desperate for Albania, but, as J. Swire puts it, *'Fortunately, Miss Durham, who, by her unselfish devotion to their cause, had won their implicit confidence, was among them.'* She helped as much as she could. At the same time she tried to get to know the Albanians and to investigate the real situation. She knew our leaders and amongst them the Abbot of Orosh, Mgr. Primo Doçi, who once was so well known in Britain. She was neither propagandist nor a fanatic. She only spoke and fought for what she considered to be the truth. She attested the real sentiments of Southern Albania, which were contested then, as they are now, by blind and short-sighted politicians.

Since then for more than thirty years her interests in Albanian affairs have never diminished. She wrote books, articles - especially in the liberal *'Manchester Guardian'* and your paper - she gave lectures and spoke her mind to public and rulers alike, having justice only in view, and with contempt and disregard for *'diplomacy'*. In that, as in many other aspects, she was like her friends the Albanians: courageous, straightforward, fearless and outspoken when justice is at stake. Her character explains why she found in our country so many friends, and why she was looked upon as one of us.

Proud and independent herself, she never ignored the dignity of her friends by assuming a condescending role towards those whom she wished to help. She was capable of understanding the Albanians and without denying the faults that every young state can commit she kept always the real sense of proportion, putting Albania's interest before everything else.

In every crisis of our life M. E. Durham stood by us; and then, when the last one came - the greatest - she resumes the struggle on Albania's freedom.

But she was then old and sick. In spite of that, she never hesitated to take part in every association which worked for Albania's rights. She opposed, personally and by fearless letters to the Press, foreign propagandists who tried again and again to mislead British opinion. Her authority and her known love for truth secured respect for her, and for Albania the opportunity to be heard.

Only a few days ago you, Madam, published a very courageous and gallant letter written in her straightforward and virile style. We believe that this was her last public action, and it was still for Albania.

To the Albanians she leaves a message of hope, and a counsel for unity, in order to face the difficulties which are ahead of us, both for the complete liberation of Albania and for its reconstruction after this terrible war.

To our British friends, who all acknowledged her authority and selflessness she leaves a message to continue her noble work, now that Albania has as much need of friends, as when she was almost alone to stand up for Albania.

We hope that these messages will be heard by all to whom Albania is dear.

It is a great pity that she did not live long enough to see Albania liberated by the exertions of her mountaineers, helped by the troops of the freedom-loving peoples, but she left us with absolute confidence in Albania's future.

The Albanians gave her the *'besa'* and considered her a true friend; she has been faithful to them in the spirit in which friendship is given and accepted in our mountains.

We can affirm that the nation will keep for her memory a special place in every Albanian heart. An the only tribute that her modesty would have accepted is that we all shall strive to make Albania worthy of friends like M. E. Durham.

Yours sincerely,

Ali Ahmeti, Halil Driçi, M. Gjoka, Q. Kastrati, S. Martini, Gj. Naçi, B. Neli, M. Noçka, Xh. Nushi, Q. Prendi, H. Sufa, Z. Shehi.

New Times and Ethiopia News, December 9th 1944
Albanian Gratitude
A Personal Tribute to Miss Edith Durham
by Dervish Duma

In the person of Miss Edith Durham the Albanians mourn a true friend and a tireless defender of their national cause.

Forty years of her life were dedicated to the struggle for the rights of the Albanian people. At the service of this human ideal she put her noble soul, her strong will, her inexhaustible energy, her sharp spirit and her outstanding artistic gifts.

It was at the beginning of the century, Albania was almost unknown to the world at large. Her neighbours had spread the absurd legend of a country inhabited by savage tribesmen who would kill a man for a loaf of bread. Miss Durham did not believe in these tales of a tendentious propaganda. As a pioneer of justice and knowledge she, a young woman coming from an intellectual English family, went alone and lived among the mountaineers of our country. She liked them and won their love and respect. With their genuine simplicity they adopted her and gave her the name of *'Princess of the Mountains'*.

In a number of books written with a passionate love for truth and right, she lifted her powerful voice in favour of a small nation threatened to be used as a pawn in the awful game of old-style diplomacy. She did not hesitate to criticise sharply even the policy of her own country when she became convinced that it was wrong. She sent back a medal to a foreign king, because his troops had persecuted Albanian mountaineers, whose terrible plight she had witnessed herself. Her books will stand as an immortal monument where moral courage, literary talent and scientific vision are combined into a harmonious unity.

'A strong and fearless woman' - wrote the *'Times'* in its obituary - *'who made a valuable contribution to the knowledge of the Balkan peoples, and especially the Albanians, among whom she lived and whose respect she won.'*

Miss Durham's struggle for the Albanian cause did not stop till the last day of her life. The tragedy of Good Friday struck her as a personal misfortune. Although burdened by her age and weakened by illness she did not miss a single meeting when she could say a good word in favour of Albania. She followed with a keen interest the struggle of the Albanian people all through the last five years

I have before me a letter which she wrote to me just a month before her death. It encloses a copy of the review published by the Manchester Geographical Association, in which a report on Albania's economic resources was printed after her intervention. In her letter she expresses her satisfaction that Mrs. Aubrey Herbert was trying to interest the British Red Cross to prepare for relief work in Albania. She added that she had written to Bishop Fan Noli, agreeing with the idea that the future régime of Albania should be decided after the war by a popular plebiscite. Her last act was a letter to the press in which she defended the right of Albania to be independent and become a member of the family of the United Nations.

The name of Miss Durham will be intimately linked with an epoch of our country's history - the epoch of our National Rebirth.

Today the Albanian people organised in the Army of National Liberation are fighting for freedom on a new a better way The British officers and soldiers who are fighting side by side with the Albanians, are continuing by other means the struggle started by Miss Durham half a century ago. Let us hope that the Allies will hear her last appeal, which sounds as her political testament.

In the liberated Albania of tomorrow, our people will immortalise the name of Miss Durham by erecting a monument worthy of the deep gratitude all of us feel for the invaluable good she has done to our country.

Dielli, Boston, May 12th 1945

Memories of Miss M. E. Durham

by V. P. Kennedy

Miss M. E. Durham, strong, capable friend to you Albanian people, has passed away but memories of her still remain in the hearts of many of you who knew her personally.

It is with many of you who did not have the privilege of making her acquaintance, that we wish to share our impressions of her personality. Just when she began to take an active interest in the struggles and aspirations of your people, I do not know, but my parents had already told us of her visits to Monastir where they were engaged for many years in missionary work previous to our going to Albania. It is my impression that it was in Monastir that Miss Durham, in her Balkan travels, first had her attention turned to Albania through her acquaintance with the Kyrias family.

'*Once a friend, always a friend*', proved true in her case. Other races in the Balkans had had her interest but there was something special in you of the Albanian race that drew upon her sympathies and awakened her admiration. Your beautiful country with its majestic mountains appealed to her artistic sense. Your noble bearing and high sense of honor pleased her. Your love of freedom and efforts to assert your independence in the face of great political difficulties appealed to her innate sense of justice.

She spent much time in travelling horseback through your rugged mountains, in order to study you that she might write and thus acquaint the world outside with your fine qualifications and latent powers and to point out what was hindering your achievement of national freedom. Discovering your difficulties and the open as well as subtler dangers threatening you on all sides, she fearlessly championed your cause.

Our paths crossed several times and it was a privilege to know her. From the record in our Guest Book, we see that Miss Durham made us a visit in Elbasan in October 1913, where we were sojourning after we were obliged to leave Korcha. It was about the time of the disaster in Dibra and vicinity when refugees from there poured into Elbasan and Tirana and gave us the opportunity to dispense relief from friends sent us for such purposes.

At one time, in these relief trips in North Albania, following the Balkan War, when Miss Durham was away, Mr. Kennedy was given permission to use her fine, well-named horse. There was such a lack of food and provender for beasts, even, in the devastated regions he visited that Miss Durham was distressed, later, when she heard how even her horse had suffered hunger and weakened visibly.

In the spring and summer of 1914, when we were staying in Durazzo, we had the privilege of seeing her often. It happened that she was in Vlora (Valona) at the time that Mr. Kennedy was in that city after he had made a relief trip in the interior. They were fortunate in being present the day that Prince Wied and Princess Sophia were accorded such a welcome to that city. They saw the enthusiasm manifested by the people, expressed not only in cheers but in effort to draw the carriage in which their '*Mbret*' and '*Mbretereshe*' were seated, up from the shores to the building in which they were to be entertained.

Miss Durham was astonished that the Prince seemed so lacking in proper emotion. She said to Mr. Kennedy, *"Why does not the Prince speak and say something in response to this beautiful welcome by the people!"* She felt he was so formal and unresponsive as he stood there bowing at the crowds below from the balcony!

Perhaps, I may add here that in speaking of this visit to Vlora, Princess Sophia told me afterwards, when I was accorded an audience with her, that their reception at Vlora was wonderful. *"It was like awakening from a bad dream,"* she added, after all the opposition they had met from certain other sections of your country.

Miss Durham was deeply moved by the need for relief work among the thousands of refugees who had travelled westward from devastated regions in the interior of Albania. We were all impressed by the patience of those sufferers, whose homes had been burned, who were hungry and sick and in need of clothing and shelter. As we looked at these groups, congregated from various parts of the interior, and noted their picturesque costumes, Miss Durham exclaimed that she wished the Albanians would retain these costumes rather than pattern after western dress.

Shkodra knew Miss Durham best for when she sojourned for any length of time in Albania, she seemed to make that city her headquarters. There she wrote; there, she endeavored to dispense relief as far as she was able - I say, as far as she was able because in a letter from her after her return to England, she wrote that she found she could not stand the physical strain of the demands made upon her by those in need who thought her funds were exhaustless and who constantly disturbed her writing. She said she had fled to England for refuge.

She has left books which show how great was her accumulation of knowledge of the people among whom she travelled in the Balkans. Her *'High Albania'* is a masterpiece and a work of art for it contains sketches she herself has made of people she met in Northern Albania. Her *'Some Tribal Origins of Laws and Customs'* is most interesting, and full of her own illustrations.

Some time we hope to read her *'Struggle for Scutari'* (Turkish, Slav and Albanian) because it is my impression that she entered Shkodra with the Montenegrins during the Balkan War when they seized that city from the Turks. She had helped in Red Cross work with that army but was loyal to you Albanians throughout her experiences.

The best way for us to remember Miss Durham and others who have contributed to the betterment of your country is to *'carry on'* in the unfinished task.

May God assign to each of us the part He wishes us to take in the reconstruction of your country so that with His help and imparted wisdom, Albania may truly have a blessed future.

INDEX

Other publications from the
Centre for Albanian Studies

The Truth on Albania and the Albanians

by Wassa Effendi
Centre for Albanian Studies, 1999
ISBN 1 873928 63 7 Price: £4 plus £1 p&p
with a new indroduction by Robert Elsie

This is a reprint of a polemical pamphlet originally published in 1879. Wassa Effendi was a secretary in the British consulate in Scutari. In this pamphlet, designed primarily to inform the European reader, Wassa Effendi argues for the unification of all Albanian-speaking territories within one province.

Scanderbeg

by Harry Hodgkinson
Centre for Albanian Studies, 1999
254 pp. Price £9.99 plus £1 p&p
ISBN 1 873928 13 0
with an introduction by David Abulafia of
Cambridge University

This is the first biography in English of the Albanian national hero Scanderbeg (1403-1468). Written by the late Harry Hodgkinson (1913-1994), a former naval intelligence officer. This book does not claim to be the definitive scholarly work on Scanderbeg, but it is informed by a deep love of Albania. Harry Hodgkinson's engrossing book is an attempt to bring the reader closer to this famous historical personage and to set him in the dramatic context of Albania and its history.

Faik Konitza

Selected Correspondence 1896-1942
Centre for Albanian Studies, 2000
204 pp, ISBN 1 873928 18 1
Price £9.99 plus £1 p&p
edited by Bejtullah Destani with an
introduction by Robert Elsie

This book contains the unpublished letters of Faïk Konitza, outstanding Albanian scholar and diplomat, who rediscovered the old Albanian flag of Scanderbeg, which had been forgotten during the four and a half centuries of Turkish domination These letters include those he sent to William E. Gladstone, Aubrey Herbert, King Zog, Nikolla Naço, Visarion Dodani, Dervish Bey Biçaku, Dervish Duma etc.

All these titles are available from Learning Design. Tel. + 44 20 8983 1944